HOW CHINESE ARE YOU?

How Chinese Are You?

Adopted Chinese Youth and their Families
Negotiate Identity and Culture

Andrea Louie

NEW YORK UNIVERSITY PRESS
New York and London

NEW YORK UNIVERSITY PRESS
New York and London
www.nyupress.org

References to Internet websites (URLs) were accurate at the time of writing. Neither the author nor New York University Press is responsible for URLs that may have expired or changed since the manuscript was prepared.

Library of Congress Cataloging-in-Publication Data
Louie, Andrea.
How Chinese are you? : adopted Chinese youth and their families negotiate identity and culture / Andrea Louie.
pages cm   Includes bibliographical references and index.
ISBN 978-1-4798-9052-1 (cl : alk. paper) — ISBN 978-1-4798-9463-5 (pb : alk. paper)
1. Interracial adoption—United States. 2. Intercountry adoption—United States.
3. Intercountry adoption—China. 4. Adopted children—United States.
5. Chinese Americans—Ethnic identity. 6. Chinese—Ethnic identity.
7. Multiracial families—United States. I. Title.
HV875.64.L646   2015
362.734089'951073—dc23   2015010014

New York University Press books are printed on acid-free paper, and their binding materials are chosen for strength and durability. We strive to use environmentally responsible suppliers and materials to the greatest extent possible in publishing our books.

Manufactured in the United States of America

10 9 8 7 6 5 4 3 2 1

Also available as an ebook

For my son, Adán Tomás "Toto" Quan

CONTENTS

ACKNOWLEDGMENTS

I would like to thank Allison Berg, Steve Gold, Kirsten Fermaglich, Victor Jew, Michael Largey, Janet Louie, Terese Guinsatao Monberg, Mindy Morgan, Anna Pegler-Gordon, Brandt Peterson, and Steve Rohs, as well as the participants in the Fall 2008 CIC Asian American Studies writing workshop, particularly Josephine Lee, for their comments on various versions of these chapters. I would especially like to thank Susan Brownell for her careful reading of larger portions of the manuscript and general guidance regarding the revision and publishing process. Sara Dorow also generously spoke with me about my research, read and commented on the whole manuscript, and suggested directions for revision and for finding a publisher. Her comments were invaluable. My work benefited from discussions with others studying international adoption, including Heather Jacobson and Eleana Kim. I am grateful to Martin Manalansan for his guidance and support. All errors and omissions are of course my own.

Two anonymous reviewers for New York University Press provided insightful comments that guided the revision of the manuscript.

Finally, I would like to thank those adoptive families and their supporters in the St. Louis area, in the Bay Area, and in China for sharing their stories with me for this research. I am sorry that I cannot thank them individually and still maintain their anonymity. I could not have conducted this research without the support and assistance in St. Louis of Melody Zhang of Children's Hope International; Jane Ogden and Donna Schneiders in their capacities as president of the St. Louis branch of Families with Children from China; Kathy Ferris, Donna Coble, and Donna Schneiders for hosting Parents' Night Out gatherings for adoption discussion; and Maggie Charity, Bob Charity, and Mary Neal for their friendship and support. In the San Francisco Bay Area, I benefited greatly from the help of Peggy Scott (FCC Northern California), Beth Hall, and Amy Klatzkin, who spoke with me and hosted a Parents' Night

Out at her home. Thanks to the families with whom I traveled to China for letting me tag along. Jo and Megan Laws have been particularly helpful, keeping in touch with me since the trip. Thanks also to the many adoptive parents in mid-Michigan, St. Louis, and the Bay Area who welcomed me and my family to various playdates and other adoption-related events.

Portions of the book appeared in my article "Pandas, Lions, and Dragons, Oh My! How White Adoptive Parents Construct Chineseness," *Journal of Asian American Studies* 12, no. 3 (2009): 285–320. A revised version of chapter 3 appeared in "Encountering a Mediated China: An Ethnographic Examination of an Adoption Trip," *Encounters: An International Journal for the Study of Culture and Society,* no. 3 (Fall 2010): 191–222, Zayed University Press, distributed by I. B. Tauris & Co.

Portions of this research were funded by a National Endowment for the Humanities Summer Stipend in 2004, and Michigan State University Intramural Research Grants in 2000 and 2008.

Ilene Kalish and Caelyn Cobb at NYU Press shared important advice, encouragement, and guidance throughout the revision process. I truly appreciate their support for the project.

My parents, Thomas and Janet Louie, provided support throughout the long process of writing this book. Finally, special thanks to Adán Quan for the warm meals, child care, and moral support, and to Toto Quan for being both a welcome source of distraction and in many ways an inspiration for this project.

1

Introduction

I sometimes feel guilty on Sunday mornings when I think about how some of my son's Chinese American friends are at Chinese school learning to read, write, and speak Chinese while he stays at home tinkering with his Legos. It's not that we have not considered Chinese school. When he was five, he expressed interest in learning Chinese along with some of his friends. I was excited that he wanted to learn the language and thought this would give him an opportunity to spend time with other children of Chinese background who were his age. We tried out a kindergarten-level class, one where parents were allowed to sit at the back of the room to monitor behavior and help children with books, supplies, and snacks. But he barely made it through the two-hour session, which was geared toward children who spoke Mandarin at home. The instructor spoke only in Chinese and assumed a working knowledge of the language, including colors and other basic vocabulary that my son did not have. The class involved the rote memorization and reading of Chinese phrases such as *duibuqi* (sorry) and *bukeqi* (you're welcome) and on-the-spot recitation. My son was lost and frustrated, only chiming in when the teacher had the class sing "Liang zhi laohu" (Two tigers), a song he had learned from watching a YouTube video.

The following year we decided to try a Chinese as a second language class run by a different Chinese school. He fit in better with this group because none of the other children were native Chinese speakers, but the class met from six to eight o'clock on Saturday evenings, and the first homework assignment, practicing the characters of the zodiac, seemed rather demanding. We could have stuck with it, and he probably would have done fine, but ultimately we did not feel strongly enough about him learning Chinese to follow through with the class. Maybe next year, we thought. Or perhaps he could learn Spanish instead.

Our ambivalence stemmed from our uncertainty about whether learning Chinese should be a priority for our son. What was it that we really wanted him to get out of Chinese language class? Was it our goal for him to become fluent in Chinese, or to merely be exposed to another language? More broadly, we wondered how important Chinese language was for fostering his sense of Chinese identity or as a general skill for him to possess as a Chinese American individual. Neither we nor his grandparents speak Chinese fluently, if at all. Our son, who is our bio-logical child, is actually three-quarters Chinese. When he was around five, he declared that since he was three-quarters Chinese, that must mean that he knows how to say three words in Chinese. Indeed, he had learned to say *ni hao* (hello), *zai jian* (good-bye), and *xie xie* (thank you) when we went to China, but has since forgotten. His first words were actually in Spanish, a language that his half-Chinese father, who grew up in El Salvador, had attempted to speak with him since birth. But Span-ish soon fell by the wayside. By age two, our son increasingly responded "Speak English!" to his father while pressing an imaginary button on his head to make him switch back to English. After all, he hears only Boston-accented English when he visits his maternal grandparents, who speak village dialects unintelligible even to Cantonese speakers; and he hears Kentucky-accented English (and sometimes fluent but Kentucky-accented Spanish) when he visits his paternal grandmother, who is of Scottish and Irish stock, was born and bred in Kentucky and later mar-ried a Chinese man from El Salvador.

As I try to help my son craft his identity, I make choices for him that reflect my own ideas about which aspects of Chinese (or Chinese Salvadoran/Kentuckian) cultural heritage he should be exposed to and about how to balance these activities with others that are not necessarily related to his heritage.

Chinese Culture Exposure

Each year since he was two, I have brought my son to the annual Chi-nese New Year celebration hosted by the local Families with Children from China (FCC) organization, which is run by adoptive parents. These celebrations have been criticized by parents I interviewed in the San Francisco Bay Area, mainly Asian American ones who were the pri-mary focus of that set of interviews but also some white parents. They had critiqued their local FCC chapter's events for being artificial and inauthentic. To them, seeing a group of white parents eating Chinese food with their Chinese children dressed in silk outfits seemed somewhat unnatural. They respected the well-meaning efforts of their fellow adoptive parents to create an environment where their children could be with other kids adopted from China, and be exposed to Chinese culture, but they thought the event seemed disconnected from other Chinese people and also from the deeper historical and cultural traditions that are ingrained within that community. Though critical of these FCC events, the Bay Area parents I spoke with did not necessarily refrain from attending them. They participated so they and their children could meet others like themselves. However, these parents felt that there were numerous other opportunities to experience Chinese and Chinese American culture in the Bay Area, from sending one's child to Chinese school to spending time with Chinese American friends.

I could see why some might view such events as lacking in historical and cultural depth. At the gathering I have regularly attended with my son, the walls of the rented church room are brightly decorated with shiny paper and foil cutouts of dragons and Chinese characters, the tables graced with centerpieces that look like miniature fireworks displays with plastic gold coins spread around them. A thirty-foot span of rectangular tables holds the potluck feast, consisting of take-out chow mein, dumplings (*jiao zi*), sweet-and-sour chicken, home-cooked dishes, and desserts. Most of the children, and some parents, are dressed in colorful, silklike Chinese outfits. Two craft tables are set up at the back of the room. The children receive red envelopes (*hong bao*) with chocolate Chinese coins inside, and more coins and other goodies are distributed at the end of the event. The entertainment program usually features a performance by a Mandarin-speaking, ethnic Chinese singer. However, the highlight of the event is the lion dance, during which the children march around the room, with three or four at a time wearing the scaled-down costumes. Next come the "faux fireworks," which involve the spreading out of an industrial-sized roll of bubble wrap and the distribution of battery-powered fiber-optic wands. At the signal, the children enthusiastically stomp on the bubble wrap and wave the wands around, creating an auditory and visual approximation of fireworks being set off.

New Traditions?

While many may not consider the FCC Chinese New Year celebration "authentic," in some ways it has become a new tradition. The celebration was meant to signify a positive identification with Chinese culture, and it was more hands-on than more formal New Year celebrations such as the parades and lion dancing that one might find in Chinatown community festivities. Through their participation, children were able to embody and take ownership of these traditions. Children remembered the lion heads, the noisemaking instruments, and the bubble wrap from past years and looked forward to partaking in the activities again. Although attending such celebrations alone is not sufficient to create a sense of Chinese or Chinese American identity, or to address issues of race, the events do represent an opportunity for adoptees to form friendships and be exposed to the variety of ways of being "Chinese."

I wonder, too, how this celebration was any different from the presumably more "authentic" lion dance my family and I attended on Chinese New Year in 2010 at a local Chinese restaurant. Hosted by the restaurant's Chinese American owners and featuring a kung fu group headed by a Hong Kong–born *sifu* (master teacher), this event focused on the consumption of dim sum and the spectacle of Chinese lion dancing. In attendance was a diverse crowd, consisting of both Chinese and non-Chinese. Interestingly, none of the performers was Chinese, though they had been trained by the *sifu* in the art of lion dancing and Chinese kung fu styles. Both the Chinese and non-Chinese restaurant patrons seemed intrigued by the kung fu demonstration, crowding around the performers, the Chinese-speaking couple behind me enthusiastically recording the performance.

I had made reservations for a group of twenty, including both adoptive families and Chinese families with first-generation immigrant parents and bilingual children. The event was a chance for families to get to know one another better in a context that disrupted certain notions of Chinese cultural authenticity. A form of "traditional" Chinese culture was being performed by non-Chinese, and appreciated by Chinese and non-Chinese alike. The social interactions among the people in our group, a third of whom were children, formed the basis for the creation of new friendships and the sharing of knowledge. In this context, the immigrant Chinese who grew up in Communist China were not necessarily the authorities because many had not previously seen the lion dance in China. After most people had left, some of the children performed their own version of the lion dance under a long, down coat with fur-ruffed hood borrowed from one of the mothers, a "tradition" that had debuted the year before to the applause of the lion dancers who were having a bite to eat after their performance.

New Identities?

Attending such events alone is clearly not sufficient to provide children with a well-rounded sense of Chinese identity. But what part do these events play in adoptive parents' efforts to expose their children to Chinese culture? The highly sensory experience of seeing, hearing, and tasting representations of Chinese culture that characterized the New Year's party resonates with how a young child explores and experiences his or her world. For better or worse, it is also consistent with how most adults experience their surroundings and understand and appreciate cultural diversity in our media-driven world, in which we are constantly bombarded by signs and symbols. How do such moments feed into the broader context of identity formation?

Like many Chinese adoptees (and other Chinese Americans) I've met, my son is still sorting out what it means to be Chinese, and being Chinese is only part of how he defines himself. At times, he has seemed alarmingly clueless about it. One day when he was in first grade, I picked him up from his after-school program. I asked one of the boys he was playing with whether they were having a battle with their toys. The boy responded, seemingly out of the blue, that he was Korean, not Chinese. Another boy then proclaimed that he was Malaysian but explained that he spoke Chinese and went to Chinese school. I then asked my son what he was, and he replied, "Nothing."

On our walk home, I asked him whether he thought he was white. "No," he replied. I asked whether he was black, and he again answered, "No." We have talked on many occasions about how he is Chinese American or Asian American. Many of his friends are also Chinese American or Asian American, and many are children of color, so his confusion raised some interesting questions. What exactly does make him Chinese American? He does not identify with mainland China, nor does he speak Chinese. Nor did he at that age identify strongly as a Chinese American or Asian American racial minority. His conception of what it means to be Chinese is likely based on popular notions of identity and culture that root Chineseness in histories, places, cultures, language, and perhaps "race." Clearly, a Chinese American identity was something that needs to be both created and reinforced.

I can understand his confusion. Though I identify strongly both as a Chinese American and as an Asian American, in the context of my daily life, I do little that could be considered specifically "Chinese." I do not speak Chinese very often (or very well), cook much Chinese food, or participate in a Chinese church or other organization. Some of the Chinese cultural practices that I follow were learned not from my parents but from friends and relatives in Hong Kong and mainland China, where I spent time teaching English and doing research. I married a man who is half Chinese but who identifies primarily as Salvadoran, or perhaps secondarily as Kentuckian. Yet I teach courses about China and in the field of Asian American studies, and my research has focused on questions of Chinese American identity and transnationalism.

I have come to understand that though there is no question as to whether my son will be seen as a Chinese American or Asian American, it is also up to me to help him understand this identity. Because of his lack of identification with China, Chinese language, and Chinese customs, I will need to help him separate Chinese identity from common notions of cultural authenticity related to language ability and descent that often become tied to it. In many ways our family already disrupts these notions of Chineseness that imply that there are specific, authentic ways to be Chinese and to practice Chinese culture. We are of Chinese descent, but my son is fourth generation and mixed race, with cultural influences from not only U.S. locations but also El Salvador.

Sometimes I wonder how important it is for me to teach him about Chinese culture at all. In the context of a multicultural United States, this question can be broadened and asked with regard to other forms of cultural heritage. But more than exposing my son to Chinese culture, I am concerned with preparing him for the complex forms of racism and discrimination he may face because he is Chinese American. He will encounter a host of stereotypes based on his "Asianness"—that he is foreign, passive, and weak; that he is good at math, plays the violin or piano, and is proficient in the martial arts; that he will become an engineer or scientist; and that he can speak an Asian language. While some of these stereotypes may not seem overtly negative, they will certainly play a role in how he sees himself, perhaps as images he tries to live up to or against which he tries to define himself. Whether or not my son learns to speak Chinese and regardless of how much he knows about China, he will be viewed as racially Asian. As Chinese American parents, his father and I hope that we may be more attuned to the multiple and often subtle ways that racism and discrimination are manifested. Though we may not always feel confident about being able to handle situations in which racism or discrimination arise, or to teach our son how to deal with them, we can draw upon our own experiences and our networks of other people of color for support.

I am also cognizant of the fact that the process of identity building is something over which I will not have total control. My son will be influenced by other family members, teachers, and peers whose views on these issues, like my own, emerge from their own experiences and identities and are framed more broadly by a shifting politics of multiculturalism and race; all of this will shape what representations of "cultural diversity" he is exposed to and how issues of race and racism will be addressed (if at all). His own ideas will also likely be reworked over time, just as my own have been, as he grows older and wants to develop and express his identity in other ways.

Chinese Cultural Authenticity?

In this sense, we represent just some of the diversity that constitutes the Chinese diaspora. Academic works on Chinese identity in mainland China and in the diaspora note that even within mainland China itself, a wide variety of cultural practices are deemed Chinese, and that these have varied across time and place (Cohen 1994; Wu 1994). Similarly, ethnic Chinese populations outside of China have been found to interpret and practice their Chineseness in a number of ways that are often framed by geopolitical factors, historical trajectories, and local racial and ethnic politics (Siu 2005). A global or diasporic perspective on Chinese identity opens up possibilities for many different ways of being Chinese that are not reducible to ideas about racial or cultural purity. Children adopted from China can be seen as representing yet another part of this diaspora.

Yet despite the actual diversity found within the Chinese diaspora, many of the white adoptive parents whom I interviewed operated on assumptions about how "real" Chinese Americans behaved: that they likely spoke Chinese at home, cooked Chinese food, spent time with other Chinese people, celebrated Chinese holidays, and practiced Chinese values of frugality, humility, respect for elders, and hard work. These ideas about authenticity to some extent also shaped the ideas of Chinese American adoptive parents, as well as their critiques of white parents' attempts to re-create Chinese American practices.

But if this is the case, how can we understand the significance of newly invented Chinese traditions, such as those created by adoptive parents and carried out by FCC organizations around the United States? Can they be seen as merely mimicking the activities of ethnic Chinese communities, or can they be understood as part of a variable and changing set of practices that constitute the landscape of Chinese and Asian American culture today? How can they be read within the broader context of Chinese American and Chinese adoptee cultural production that I address as part of my reframing of Chineseness as something produced rather than just inherited?

In order to understand Chinese cultural identity as something produced, I share an example from my own family. Every year that her health allowed, my grandmother used to make *faat-go-ti* (a type of brown sugar–sweetened muffin eaten during Chinese New Year) and distribute them to family members. A few years ago, my aunt, who had learned the recipe from my grandmother, invited a group of my cousins and their children over to her condo after they asked her to show them how to make them. My cousins paid close attention, and though they are still never sure whether the muffins will turn out correctly, making them represents the continuation of a tradition started by my grandmother. In this sense, the production and performance of Chinese identities involves a degree of reflexivity about how to translate a family's past so that it becomes meaningful for its future. In the context of adoptive families who are incorporating aspects of cultural tradition and identity that are not part of their own family traditions, Chinese identities are worked out through the imagination and reinvention of both parent and child identities as they "triangulate" with Chineseness.[1] I argue that this is by no means unique to Chinese Americans but can operate within other ethnic and religious traditions.

Preemptive Parenting and the "Privilege of Authenticity"

As I grapple with how to expose my son to the various aspects of his heritage, I do so within the context of broader questions about parenting. In this age of conscientious child rearing, activities such as sports, dance, and playing a musical instrument are carefully selected to produce a well-balanced child by middle- and upper-class parents trying to provide their children with a competitive head start (Hays 1996; Friedman 2013). But where do Chinese language, cultural events, and the making of *faat-go-ti* fit in? These questions surrounding Chinese language and culture are not unique to our family but become part of a broader set of decisions that go into raising a child with attention to his or her developing identity, as well as family heritage and identity as whole. Furthermore, they become intertwined with parents' own values and perceptions regarding both parenting and identity, Chinese or otherwise.

I have realized that many issues I have faced as a Chinese American parent relate to the experiences of adoptive parents and their children, and to parenting more broadly. First, how can one as a parent proactively and preemptively address issues of cultural and racial identity to meet the challenges of parenting a Chinese American child in today's world? Second, what combination of self-exploration, family tradition, and invention characterizes the formation of today's Chinese American identities and cultures? And how do these processes of identity development and negotiation work, initially under the guidance of parents and later on one's own? Third, how do these identity formations work in relation to other discourses defining Chinese, Asian American, and other aspects of identity, as well as within the broader structures of a changing U.S. racial politics?

Being a parent presents numerous challenges that accompany the decisions that must be made in shaping one's child's future. I acknowledge that raising an adopted child creates additional challenges and sparks a host of anxieties for parents. After all, adoptive parents, whether Asian or white, negotiate issues of culture, race, and adoption not as discrete and compartmentalized issues but as interconnected within a broader context of meanings and practices. The interplay of these issues is shaped by parental class, racial, and ethnic identities; ideas about "family"; and, most important, the ways that the racial and cultural "difference" of Asians, particularly Asian females, has historically been understood and acted upon in the United States.

My son does not have the close ties to China that many children adopted from there have, though if he decides he wants to connect with his roots, he will have access to relatives, as well as information about family history, genealogy, and the ancestral village. He will not have to grapple with the weighty issues of abandonment and of being transracially adopted that many adoptees may encounter. As a male, he will have to deal with a very different set of stereotypes than those that impact Asian women and female adoptees. The adoption of children from China is highly gendered. Not only are there misconceptions about the position of women and girls in Chinese society that appear to be verified by the fact that a high percentage of adoptees are female, but there is also an abundance of stereotypes regarding Chinese and Asian women that circulate in the Western media and popular culture to which these children will be subjected, both as Asian Americans and as Chinese adoptees more specifically. Particularly strong are discourses about female Chinese adoptees having been rescued from a culture and society where the only thing they did "wrong" was to have been born a girl (Evans 2008). As I discuss in chapter 3, the China-based adoption coordinators I interviewed lamented the fact that many adoptive parents did not fully understand the complex circumstances that led to Chinese people relinquishing their children. While there have been notable efforts to counter these discourses with more informed readings of the situation in China, such as Kay Johnson and Amy Klatzkin's *Wanting a Daughter, Needing a Son* (2004), less nuanced notions of the gender oppression that Chinese girls and women face fit more neatly with the Orientalist ideas that pervade Western understandings of Asia and Asian people as exotic and "other" (Said 1979). As Chinese adoptee girls grow up in the United States, they continue to be subjected to assumptions based on their race and gender. As Dorow observes, "'Identity issues' of postadoption are not just the result of leftover feelings of loss and rejection or individual experiences with racial prejudice; rather they surface because the historical raced, gendered, and classed conditions of abandonment and adoption are still present" (2006b, 25). From being referred to as "China dolls" as young children to being stereotyped as exotic and submissive as teens, Chinese adoptees are exposed to ideas about Chineseness that are powerfully gendered, and these ideas are repeatedly imposed on them, whether consciously or not, by well-intentioned parents trying to cultivate an "authentic" sense of Chinese identity or, on a number of other levels, from everyday interactions with teachers, peers, and strangers.

In addition to not having to be concerned with gendered and sexualized constructions of Chineseness in relation to my son in the way that parents of female Chinese adoptees must be, as a Chinese American biological parent, I have what I call the "privilege of authenticity," the flexibility to shape my son's exploration of his identity without my intentions or authenticity being questioned. We can choose to teach him Spanish, Chinese, or nothing at all, and his identity as a Chinese American will likely not be questioned, nor will my parenting choices regarding his Chinese cultural education be scrutinized.

My Research

The experiences I have just described inform the ethnographic study of Chinese adoption that I present in this book. I certainly did not begin this study thinking about parenting and identity issues in the same ways that I do now. Rather, this study developed in tandem with my experiences of being a parent to a child whose identity I now realize is so much more than just "Chinese," along with my own developing academic interests and interactions with adoptive parents and their children. While I was initially hesitant to bring my personal background and experiences into my research or this book, I have realized that this context provides a reference point from which to lay out the main themes of my study and the development of the questions I ask within it. My positionality as a Chinese American parent frames this study. In my relationships with adoptive families, their preconceived notions about "Chineseness" and Chinese people shaped our interactions. These ideas included conceptions about the ways Chinese American parents with biological children raised their children. In many ways, Asian Americans constitute an "other" to white adoptive parents. As a group that possesses an imagined "authenticity" against which adoptive parents' practices are implicitly compared, Chinese American families, both adoptive and not, served as a model of comparison for many white adoptive parents as well as those who observe them.

Parents' approaches toward creating Chinese culture are shaped by their understandings of how "authentic" cultures can be created, "passed on," and practiced, and thus shed light on parents' conceptions of ethnicity (and its relationship to race and racism), identity, and family (Dorow 2006a, 2006b; Jacobson 2008). In many ways, adoptive parents' improvisational yet strategic approaches to Chinese culture may make these processes of cultural production seem too slippery and flexible, without acknowledgment of their limits. However, I argue that it is necessary to move beyond debates about cultural authenticity to examine what is actually being produced, how it reflects broader contexts and processes for identity production, and how it affects adopted children and their parents, perhaps in different ways. I want to delve further into the ways adoptive families' expressions of Chinese culture reflect broader processes of cultural production in the context of contemporary multiculturalism and ask whether it is possible to understand these constructions of Chineseness so that they can be seen not as devoid of meaningful content but as potentially both reflecting and reshaping contemporary discourses on race, culture, and family. What can we learn from examining how they play out as part of a broader set of discourses of Asian American identity as parents and children negotiate, contest, and revise these meanings as they practice Chinese culture in the context of their daily lives?

Throughout this book, I discuss how new family identities—incorporating forms of whiteness and Chineseness, and ideas about multiculturalism and race—are being created out of the practices surrounding Chinese adoption. Chinese adoption can also be seen as leading to new forms of Asian American cultural production. But what is being produced, how, and by whom? How are these processes both similar and different for white versus Asian American adoptive parents, and how are the meanings of these productions renegotiated over time by their children? To answer these questions, we need to rethink what constitutes Chineseness in the context of U.S. and broader global society and consider how parents, both white and Chinese, approach the construction of Chinese cultural and racial identities for their children. How is the "difference" of Chinese adoptees as Chinese or as Chinese Americans (people racialized as Asian living in the context of a white America) conceptualized as adoptive parents imagine and construct Chinese identities for their children? These questions have implications for new possibilities for defining whiteness and its relationship to nonwhiteness.

Rooted in extensive ethnography, this book takes as its core premise that all Chinese Americans, including Chinese adoptees, craft their own forms of "Chinese and Chinese American" cultural capital as they negotiate the politics of race, class, and culture in the United States. Chineseness is not produced in a vacuum, nor does it play out in a vacuum. Therefore, parents' productions of Chineseness become part of, but not the entire, context within which their children will sort out their own relationships to their Chinese identities. I focus on the complex and varied ways that parents approach these issues and explore how adoptive families work within and around the constraints of U.S. racial and multicultural politics.

Through my ethnographic research, I also aim to unpack the imagined "authenticity" of the Chinese American "other" found in public discourses regarding issues of cultural authenticity, and against which adoptive parents implicitly compare themselves. The idea that there is a correct context for Chinese culture misrepresents and misunderstands the heterogeneous practices that constitute what is considered to be "Chinese culture" and the processes through which it is dynamically produced and negotiated over time and within various contexts. Yet discourses of Chinese culture in the West essentialize ideas about Chineseness in ways that do not leave room for multiple ways of being Chinese or practicing Chinese culture, and do not consider the context of unequal power relations that shape productions of Chinese culture and racial identity. The objectification of Chinese traits and values can be viewed as part of a strategy to lay claims on Chinese cultural authenticity and in the process deny it to others. Taking ownership of Chineseness and turning it into a form of cultural capital may be a way to revalue Chineseness in relation to the negative stereotypes associated with it as a racialized label in U.S. society. Lok Siu's book *Memories of a Future Home* (2005) discusses the role that varying ideas about Chinese cultural authenticity played in a Central American Chinese beauty pageant. The debate that arose between the newer immigrants who valued markers of "pure" Chineseness such as Chinese language fluency and stereotypical "Chinese" physical features, and those who appreciated the hybridity of the mixed-race contestant who was born and raised in Central America, illustrates the divergent interpretations of Chineseness as a form of cultural capital.

In my ethnography, I examine the ways that both Chinese American and white adoptive parents, and their children as they become teens, approach issues of Chinese identity, as they draw on a variety of resources in crafting "Chinese" identities. I explore the ways that even those productions of Chinese culture that may appear to be constructed out of traditional Chinese historical and cultural contexts become salient for those Chinese adoptees who are living them, particularly as they bump up against alternative forms of Chinese identity and are negotiated in relation to other axes of identification. I show that these productions become "messier" than originally conceived as they play out in the context of everyday lives, reflecting the complex and multilayered nature of families, culture, and identity. In other words, I explore the forms that representations of Chineseness take and the work that they potentially perform as they are employed by adoptees and their families.

Examining the ways that Asian American parents engage in these processes of cultural and racial identity production provides comparative insight into the ways that culture, race, and adoption intersect for different groups. Asian American parents' negotiations of Chinese culture and identity may be seen as emerging from but not wholly constituted by existing Asian American and Chinese American subcultures. In analyzing their practices, we can also begin to understand how white adoptive parents and their families fit into this mix, as they produce their own forms of Chinese American culture that interact with other forms created by a heterogeneous group of Asian Americans. More broadly, a comparative examination of Chinese adoption can help us understand how the racial positioning of Chinese Americans and Asian Americans may be changing vis-à-vis other minority groups and whites. I focus on how the construction of identities for adopted children by white parents reveals parents' assumptions about how race works and how to defend against racism, about culture and its relation to race, and about identity and how to shape it. The celebratory focus on Chinese culture is often presumed to occur at the expense of teaching children about race and racism, with these two processes being mutually exclusive. However, I argue that some parents can come to new, more nuanced understandings of how race affects their children's lives and that what may begin as essentialized, symbolic forms of culture in the lives of adoptive families may have the potential to become something more complex and subject to negotiation.

The adoption of children from China into U.S. families has implications for the changing future of U.S. racial and cultural diversity, as it plays out on an everyday level in the ways that parents and children experience, interpret, and reshape meanings of race, culture, and family. Parents draw on both local and global sources, crafting identities that are on the one hand flexible and inventive, and on the other, weighed down by historically rooted discourses defining family, race, and cultural difference. While parents' understandings of Chineseness may both be shaped by and reproduce existing power hierarchies and racial meanings, in the process of the everyday parenting of their children, adoptive parents are negotiating broader issues of difference, both racial and cultural, or what Dorow terms "the impossible contradictions of colorblind or even multicultural projects of identity" (2006a, 360).

My project focuses specifically how white and Asian families deal with the attention brought to Chineseness as a form of both racial and cultural difference, and how they imagine the Chineseness of their children both in a midwestern context and in a Pacific Rim city, in relation to blacks, whites, Asians, and other groups. Relationships to China and Chinese culture will differ dramatically for these two groups, as well as within them, shaped by factors such as immigrant generation, location of residence, religious affiliations, exposure to other Chinese and Asian Americans, experiences with China, and ideas about China and Asia more broadly that circulate within popular culture and history. The Asian American adoptive parents I interviewed approached issues of Chinese cultural heritage and race in diverse ways, and this reflects the fact that even the practice of "birth culture" by Chinese Americans who did not adopt from China is highly variable.[2] However, the approaches of Asian American adoptive parents were characterized by a flexibility that stemmed from the fact that as Asian Americans, the authenticity of their practices is not questioned in the same way that the activities of white parents is scrutinized (Jacobson 2008). In reading Chineseness as a form of cultural capital that can be invoked in a variety of ways, we can shift the discussion from viewing Chineseness as an essentialized, biological trait and set of practices and traditions to something that can be understood as a performance and assertion of identity. This is not to say that Chineseness does not include cultural practices and family traditions that have been passed down, nor that the ways that Chinese Americans are racialized as Asian does not affect their daily lives. But Chinese cultural practices are also reinterpreted and recontextualized as they are practiced by each new generation.

An Ethnography of Chineseness and Parenting: Key Themes

Racial and cultural origins of Chinese adoptees are a central focus of their upbringing for many adoptive parents. But where did these concerns originate? And what forms do the cultural and racial identities being fostered in these children take? As noted earlier, concerns about raising a child with a strong sense of identity affect almost all parents. Nevertheless, many scholars and adoption professionals have emphasized the importance of cultivating a sense of racial and cultural identity for adoptees. They, along with adult adoptees, have also expressed concern that adoptive parents' focus on abstracted forms of Chinese culture may make racial difference and the system of inequality within which it is made meaningful less visible to them (Anagnost 2000; Dorow 2006b; Freundlich and Lieberthal 2000).

Thus, three key issues emerge:

1. What conceptions of China and Chinese culture inform the symbolic, flexible, and performative ways with which many adoptive parents construct Chinese culture for their children? For white parents, in what ways do these constructions reflect the position of white privilege from which they approach cultural and racial difference on behalf of their children? For Asian American par-

ents, in what ways do these constructions reflect their "privilege of authenticity"?

2. What are the limits and potentials of these constructions to effectively address issues of cultural and racial identity for children adopted from China? More specifically, how does the focus on cultural construction relate to, or perhaps distract from, attention to issues of race?

3. How do parents and children negotiate, contest, and revise these meanings as they practice Chinese culture in the context of their daily lives? And how do these identities reflect the production of new Asian American forms of culture and identity?

This ethnographic study builds upon the body of important work by scholars who have examined the production of Chinese cultural and racial identities by white adoptive parents (Anagnost 2000; Dorow 2006a, 2006b; Eng 2010; Jacobson 2008). Some studies on adoption are optimistic about new, hybrid forms of identity that these families create as they explore birth cultures, and the work that these cultural productions may do in resolving important adoption-related issues such as the longing for the birth mother (Volkman 2005).[3] Another body of critical social science literature examines the practices of adoptive families within the politics of race and culture in the United States, noting that white parents' performances of Chinese birth culture may exercise a flexibility in constructing identity that their racial minority children may not actually have. Written by academics, adoption professionals, adoptees, and adoptive parents themselves,[4] these works interrogate the broader contexts of power and privilege that shape relations between adoptees and others, including their parents (Anagnost 2000; Dorow 2006a, 2006b; Eng 2003; Shiu 2001). Some works focus specifically on how white adoptive parents deal with issues of "culture-keeping" (Jacobson 2008) and the ways they are positioned within a broader political economy and in relation to ideas circulating about race, gender, and citizenship (Dorow 2006b).

Dorow and Jacobson lay an essential groundwork that enables me to pursue the questions I explore in my own study. Dorow's multisited, ethnographic project focuses on the construction of racial and cultural identity for Chinese adoptees within broader social and historical contexts. She analyzes the political economy of adoption and the narratives surrounding Chinese adoption, focusing on the "impossible contradictions" created by transnational adoption. She astutely observes that regardless of which strategy parents use in creating Chinese identities for their children, "they must all deal with the ghosts of difference and unsettled relationships of power . . . stirred by the dislocations and relocation of their children" (2006b, 32).

She notes that key to parents' approaches to crafting Chinese identities for their children is the "imagined 'flexibility' of Chinese children that figures into adoptive choices" (2006b, 212). Importantly, she asks, "How flexible are they, really? When is there 'too much' difference?" (212). Like Dorow, I explore the contradictions and tensions that arise from transnational adoption and the variety of approaches that parents use to deal with the cultural and racial "difference" of their children. Many of my findings not surprisingly echo Dorow's, particularly those on the ways that these questions may "reflect, reproduce, and potentially challenge" existing power relations (214). However, I am particularly interested in issues of cultural authenticity and processes of cultural production that operate within the cultural and political economy of Chinese adoption that Dorow so nicely lays out. Although I share concerns with those who worry that Chinese culture is being decontextualized or observed in celebratory ways without sufficient attention to historical context, race, or contemporary Chinese communities (Anagnost 2000; Eng 2010), I am also interested in looking at what is being produced out of these often limited representations and understandings of Chineseness.

Jacobson's work on "culture keeping" also employs a methodology that is comparative and ethnographically based, focusing on adoptive parents of children from China and Russia in the Boston area. Her inductive study focuses on how white adoptive mothers' ideas about "culture keeping" are a product of broader societal ideas about race and kinship (Jacobson 2008, 12). Her comparative perspective is important in that it focuses on the adoption of same-race versus transracial adoptions, and the ways that white middle-class mothers' assumptions about how race and ethnicity work shape their approaches to "culture keeping." She argues that white mothers of Chinese adoptees feel compelled to expose their children to a form of birth culture that is also meant to double as a defense against racism. They do this in part because of their perceived loss of their children's Chinese homeland, what she terms an "interrupted ethnic identity" (78), and in part due to their assumptions about the "ethnic expectations" (citing Tuan 1999) that Asian Americans possess rich culture, even those raised by white American parents. She also notes that while parents viewed their children's Chinese identities as fixed and primordial, they also exercised "ethnic options" in how they crafted these identities. In contrast, the parents of Russian adoptees were less compelled to engage in "culture keeping" because they did not feel the same sense of urgency to provide their children with a cultural identity as did parents of children from China.

Jacobson's insightful ethnography covers many of the issues I explore in my own study and provides a valuable framework for understanding what motivates and structures "culture keeping" for white adoptive parents, particularly the way that the racial origins of the child fit in. However, in my research, I bring in a different comparative focus, looking at both white and Asian American parents, in both a midwestern site characterized by white and black racial politics and a West Coast site with a large Asian population. I also look longitudinally at how these conceptions of Chineseness are negotiated by parents and children over time.

Thus, despite there being some overlap with the work of previous China adoption scholars, my positionality and the framing of my study enable me up to focus on different but related questions that build upon and complement their work. Dorow's primary research was conducted beginning in 1998, and though she has done follow-up work, most of the data in her book *Transnational Adoption* (2006b) are based on interviews conducted during that very important period when many families had young children and many more were in the process of adopting. Jacobson's research was conducted during a slightly later period, in 2002–3. My data come from an even later time, from 2001 to 2009, and encompass both parents who had adopted in the middle to late 1990s and those who had just brought their children home. Toward the end of my study in 2009, the rate of new adoptions had begun to slow as waiting times increased. The children who had been six or seven during the early years of my study were now in their teens, and I was able to interview some from this cohort, some of whom I had met earlier when

I interviewed their parents. My study had become longitudinal, necessitated in part by funding issues as well as job and family responsibilities. In many cases, this longitudinal time frame allowed me to talk to some adoptive parents and their children at multiple points in their lives and to gain insight into how identity issues shifted as children grew older and they and their parents gained new experiences, both individually and as a family. While Dorow also interviewed both Asian American and white adoptive parents in both the San Francisco Bay Area and the Midwest, I structured my study more deliberately around a comparison between white and Asian American adoptive parents in these areas and from that vantage point focused on the processes surrounding the construction and negotiation of Chinese cultural identities.

My previous work on renegotiations of "Chineseness" among American-born Chinese American youth involved an exploration of issues of identity construction in the context of changing discourses of race, multiculturalism, and belonging in the United States, and of changing attitudes toward the Chinese abroad in the wake of the Open Policy and Economic Reform (Louie 2004). In many ways, my current study's approach follows my previous inquiries into the construction of Chinese identities as shaped by discourses of family, kinship, and nation. China is a product of the imagination, as a place of origin and ancestral homeland.

China is also very real in its continued influence on Chinese Americans, particularly in the form of discourses created about and by China (Said 1979). In the United States, both past and present, Chinese Americans, whether adopted or not, are often involuntarily associated with China, and much of what they learn about China is filtered through a Western lens. In both studies, I am interested in exploring processes of identity construction and negotiation. However, for Chinese adoptees, relationships to issues of race, ethnicity, and nation are complex and multilayered in a different way than for the nonadopted, American-born Chinese Americans I studied previously. This is in part due to their histories as adoptees but also to the practices of their parents, which, though varied, are enacted in specific ways because of the fact of their adoption.

Background Literature

The second half of this introduction focuses on providing a context for my study by reviewing some of the literature on transnational adoption on China that frames my research and by laying the foundation for my examination of Chinese adoptive families. I discuss the production of new forms of Chinese adoptee identities, with special attention to ideas of Asian cultural authenticity and cultural difference within contemporary racial and multicultural politics. I then examine how these identities are crafted as part of preemptive parenting strategies. Finally, I provide an overview of my use of the concept of ethnic options for both white and Asian American parents and lay out the multilayered (local, national, and transnational) contexts for understanding Asian American cultural production.

White and Asian American Adoptive Parents

At the center of this analysis is a comparison between white and Asian American adoptive parents.[5] Though 92 percent of U.S. parents who adopt internationally are white (Vandivere, Malm, and Radel 2009),[6] as mentioned previously, Asian American adoptive parents are an important comparative group. I investigate the ways that both Chinese American and white adoptive parents engage with issues of Chinese cultural authenticity in different ways, as they draw on local, national, and transnational resources in crafting "Chinese" identities for their children. By more closely examining the experiences of Asian American adoptive parents, we can further examine how they address race and ethnicity in their parenting choices. While I initially began doing ethnographic interviews with white adoptive parents, I soon realized that parents' approaches to crafting Chinese cultural identities were informed in part by their perceptions of how "real" Chinese or Chinese American parents raised their children. Many parents expressed concerns about whether their children would fit into the larger (if imagined and homogenized) Chinese community, whether in China itself or among Chinese immigrants to the United States. They also expressed concern about whether or not children would be raised with a strong sense of Chinese identity, and they believed this sense of identity was important to retain as a form of birth culture. What this Chinese identity should consist of was another question, and this ambiguity only added to the anxiety that many adoptive parents felt about raising their children. This concern stemmed in large part from parents' attention to critiques made by earlier generations of transracial adoptees, many from Korea, regarding their general lack of exposure to information about their countries of birth (Tuan and Shiao 2012).

In my interviews, I found that many Chinese American adoptive parents engaged in practices that essentialized Chineseness. However, because they enjoy the "privilege of authenticity," they exercised more freedom and flexibility in making choices for their children and escaped some of the pressures that white adoptive parents faced. Therefore, examining the ways that Chinese American adoptive families approach culture may help demystify some of the unrealistic standards to which white adoptive parents are being held, or are holding themselves. The comparison of white and Asian American parents' approaches to Chinese identities allows us to further examine how their respective understandings and experiences of racial and cultural difference affect parenting practices. It also allows us to examine assumptions about similarities and differences between Asian American and white communities, particularly in light of the in-between (neither black nor white) racial status of Asians in America (Dorow 2006a; Zhou 2004), and to examine notions of Chinese cultural authenticity circulating in U.S. society.

The Production of Chinese Adoptee Culture and Identities under Multiculturalism

Many adoptive parents, both white and Asian, have engaged in concerted efforts to address both the racial and the cultural aspects of their children's identities. Having sought out resources from adoption experts, fellow parents, adult Korean adoptees, and others, many of today's adoptive parents are engaging in a type of preemptive parenting. They have numerous resources at their disposal, including a growing market (often including goods marketed for and by adoptive parents themselves) of Chinese educational materials (Dorow 2010; Traver 2007), clothing, toys, books, and adoption-related goods. The most active and visible of these parents organize playgroups, guest speaker events, and cultural events.

As Jane Brown, a social worker and white adoptive parent of children from Korea and China who specializes in adoption issues, observes: "Sometimes parents want to celebrate, even exoticize, their child's culture, without really dealing with race. . . . It is one thing to dress children up in cute Chinese dresses, but the children need real contact with Asian-Americans, not just waiters in restaurants on Chinese New Year. And they need real validation about the racial issues they experience" (quoted in Clemetson 2006).

As reflected in Brown's words, in constructing Chinese cultural identities for their minority children, white parents may merely be reproducing the myth of contemporary multiculturalism, which focuses on the celebration of diversity while avoiding issues of white privilege, racial politics, and power. Though the narratives that adoptive parents construct for their children attempt to do the important work of creating a past for the child that connects her to both her birth parents and her adoptive parents, some scholars worry that parents' focus on the visible, commodified aspects of Chinese culture may occur at the expense of more contextualized, deeply rooted understandings of race and power. Anthropologist Ann Anagnost (2000) calls these bits of commodified and decontextualized Chinese culture "culture bites."

Cultural studies scholar David Eng discusses the broader discourses that frame parents' approaches. He argues that in the context of what he terms "neoliberal multiculturalism," "which is based on the rhetoric of choice, the idea of abstract individualism, and the premise of race constantly appearing as disappearing" (Eng 2010, 110), the racial difference of adoptees is "absorbed" or erased within the context of white adoptive families. Eng asserts that Asian adoptees fulfill specific needs for the white families who adopt them, performing what he calls "affective labor" as they help create families and the "feeling of kinship." This "work" stands in contrast to that of previous generations of Asian immigrants who engaged in wage labor (108). According to Eng, the deep losses experienced by adoptees, of "homeland (126), family, language, property, identity, custom, and status, "combined with the inability to mourn these losses within the exclusionary context of U.S. racial politics, lead to a permanent state of "racial melancholia" (126), which he defines as a "psychic condition by which vexed identification and affiliation with lost objects, places, and ideas of Asianness, as well as whiteness, remain unresolved."

Here, Eng is speaking primarily of Korean adoptees, many of whom he encountered as teens or young adults, but he extrapolates his arguments to include young Chinese adoptees today, as in his analysis of the John Hancock commercial showing a lesbian couple bringing their baby home from China. However, while his argument is compelling on many levels, it also presents a rather dismal picture for Asian adoptees, whose racial and cultural origins are largely absorbed and erased within the intimate realm of kinship and family. Furthermore, because he relies more on secondary sources, he does not employ an ethnographically grounded, inductive approach to examine how things may play out both within and outside of the home and over time. Nor does he engage with the ways parents and children may rework discourses of multiculturalism and cosmopolitanism, whiteness and Asianness, family and identity as the children grow older.

In my study, I turn my attention to the ways that these discourses unfold in a variety of ways as they are enacted within parenting strategies and children's responses to them, some of which may reflect more flexible processes of the negotiation of identity production. Will these children have the same vexed relationship to both Asianness and whiteness that some have characterized for Korean adoptees of an earlier generation? Are their Chinese origins being erased or absorbed, or is something else happening?

Anagnost both cautions us about invented, celebratory approaches to cultural difference seen in some of the decontextualized representations of Chinese culture produced by adoptive parents, and points to the ways that this flexibility may represent a potential area for the production of new Chinese adoptee cultures:

> Celebratory representations of cultural difference, which are often detached from immigrant histories in the United States, may not only pose problems for adopted children in developing an understanding of their racialization, but this dehistoricization also maintains the separations that constitute racialized boundaries in US society historically. . . . If constructions of race and culture are contingent processes that are his-

torically open-ended, then we need to consider how current adoption practices do not merely fit in to what is historically given, but in themselves produce race in a new form. This process is rife with possibilities, some of which may be politically progressive in exploring the problem of identity and difference, but it also presents the danger of producing it anew. (2000, 390, 412–13)[7]

The tension between the reproduction of existing racial structures versus the potential for "politically progressive" change that Anagnost points out is one that is carried throughout this book. In noting its "ever-widening circulation as a powerful discursive tool," Anagnost also asks, "What is at stake and who is empowered when culture is invoked?" (2000, 412–13). Another way to frame this question is to ask how we can move beyond rigid ideas about Chinese cultural authenticity to acknowledge culture's potential to both reproduce and transform existing structures.

To further understand what the future may hold for Chinese adoptees and their families, it is important to ask how, why, and for whom "Chineseness" is produced, and investigate how formations of Chineseness play out within the context of family, community, and nation. While these productions may be framed by white privilege and Orientalism, it is nevertheless necessary to more fully examine how the constructions of Chinese culture and identity created by white adoptive parents can shed light on the broader dynamic between race and culture, whiteness and Chineseness. After all, how can we understand the multifaceted nature of whiteness and the modes of power within which it operates without looking at productions of Chineseness crafted in relation to it? These productions are not mutually exclusive, particularly if we consider that adoptees' identities are being integrated into those of their adoptive families. However, few studies of whiteness or adoption have examined Chineseness, and I assert that by examining productions of Chineseness and Asianness by Asian American adoptive parents, we can gain comparative perspective on the relationships between parenting, ethnic and racial identity, and adoption.

Rebecca Chiyoko King-O'Riain's work on mixed-race Japanese American beauty contestants shows that these young women continue to be affected by notions of race both as whiteness and as "Japanese

Americanness," and that these ideas of race as both social and biological are enmeshed with ideas about gender and ethnicity (2006, 33). She addresses the ways that these young women who wish to gain access to Japanese American cultural capital through claiming Japanese American identities negotiate meanings of "race" and "culture." Though as mixed-raced individuals their racial legitimacy is sometimes questioned, they engage in "race work"—a series of social actions related to "deportment, dress, action, language, food practices, accent" (23)—to perform their Japanese identities.

Though Chinese adoptees are usually perceived to be phenotypically Chinese, their parents and others may ascribe to them both racial and cultural characteristics based on their Chinese origins, which are also imagined as both racial and cultural. This "race work" is performed by parents, and others, on their behalf, with the hope that it will enable adoptees to fit into an imagined Chinese or Chinese American community. Notions of race as whiteness and Chineseness/Chinese American-ness thus affect them in ways similar to those that affected the young women in King-O'Riain's study. They may identify with the white culture (and perhaps the racial phenotype) of their white parents but also may view Chineseness as a form of cultural capital in which they can selectively participate.

Ethnic Options?

Most white ethnics, including white adoptive parents, think of race and ethnicity as separate from one another. They are used to viewing ethnic identity as something that can be crafted as one chooses, and race as something that they themselves do not have. However, the idea of ethnic options works in different ways for white and Asian American adoptive parents.

Mary Waters (1990) originally developed the term "ethnic options" to describe the flexibility with which white ethnics approach ethnicity, with the ability to pick and choose aspects to display as forms of symbolic ethnicity. According to Waters, white ethnics perform practices that symbolically represent the aspect(s) of the cultural heritage with which they choose to identify. For example, Irish Americans may eat corned beef and cabbage or wear green on Saint Patrick's Day because these practices effectively represent Irish culture in the context of the United States.[8] But Waters emphasizes that while white ethnics have the luxury to choose these representations of their heritage, and where and when to perform them, racial minorities do not. Rather, their "racial" features connect them to historical legacies of racism and oppression, which may leave them few options for selectively creating and displaying ethnic and racial identities. In a later piece, Waters observes how many white ethnics tend to attribute the flexibility that they are able to exercise as white ethnics to racial minorities, thus conflating racial and ethnic differences:

> The symbolic (white) ethnic tends to think that all groups are equal; everyone has a background that is their right to celebrate and pass on to their children. This leads to the conclusion that all identities are equal and all identities in some sense are interchangeable—"I'm Italian-American, you're Polish-American. I'm Irish-American, you're African-American." (1996, 449, quoted in Song 2003, 15)

However, while it is a privilege for white parents to be able to consider their racial and ethnic identities as separate, for their racial minority children, these identities are inextricably intertwined.

So what happens when the dimension of transracial adoption is added in, with white parents adopting nonwhite children? How might the idea of ethnic options apply to white adoptive parents who are used to having options in thinking about and enacting their ethnic identities?

It is important to consider how the concept of ethnic options works within new contexts, as whites embrace nonwhite identities, whether more generally or in the context of transnational adoption, and as they use their privilege for the production of what they view as cosmopolitan identities. In other words, the terms have changed for white ethnics who are crafting their relationships in response to multiple factors, both within the family and beyond.

As discussed previously, Heather Jacobson's research examines how white middle-class mothers in Boston both attributed an essentialized sense of Chineseness to their children adopted from China and also exercised flexibility in how they symbolically implemented Chinese culture in the home. Building upon the work of other scholars on symbolic ethnicity, Amy Traver similarly focuses on the relationship between the symbolic approach of white ethnics toward their identities and the application of those ideas to their nonwhite children in the context of Chinese adoption. Citing an earlier source by Waters (2004), she notes that "whites tend to interpret all ethno-cultural/ethno-racial identifications through a symbolic ethnic lens" (Traver 2007, 211). Traver links the consumption practices of white adoptive parents to both their tendency to celebrate diversity through the consumption and display of "ethnic" objects and the positionality of adoptive mothers seeking to gain legitimacy as mothers in the absence of a biological child. She also demonstrates how race continues to structure these practices that parents often think of in ethnic terms. My research also shows that white parents to some extent try to follow the same flexible approaches to crafting identities with their transracially adopted children, even as they are earnestly trying to address their "difference." Unlike previous eras in which racial and cultural difference was not as readily acknowledged, these parents are raising their children during a time when this exposure to and acknowledgment of racial and cultural difference are seen as necessary and positive by many people. White adoptive parents apply a parenting strategy that is shaped both by the privilege of exercising ethnic options that they are used to employing and by their conceptions of what Chinese culture is and how both cultural and racialized identities are acquired and enacted. However, given the differences in the ways that ethnic options apply to nonwhites, and their understandably incomplete information about the ways that ideas about Chinese and Chinese American culture and race operate in U.S. society, they may run up against limitations in their ability to fully exercise their ideas about cultural and racial difference. Dorow writes: "I have said that race 'condensed' the range of cultural identity possibilities parents imagined, and by that I mean that race constrains the imagined free play of ethnic options" (2006b, 235–36). She also notes that transnational adoption may expose parents to experiences that may lead them to think about race and inequality in new ways.

But what ethnic options are available for Asian American adoptive parents of children from China who racially "match" their children? In providing background for the culture-keeping activities of white adoptive parents, Jacobson cites research on how women of color in the

United States engage in their children's ethnic socialization while also attempting to create "racially safe" (2008, 62) environments for their children. Biological mothers of white children, however, are used to exercising much more flexibility in the environments they construct for their children. They do not have to worry about their "racial safety" and are able to pick and choose from a variety of elements of ethnic identity (63). So what about Asian American adoptive parents of children from China? Do they engage in similar strategies of ethnic socialization and racial safety? Jacobson observes that white parents who adopted from Russia enjoy what she calls "biological privilege" (158), referring to the privilege not only of being able to give birth to biological children but also of appearing to be the biological parent of a child. As I discuss further in chapter 4, the biological privilege of Asian American adoptive parents of children from Asia allows them to also exercise their "privilege of authenticity" in terms of their flexibility in constructing racial and cultural identities for their children. Does this mean that they are employing ethnic options in the same way that white parents of white adopted children or white ethnics as a whole do?

Sociologist Miri Song has explored the question of whether racial minorities are indeed able to exercise some degree of ethnic options. Based on a comparative analysis of racial and ethnic politics in the United States and Britain, Song concludes:

> Ethnic minority individuals and groups can exercise some degree of agency and control in their assertion of ethnic identities, including claims to belonging within the nation, on their own terms. Although significant constraints structure these processes, the conscious and deliberate choices made by minority groups and individuals regarding their ethnic identities have tended to be overlooked, particularly in the USA, where there is much emphasis on the dynamics of racial assignment by the broader society. . . . Minorities do have some ethnic options, but these can differ across and within groups—for example, according to class, length of settlement, and gender. (2003, 142)

In my ethnographic discussion of Asian American adoptive parents, I show the varied ways that constructions of Chinese and Asian culture are (often strategically) cultivated or flexibly employed in parenting their children and shaping their identities. Echoing Song's findings, these efforts reflect broader processes of how Asian Americans rework their identities throughout their life course, including changing relationships to their families of origin and conceptions of what it means to be Chinese American, and changing relationships to China and America. However, because of my focus on adoption, I look at what unfolds in the intimate realm of family identity and at individual expressions of identity.

Finally, there is the important question of how adopted children exercise options in expressing both their racial and cultural identities as Chinese. In demonstrating that ethnic options exist for racial minorities (and therefore that both race and ethnicity factor into how they identify), Song calls for a broader conceptualization of ethnicity, moving beyond the equation of ethnicity with "ethnic origins and heritage" (2003, 32) to something that takes into account "ethnic labels and images" as being "rather ambiguous, or inflected in changeable ways" (36).

The potentially contested nature of ethnic identities is key to the question of how Chinese adoptees, along with Asian Americans more generally, can exercise agency in creating and claiming new forms of identity that may serve to define new group boundaries and challenge existing notions of both racial and ethnic identity. This idea of ethnicity (and race) as multifaceted and a basis for politicized identities is also consistent with Lisa Lowe's (1996) model of Asian American cultural production, which I use to frame my discussion of Asian American cultural production later in this book. Within this context, Chineseness, as crafted and recrafted in specific ways by Chinese adoptees, can become something over which they have some control in defining, rather than remaining an identity that is merely ascribed to them, often with negative connotations. Writing more generally of racial minorities, Song observes that we should examine how "the possession (or lack) of cultural capital . . . has mediated groups' range of ethnic options, as well as their selective inclusion and exclusion across many social contexts" (2003, 40). I explore the processes through which ethnic options are constrained and exercised within a broader politics of race and multiculturalism, both locally and globally, in the following section.

Preemptive Parenting and Asian Difference

Today's negotiations of identity by adoptive parents are marked by a preemptive and proactive quality. Like all parents, they make conscious choices regarding their children's friends, schools, and extracurricular activities. My ethnographic findings show that many families who adopt from China are actively creating new forms of Chinese American culture—and new forms of Chinese adoptee culture—that play out within a broader nexus of race, culture, and adoption.[9] Many white adoptive parents are finding that they need to address issues of both race and culture in ways they have not had to do previously. Having accepted the color-blind discourses that have come to define approaches to both race and culture in the United States (Bonilla-Silva 2009), some adoptive parents, like National Public Radio's *Morning Edition* host Scott Simon (2010), claim that the color of Chinese adoptee children's skin and their "ethnicity" do not matter. In this case, as with color blindness more generally, racial and ethnic difference are seen as one in the same, and as not playing a role in how an individual is treated. But for many parents, experiences with their nonwhite children and the advice of adoption advocates have pushed them to go beyond these color-blind approaches that they fear overlook culture, power, and race (Steinberg and Hall 2000; Register 2005).

Parents who adopt from China, whether of white or Asian background, must grapple with the tension between embracing and managing the "difference" of their children. While what this "difference" means may differ from family to family, all adoptive parents engage in reimagining themselves as a family upon adopting their children while simultaneously reworking their own identities in relation to the presence of "difference" in their lives (Dorow 2006b; Jacobson 2008; Volkman 2005). They are reminded in a variety of ways of the "difference" of their children and of their families as a whole. The adoption process scrutinizes parents' backgrounds, while the trip to China, during which parents complete adoption paperwork for the Chinese and the U.S. governments, encourages parents to experience "Chinese culture" through touring local sites and purchasing souvenirs. For transracial families, their visibility as adoptive families, beginning in China and continuing into their everyday lives in the United States, often means that they face intrusive questions about the origins of their children ("Where did you get her?" "Isn't she lucky that you saved her?" "Are they real sisters?" "How much did she cost?"). Furthermore, the Orientalist lens through which the West has historically conceived of the East also shapes the ways adoptive parents and others, whether white or Asian American, view their children's origins. As discussed in Edward Said's classic work *Orientalism* (1979), rather than merely constituting an objectively defined geographic location, an examination of the history of ideas about the East, produced in and by the West, illustrates how the East has been constructed as simultaneously exotic, mysterious, dangerous, and "Other" to the West. These ideas about the difference of the East have been used to justify attempts to tame or control that region (Said 1979; Rana 2011; Maira 2009) and have also framed the portrayal of people in the region in ways that are often highly gendered.

In the U.S. context, the emphasis of these discourses has shifted over time. During the Chinese exclusion era, they stressed the idea of a "Yellow Peril" (Tchen and Yeats 2014) to justify immigration restrictions in the form of the Chinese Exclusion Act (1882–1943) based on Chinese people's unassimilable and barbarian nature (R. Lee 1999). During the Cold War, China was seen as a communist threat to U.S. democracy, forcing Chinese Americans to disassociate themselves from China (R. Lee 1999). Contemporary discourses about "the East" have become even more complex as these widely circulating ideas about Asian difference coexist with the celebration of and fascination with Asian popular culture. The spread of "Asian" culture, from food to popular culture (kung fu films, Japanese anime, Hello Kitty), to opportunities to learn "Asian" languages, is facilitated by transnational media flows and a general increased openness to exploring Asian things. However, this exploration can also overlap with new forms of Orientalism, as part of the appeal derives from how these things represent forms of often exotic or mysterious Asian difference. And this positive interest coexists with continued portrayals of the East as a threat to the West, whether in the form of terrorist threats from Asian Muslims (Maira 2009; Rana 2011), the outsourcing of jobs from the United States to Asia, Asian economic competition, or even the threat of new immigrants and international students from Asia arriving on U.S. soil. These ideas are often reinforced by stereotypes that portray Asians as perpetual foreigners, a new form of Yellow Peril, or an "Asian invasion."

Given the numerous and contradictory messages about Asia that circulate daily and on a number of levels through the lives of U.S. adoptive parents and their children, it is not surprising that parents might try to control what children see and how they experience "Chineseness" as a form of protection. In this context, Asian "difference" is seemingly knowable but also frighteningly unknowable. In Dorow's words, Asian adoptees are "at once strange and familiar, different yet knowable" (2006b, 56).

Ironically, while parents may wish to control what their children see and experience in terms of information about Asia and Asian people, while these very images continue to shape their productions of Chinese identity for their children, and their ideas about what it means to be a "different" kind of family more broadly. Despite the fact that they may "match" racially, even Asian American parents may view their children as being different by virtue of their history, having been born in Asia under circumstances much different than their own family backgrounds and thus having particular ties and unanswered questions relating to these origins (Dorow 2006b). While they may exercise a certain degree of flexibility in how they practice Chinese culture, most adoptive parents remain aware that their children have direct connections to China that may need to be addressed. On the one hand, these direct connections may provide exciting opportunities to connect with Chinese and Chinese American culture and people in new ways; on the other hand, they may represent something that differentiates parents from their children and in that sense threatens the coherence of family identity.

Images and stereotypes about Chinese adoption provide an additional layer of complexity, as these also circulate widely in the U.S. media and are therefore easily accessible to parents and to their children as they grow older. These stereotypes may also heighten perceived differences between adoptive parents and their children. They include misunderstandings of the one-child policy itself, why the Chinese government implemented it, and what the high rate of infant abandonment of females reflects regarding the status of girls and women in Chinese society. Wanting to portray adoption in a positive light, some adoptive parents may perpetuate ideas about an oppressive Chinese government and a society that does not value girls or orphans in providing explanations for why birth parents may not have been able to raise them. In many cases, parents may believe these ideas to be true. What becomes challenging for parents is how to manage these ideas of Asian difference in order to protect their children, yet also ensure that children remain aware of their origins. On the one hand, in public discourses, Chinese children are seen as exotic, desirable, and sometimes in need of rescue (Dorow 2006a); on the other, they are seen as children whose difference must be managed so that they can be incorporated into their adoptive family households. In light of increasing contact within China and Asia more broadly in the context of globalization, and their own experiences traveling to China as part of the adoption process, parents begin to engage in the process of reimagining the West in relation to the East. Parents may even see the new connections to the East that adoption creates as providing them with opportunities to participate in a cosmopolitan world (Werbner 2009) rather than, as some parents I interviewed mentioned, remaining generically white. Adoptive parents may be more attentive to parenting because of the public scrutiny their children receive as visibly adopted children who are part of adoptive transracial families (Jacobson 2008).[10] These tensions between embracing and controlling the difference that their children represent come to the fore in both daily family activities and broader process of identity negotiation faced by both parents and children. For example, as I discuss in chapter 6, parents place importance on fostering a sense of familial ethnic identity in their children, along with a sense of Chinese origins. This can play out in multiple ways and reflects the challenges of how to instill a healthy and prideful identity in a child, particularly one, in the case of transnational and transracial adoption, that parents themselves do not entirely share. This issue was highlighted in a New York Times video feature on the Cough family in Maine, which touched upon both parents' and children's attitudes toward Chinese culture activities. The video showed the children's attitudes toward Chinese school and dance to be varied, with one daughter embracing these activities but admitting that she still only feels "Chinese on the inside," and the other expressing her dislike for Chinese school and dance (Mak 2014). And as illustrated by my ethnographic interviews with both white and Asian American adoptive parents, while identity-making practices initially reflect parents' own conceptions of how they identify with China and Chinese culture, and their conceptions of race and culture, they continue to evolve over time.

As adoptive parents engage in the process of exploring "difference" and in reevaluating their own, they are reimagining themselves in relation to both their nonwhite children and a cosmopolitan, multicultural world to which many feel their children are giving them access. Cosmopolitanism is an ideal that encapsulates cross-cultural exchange and worldliness that goes beyond previous models of multiculturalism and diversity in its global scope, yet localized execution (Werbner 2009). Cosmopolitanism enables adoptive parents not only to imagine themselves as attached to other parts of the globe through their adopted children but also to take steps to craft these connections. Adoptive parents have formed charities that work to improve conditions in Chinese orphanages by bringing in Western educational techniques, volunteers, goods, and capital.

Parents enroll their children in Chinese language classes and sometimes learn Chinese themselves with the idea that it will expand their ability to communicate with Chinese people, with many parents citing the utility of knowing Chinese in the twenty-first-century global world. Both Asian American and white parents draw flexibly and creatively on a variety of resources and connections, both local and nonlocal, in shaping and justifying their approaches to crafting Chinese identities for their children and to some extent for themselves as well. Within these cosmopolitan imaginaries, adoptive parents can flexibly interpret how activities such as dining out at a Chinese restaurant, purchasing Chinese decorations, befriending Chinese and Chinese American people, traveling to China, or even visiting Chinatown contribute to their child's Chineseness. But while this flexibility is potentially liberating, on some level it is also disconcerting from an outsider's perspective because it signifies the degree of control that parents have in not only shaping but to some extent interpreting their children's worlds. Again, while this is not unique to white adoptive parents or to adoptive parents in general, for white adoptive parents who adopt from China, this may at times involve co-opting or at least selectively drawing from cultures that are not entirely their own. Asian American parents can selectively draw upon elements of their family "traditions" and bring in new ones as described earlier; they are backed by their "privilege of authenticity" that enables them to appear to seamlessly incorporate new traditions into their lives. As discussed earlier, this flexibility stems in part from their ability to interpret whatever they do as "Chinese," but also from the fact that they may not feel as much pressure to demonstrate their "Chineseness."

Both white and Asian American adoptive parents are working with and responding to external discourses about family, culture, Chineseness, adoption, and difference. Much of this work takes place within the context of the home, and in this sense often in private and isolated ways. In his analysis of the "racial forgetting" in transnational and transracial adoption, David Eng (2010) notes that adopted children can be seen as fulfilling a labor of intimacy for their parents, for whom the adoption of children enables them to complete their nuclear family. Simultaneously, their children's difference is sacrificed, as they are made to forget their origins and, more specifically, their racial difference. While this is a compelling model to explain the dynamics of what Eng calls "queer liberalism" and the broader context of neoliberalism within which it is crafted, I believe there are other ways of taking into account the complicated tension between achieving intimacy within the family and handling the "difference" of transnationally or transracially adopted children.

To more fully understand the factors that shape the production and negotiation of identities in today's adoptive families, it is necessary to consider Chineseness not as a naturalized or inherited form of identity but as a form of cultural capital that parents try to cultivate for their children in light of multiple factors. Many parents viewed Chineseness not only as a cultural and possibly a racial identity but also as a form of potential cultural capital in a cosmopolitan world. Chineseness has become a highly charged and multivalent symbol and form of identity, something that both adoptees and their parents try to carefully craft and manage. I suggest that on a certain level, some parents may see developing this form of Chineseness as a means of shaping or controlling the Chineseness of their children. Both white and Asian American adoptive parents engaged in these processes to different degrees, and in different ways, because of their different relationships to Chineseness. Chineseness carries its own weight as a generic term standing for all Asians,[11] and thus encompasses a powerful set of stereotypes.

For white adoptive parents, ideas about what it means to be white or Chinese have been shaped by models of racial and cultural diversity that circulate within broader U.S. culture but that also encompass global flows of information. However, these models are limited in terms of their ability to encompass the coexistence of multiple racial and ethnic identities within both individuals and families, that is, if these differences are recognized at all. The pervasive discourses of color blindness and the "melting pot" tell us that race and ethnicity no longer matter because we are all becoming part of a blended culture. But it has become clear that race and ethnicity do not disappear. As discussed earlier, in connection with the idea of ethnic options, models of multiculturalism emphasize ethnicity as a choice, something that can be explored and cultivated. These approaches easily slot into neoliberal identity projects that broaden the scope of identity production to a global scale, making the incorporation of Chinese adoptees into U.S. families apparently even more seamless and emphasizing the ability of the individual to engage in such projects. These celebratory approaches often push race or other structural factors aside, as the responsibility for the "self-fashioning" of identity is placed on the individual, further rendering the broader social, cultural, and historical contexts that shape them invisible (Zhang and Ong 2008). But what differentiates the negotiation of adoptive family identities from other projects of identity formation is that parents are attempting to understand and negotiate notions of "difference" while also incorporating this difference into their family identities. They must negotiate contradictions between the idea that identity projects are driven by internally constructed choices that one can craft for oneself and one's children (Bondi 1993), and the powerful societal discourses about race, gender, family, and adoption that actively shape these identities. The same global flows that allow parents access to the information about China, Chinese culture, and international adoption that they selectively use in these processes of reshaping their own and their families' identities also have much broader ramifications for how these identities will play out in everyday life and over time.

The adoption of children from China into U.S. families has implications for the future of U.S. racial and cultural diversity, as it plays out on an everyday cultural level in the ways that parents and children experience, interpret, and reshape meanings of race, culture, and family. Parents draw on both local and global sources, crafting identities that are, on the one hand flexible and inventive and, on the other, weighed down by historically rooted discourses defining family, race, and cultural difference. While parents' understandings of Chineseness may both be shaped by and reproduce existing power hierarchies and racial meanings, in the process of the everyday parenting of their children, adoptive parents are negotiating broader issues of difference, both racial and cultural. We need to consider how white and Asian families deal with the attention brought to Chineseness as a form of both racial and cultural difference, and how they imagine the Chineseness of their children both in a midwestern context and in a Pacific Rim city, in relation to blacks, whites, Asians, and other groups.

A Background on Transnational and Transracial Adoption

My Ethnographic Study

This book is based on ethnographic interviews and extensive participant observation and focus group discussions with more than seventy-five individuals conducted intermittently over an eight-year period (2001–9), representing white adoptive parents, adoption professionals, Chinese American adoptive parents, and teens adopted from China in St. Louis, Missouri, and in the San Francisco Bay Area.[1] I examine the processes by which Chineseness and Chinese culture are negotiated by adoptive parents within the politics of race, class, and culture of the Midwest, an area that I argue represents the majority of the United States, and also in the San Francisco Bay Area, an area that prides itself on its cultural diversity and where I interviewed the majority of the Asian American adoptive parents in my sample.

I conducted participant observation at more than twenty adoption-related events, including playgroups, adoption agency events, Families with Children from China (FCC) events, and other small gatherings and informal dinners with families. In 2002, I accompanied a group of adoptive parents to China when they traveled there to meet their children. I also conducted approximately six focus groups or informal group discussions in both locations, sometimes in the form of Parents' Night Out gatherings in which I led open-ended discussions with parents on a variety of topics, from cultural identity to parents' concerns about attachment issues. Finally, I have followed China adoption narratives and videos, as well as Internet data (blogs, organization websites, personal websites, and Facebook pages).

Research trips to St. Louis ranged in length from a week to two months in 2001, 2004, and 2009. The San Francisco Bay Area portion of the research took place primarily in 2006 and 2008, with trips ranging in length from ten days to one month. In both cases, interviewees were recruited through e-mail announcements that were circulated among local adoption communities through parent organizations such as FCC and other groups that focus on transnational adoption. Snowball sampling was employed, with interviewees recommending others who might be willing to speak with me. I also met additional families through attending local adoption agency or Chinese Culture Day events, and through giving talks in the area.[2] Because the Bay Area portion of the research was initiated later during my project (though I had done some preliminary interviews there in 2000), the majority of my interviews there focused on Chinese American or Asian American parents and on families with teens. However, I did interview white adoptive parents in the Bay Area and interacted with them extensively during the numerous talks I gave or at events such as playgroups where I conducted participant observation.

Because adoptions from China to the United States greatly increased around 1995, after China's adoption system was restructured to facilitate international adoptions, in the early years of my study, the majority of the children were around seven years or younger, and therefore too young to be interviewed for the study. Over the years, I had multiple opportunities to interact with families and do participant observation at various events, both formal and informal. In some cases, I was able to interact with the same families over a number of years, interviewing some two or three times, with later interviews also including conversations with their teenage children. In other cases, I met and interviewed adoptive parents and their teenage children for the first time without having previously met the children when they were younger. My primary research method involved open-ended, semistructured interviews, in which individuals were asked to provide their adoption stories and discuss issues of racial and cultural identity regarding themselves, their children, and their families as a whole. Despite the flexibility of the interview process, which was designed to make interviewees comfortable and able to share issues in a more natural and spontaneous manner, I made sure to cover the same topics in each interview. Interviews conducted with teens, aged thirteen to seventeen, took place without parents being present and focused more broadly on teen identities. I asked them questions about how they viewed themselves in relation to Chinese and other cultural influences, and questioned them about experiences related to their racial backgrounds.

In the sense that my project was a multisited study of a dispersed "community," it represented a challenging and nontraditional form of ethnography. Although no community is ever completely bounded, I found that a particular challenge of this fieldwork was understanding how knowledge circulated and networks formed within this dispersed "community" and how families differentially negotiated these broader pressures within their evolving family culture and values. While they may share the experience of adopting and raising a child from China, it is difficult to call the Chinese adoptive families a "community." They may interact with one another only at particular moments and on a variety of levels, sometimes only at FCC events or on Internet forums, or sometimes as part of deeper, long-term friendships. Some members of the "community" may not associate with others at all, and in this sense the Chinese adoption community is not a cohesive one that interacts on a regular basis or even participates in the same activities. At times adoptive parents may work in cooperation with one another in adoptive parent organizations, but at other times they may be responding to fears or concerns generated by one another and shared through a discussion board, panel, or other events. This made the logistics of fieldwork challenging. Besides attending specific group events and analyzing newsletters and discussion board content, I conducted my fieldwork primarily through individual interviews with adoptive parents, in which they discussed issues specific to their family situations, and participant observation in more informal settings.

A Chinese American Anthropologist Studying Chinese Identity

When interviewing white adoptive parents in St. Louis about their attitudes toward teaching their child or children about China and Chinese culture, I introduced myself as a Chinese American academic interested in adoption issues. I attended numerous adoption-related events and was often the only nonparent present. As a Chinese American researcher with expertise in China and Chinese Americans, I occupied a liminal position in relation to parents and their children (Turner 1967). Like the children, I was a person of Chinese descent, raised in the United States. Like the parents, I was an adult, but though I was old enough to be a parent, I was not yet one. Because most of the adoptive parents were white,

I was often one of a handful of adult Chinese present at these events; the others were usually first-generation immigrants who were adoption agency workers or people from the local community who taught the children about Chinese culture or language.

During research interviews, I wondered whether I was unintentionally influencing parents' thinking about issues of Chinese and Chinese American culture, as well as adoption issues. As I asked parents to tell their adoption stories and discuss whether, how, and why they would or would not teach their children about China and Chinese culture, I realized that by framing my questions in relation to China and Chinese culture, I was to some extent shaping the context for their storytelling. Many parents thanked me for the chance to think and talk about issues that they previously may not have had a chance to directly address.

I remember saying hello to nine-year-old Sarah Martello when I arrived at her home for my interview. Her parents had explained to Sarah that I was there to talk about Chinese culture. She asked what my name was, and when I replied "Andrea," she said, "Andrea, that's not a Chinese name." Her parents said, "Neither is Sarah." She responded, "But I have a Chinese name." I did not mention this to Sarah, but I also have a Chinese name. Though I did not interview Sarah herself, because I was not then interviewing children as part of my research, my interaction with her touched on an issue that came up repeatedly throughout my fieldwork: the question of how my background as a Chinese American may have affected the interactions that constituted my research. I often speculated whether, as a Chinese American scholar of China, Chinese Americans, and adoption issues, my questions may have seemed "loaded" to parents. What types of answers might I expect to receive when I asked adoptive parents about teaching their children about China and Chinese culture? Knowing my background, might parents (over)emphasize the amount of attention they give to Chinese culture? Of course, parents who were not interested in these issues probably would not want to talk to a researcher, particularly one with my "Chinese" background.[3] However, my presence and presentation of self may have figured into or refigured adoptive parents' conceptions of what a Chinese person may be like. Most adoptive parents I interviewed appeared to construct their notions of Chineseness for their children in reference to other Chinese or Chinese Americans they knew, and also in relation to media and popular culture portrayals of Chinese and Chinese Americans.[4] Though I was not central to their lives, I wondered how I might fit into the picture, particularly as someone who, as Sarah noted, did not seem all that Chinese.

My intervention into parents' constructions of Chinese culture was more direct in other ways. At various points in my research, I participated in informal Parents' Night Out conversations, hosted by local adoptive families, on Chinese culture or on similarities between the experiences of Chinese adoptees and Chinese Americans more broadly. Though these discussions were open-ended and informal, I saw them as an opportunity to reciprocate the parents' assistance by sharing some of my knowledge and viewpoints on issues related to Chinese and Chinese American culture. In one discussion I introduced parents to the model minority and perpetual foreigner stereotypes and discussed my views about the flexibility of Chinese culture.[5] I also contributed an article on my research to a local Chinese American newspaper in St. Louis.

During my research trip to China, parents would sometimes ask me questions: Would their daughter be eligible for scholarships for minorities in the United States, even though her parents were white? How did I define Chinese "culture"? What did I think of the one-child policy? Would China remain united in the future? Some parents asked me how I felt about my experiences with the group, or what my favorite part of the trip had been. In sharing this information with parents, I often wondered whether I was unintentionally influencing their perspectives by sharing my anthropological views regarding the changing and variable nature of Chinese culture in China and abroad (Cohen 1994). Some asked questions specifically about me: about my research, where I went to school, whether I spoke Chinese. Some questions were more personal: Was I married? Did I have children? (No.) Was I thinking of having children? (Yes, perhaps someday.) I shared that my husband was half Chinese and half white but had been raised in El Salvador speaking Spanish and English, but no Chinese. I mentioned that if we became parents, we would most likely teach our child Spanish, a language in which my husband was fluent, rather than Chinese. Again, I wondered whether my positionality, as manifested in my personal relationships and the flexible and sometimes unconventional forms of Chinese culture they represented, were in some ways shaping parents' conceptions of Chinese culture. Did the fact that I spoke some Chinese reinforce the importance of teaching their children to speak Mandarin? Did my lack of total fluency convince them of the need for more comprehensive language training? Or did the fact that I did not grow up speaking Chinese open parents to the possibility that not all Chinese Americans actually speak Chinese at home?

A Midwestern Field Site

Having discussed my methods and positionality, in this section, I would like to delve further into the specifics of my field sites. My choice of St. Louis as a research location was the result of a fortuitous set of circumstances. While on a postdoctoral fellowship at Washington University, St. Louis, in 1997 and 1998, I came to know some local adoptive families and was asked to speak on a panel at a local adoption agency on Chinese American culture and identity, along with journalist Mei-Ling Hopgood.[6] After completing my postdoc, I decided to return to St. Louis to develop my project on Chinese adoption.

While most adoptive parents in St. Louis were white, middle-class, and originally from the Midwest, there was some diversity in terms of age and family type among the parents I interviewed. Some were older parents in their late forties or fifties who had married or remarried later in life. Some families had biological children in addition to adopted children, and in some cases the biological child was much older (fifteen to twenty years) than the adopted child or children. Many families had adopted children from other countries or with other "racial" and ethnic backgrounds in addition to China, often from Vietnam or Korea. Some of the parents were medical doctors, while others held PhDs. Adoptive parents also worked as businesspeople, military personnel, and store managers. Their homes ranged from two-bedroom apartments to spacious, newly built houses. Some adoptive families told me that they had made conscious efforts to live in more racially diverse areas such as the city of St. Louis or University City, but most lived in majority-white middle-class suburbs. The divide between "city" and "county" was something that came up in many interviews and general conversations with St. Louisans, with "city" often serving as code for lower-income, nonwhite neighborhoods, and "county" for wealthier, predominantly white areas.

As a midsize midwestern city, St. Louis may in many ways be more representative of the experiences of the majority of adopted children from China than are large, highly diverse metropolitan areas such as the Bay Area or New York. And while St. Louis may not have as many resources about and connections to China as do larger metropolitan regions, it does have a visible Chinese population with historical roots in the area. According to Huping Ling (2004, 2), unofficial estimates place the dispersed Chinese "cultural community" in the greater St. Louis area at between 15,000 and 20,000 people. She notes that the lack of a Chinatown after 1966 resulted in the creation of a primarily suburban and professional Chinese "cultural community," observing that "by 1990, 80 percent of the Chinese in the St. Louis region who were working were either professionals or entrepreneurs. . . . Also by that time, 83 percent of the Chinese in the St. Louis region were living in the suburbs" (17). St. Louis is additionally marked by its black-white race relations. According to the 2000 U.S. census, the population of the city of St. Louis was 43.8 percent white, 51.2 percent black, 3.6 percent Hispanic and Latino, and 2.0 percent Asian. In contrast, the population of the St. Louis counties was 73.5 percent white, 21.8 percent black, 3.7 percent Hispanic or Latino, and 3.0 percent Asian.[7] These statistics reflect not only the racial segregation between city and county but also the primarily black and white racial politics of the area, with Asians representing only 1.5 percent of the total population of Missouri. In 2012, the population of the city of St. Louis was 45.9 percent white, 48.5 percent black, and 3.0 percent Asian, while the counties were 83.9 percent white, 11.7 percent black, and 1.8 percent Asian (U.S. Census Bureau 2012).

This study's ethnographic focus on the Midwest makes a contribution to the Asian American studies literature (E. Lee 2009) by providing a more nuanced and complex view of the processes by and contexts within which identities of middle-class white midwesterners are both maintained and challenged through the experience of adoption. The Midwest is often viewed as a homogeneous cultural desert, in contrast to larger metropolitan areas on the coasts, with the implication being that midwestern adoptive parents may have fewer resources upon which to draw in creating a sense of Chinese community for their children. However, as a region characterized by black-white race and power relations, largely segregated residential patterns, and scattered Chinese American populations, the Midwest is representative of the context in which the majority of Chinese children adopted into white families live, in communities that, unlike San Francisco or New York, are not home to large numbers of Asian Americans.

Aside from small strips of Chinese stores and restaurants in more urban areas such as Olive Street in St. Louis County, not far from the St. Louis city border, and on Grand Street in St. Louis, the Chinese "cultural community" was spread throughout the surrounding suburbs. Churches and Chinese schools served as gathering places for many local Chinese Americans. There were two Chinese language newspapers in St. Louis, a local chapter of the Organization of Chinese Americans (OCA), and groups that organized special events such as the Chinese New Year celebration and the annual Chinese Culture Days (usually in mid-May) at the Missouri Botanical Garden.[8] Many of the children adopted from China attended language classes either at the Taiwanese-run St. Louis Chinese Language School, which offered Chinese language classes for English speakers, or through private lessons from local Chinese teachers. Many adoptive parents made efforts to attend community cultural events and to patronize local Chinese restaurants to expose their children to Chinese food.[9] In other words, although Chinese culture was accessible, it was also something that parents had to consciously seek out. In contrast, the unusual demographics of the San Francisco Bay Area, where I also carried out adoption research, made it much more likely that Chinese people would be a daily part of white middle-class family lives as bus drivers, teachers, store employees, and so forth. In this sense, for parents in St. Louis, the Chinese community might be viewed as a resource but also as a population that was not necessarily a familiar, everyday part of family lives—as something that could be drawn upon and partially incorporated into family activities but that remained somewhat foreign and separate.

In St. Louis, it became clear that the community of adoptive families took part in a number of overlapping networks and drew informally on these resources in different ways and at different times. In comparison to the Bay Area, the relatively smaller size of the adoptive community and comparatively limited range of Chinese resources created opportunities to study these overlapping organizational networks, as I was able to see families multiple times in varied settings. I was able to readily identify the key sources of "Chinese culture" upon which adoptive families drew, including adoptive parent organizations, adoption agencies, foundations focusing on adoption from China, local and virtual informal networks of adoptive parents, and local Chinese and Taiwanese community members. The presence of a major adoption agency in the area that provided both pre- and postadoption services for adoptive families served as another basis for networking and created opportunities for me to meet with adoptive families at agency reunions and other events.

Most of the parents I interviewed were members of the local Families with Children from China, a national organization for parents who have adopted from China. At the time the majority of my interviews were conducted, the St. Louis chapter of FCC had approximately 200 member families. Some families attended one or two events a year, while others only received the group's mailings. The most active members served on the board and organized activities such as the annual Chinese Culture Days. At this event, children learned Chinese songs and calligraphy and listened to Chinese stories. Parents attended panels about raising adopted children, and local members of the Chinese community often gave cultural performances and sold items at the vendor tables. FCC had its own booth, selling T-shirts, Chinese dresses (qi pao), panda purses, stationery, Chinese jump ropes, and other trinkets for children. FCC was a key resource around which parents gathered and shared information about China and Chinese and Chinese American culture and utilize this information through various Chinese culture–related activities. It also served as a network for adoptive parents to discuss childrearing matters, from issues specific to adopting children from China to more general parenting issues. Overall, mothers were more involved than fathers in FCC activities, which is consistent with studies that have examined parental participation in adoption-related issues (see Tessler, Gamache, and Liu 1999; Traver 2007; Jacobson 2008). Indeed, when I asked why mothers were more involved, both mothers and fathers replied that perhaps it was because attending such activities was part of child care responsibilities, and because transmitting culture and values has traditionally been a women's job. Jacobson emphasized the role of mothers in "educating children about cultural heritage and cultural tradition" (2008, 8–9), citing numerous other scholarly works that address the gendered nature of the ethnic socialization of children. In my sample, however, some fathers were very active in FCC, for example, serving on the board and participating in FCC events and language schools.

The FCC parents in my study formed close friendships with other adoptive families, often with those that had children of the same age. They also formed networks around other organizational nodes such as their China travel group and held periodic reunions so that the children could keep in touch with their orphanage-mates. They created their own Chinese New Year celebrations, which sometimes involved decorating their homes in elaborate ways. As noted by Volkman (2005, 83), these diverse and highly visible practices crafted around Chineseness and Chinese culture are perceived by the parents who organize them as contrasting with the lack of attention given to Korean culture by previous generations of Korean adoptee parents. It should be noted, however, that parents who adopt from Korea today engage in many of the same practices, often under the advisement of and sometimes under the continued scrutiny of adult Korean adoptees.

The Chinese adoptive parents I interviewed in St. Louis sought out Chinese or Chinese American friends, acquaintances, and experiences. Some adoptive families, particularly those with multiple children adopted from different countries, attended an international families adoption group. There was another group, which I was invited to observe, that was open to all adoptive single mothers, regardless of where their children were from.

San Francisco Bay Area

Located in Northern California, the San Francisco Bay area includes nine counties: Alameda, Contra Costa, Marin, Napa, San Francisco, San Mateo, Santa Clara, Solano, and Sonoma. The 2000 census puts the population of the Bay Area at 6,783,760. In 2010, the population had risen to 7,150,739. In 2000, approximately 19.0 percent of the population was Asian, 58.1 percent white, 7.5 percent African American, and 19.4 percent Hispanic/Latino (U.S. Census Bureau 2012). By 2010, at the end of my fieldwork there, it was 23.3 percent Asian, 52.5 percent white, 6.7 percent African American, and 23.5 percent Hispanic/Latino (U.S. Census Bureau 2012). Thus, Bay Area racial politics were more complex than the primarily black-white dynamic in St. Louis due to the larger Asian and Latino presence and the proportionally smaller black population. For the city of San Francisco itself, the 2006–8 American Community Survey (U.S. Census Bureau 2012) showed that Asians constitute 31 percent of the city's total population, with Chinese constituting 20 percent. Other areas of the Bay Area vary in their racial and ethnic makeups, and the Asian population itself is diverse, with both newer and older Chinese immigrants from various parts of China and the diaspora (Southeast Asia, Latin America, etc.).

The first Chinese migrants arrived in the Bay Area in the mid-1800s from Guangdong Province in southern China, an area that had been devastated by environmental disasters, political turmoil, and overpopulation, and which resorted to sending its men abroad to make a living (see Hsu 2000). The third-, fourth-, or fifth-generation descendants of these migrants now constitute a portion of the Bay Area's Chinese American population, along with newer immigrants who hail from all over China. Many of these later immigrants came after 1965, when the annual immigration quota of 105 that had been in effect since the end of the Chinese exclusion period (1882–1943) was lifted as part of the Immigration and Nationality Act (Hart-Celler Act). Although some of the newest immigrants arrive with few resources, others, such as wealthy businesspeople from Hong Kong, bring large amounts of capital (Ong 2003). The Chinese American adoptive parents I interviewed as part of this study reflected these diverse immigration trends, though they tended to be somewhere in the middle, neither very poor nor very wealthy. They worked as freelance consultants, lawyers, and business managers, in high-tech fields, and in numerous other occupations.

As a result of its large and fairly established Chinese American population, as well as its location on the Pacific Rim, the Bay Area boasts abundant Chinese and Chinese American resources, including bilingual Chinese preschools and bilingual Mandarin immersion schools such as the Chinese American International School (CAIS) and the Pacific Rim International School, which offers both Japanese and Chinese language. The scope and variety of Chinese and Chinese American influences and resources in the Bay Area are too great to detail here. In addition to formal institutions such as Chinese Culture Center, the Chinese Historical Society, and the Asian Art Museum, there are also advocacy groups such as the Asian Law Caucus, and arts organizations such as the Center for Asian American Media, which organizes the annual San Francisco International Asian American Film Festival. In addition to the annual Chinese New Year parade, there are numerous other opportunities to engage in Chinese practices, such as dragon boat racing. While Chinatowns in downtown San Francisco, the Richmond District, and Oakland may serve as ethnic enclaves for newer immigrants, there are Chinese-owned businesses scattered throughout the area. It is not unusual to see Chinese Americans in daily life, in both stereotypical and nonstereotypical occupations and roles.

The FCC's Northern California branch has three regional chapters with local coordinators and a large membership. When I offered to give a talk on my research in the summer of 2008, I ended up giving versions of the same presentation to small FCC audiences in Berkeley (in the East Bay), Mountain View (in the South Bay), and Pleasant Hill (in the East Bay, inland) to accommodate parents who did not want to travel too far to other parts of the Bay Area to attend the talk. However, just as in St. Louis, not all adoptive families I interviewed were involved with FCC, and there also existed alternative organizations related to adoption issues, such as Pact, An Adoption Alliance, which focuses on transracial adoptions, both foreign and domestic, and provides resources as well as summer camp opportunities for families and children; and Families Adopting in Response (FAIR), which addresses adoption issues more broadly. Many Bay Area parents, both white and Asian, felt that they did not need to go out of their way to provide Chinese cultural resources for their children, given the great diversity and cultural resources that the area offered.

Adoptive parents are a diverse group, shaped both by geography and by racial, ethnic, and class positioning. The respective demographics and local resources of these two areas are important in shaping the Chinese adoption cultures.

Transnational Adoption from Asia

Transracial adoption in the United States has long been a debated and controversial issue, particularly in the context of the adoption of African American children by white parents and the adoption of Native American children by white families. In 1972, the National Association of Black

Social Workers (NABSW) published a statement outlining its stance against the transracial adoption of black children by white families. The NABSW, and other critics of transracial adoption in a domestic U.S. context, have focused on the potential difficulties resulting from the removal of adopted children from their birth cultures (Patton 2000; NABSW 1972). They cited their concerns about the inability of white families to effectively understand and address issues related to both the racial and the cultural identities of these children. Black children needed to be raised not only with knowledge of African American culture but also with the tools and community connections needed to combat racism.

But in recent years, attention to multiculturalism, racial "tolerance," and diversity appears to have produced a new openness to transracial adoption. Most adoption professionals cautiously emphasize that transracial adoption can work if adopted children are educated about the circumstances of their adoption and about their birth culture, stressing that adoptive parents have a responsibility to provide their children with this information (R. Simon, Altstein, and Melli 1994; Melina 1998; Steinberg and Hall 2000). Indeed, parents receive messages on a number of levels about the importance of "culture keeping" (Jacobson 2008). Jacobson describes how from the very beginnings of the international adoption process, prospective parents are presented with images of children that portray them as "innately and desirably (and manageably) ethnic" (2008, 54). She recalls an adoption agency director for a Russian adoption program saying, "You are not only adopting a child, you are adopting a culture. You need to know that" (4) and also notes that "this framing of culture as attractive, necessary, and innate to the child is the professionally prescribed position of the adoption industry" (54).

The adoption process itself emphasizes that being a good parent involves addressing your child's cultural identity. Adoptive parents must go through numerous steps throughout the adoption process that are designed to verify that they are fit to be parents. These include everything from a home study conducted by a social worker to a fingerprint check by the FBI to ensure that the parents have no criminal history. The adoptive parents' finances are also scrutinized. Preadoption programs run by adoption agencies stress the importance of honoring the child's birth culture, and resources on adoption written by adoption experts (including fellow adoptive parents) also emphasize this.

Attitudes toward transracial adoption have also shifted, as reflected in increasing numbers of international transracial adoptions from Asia. Internationally adopted children are seen as culturally distinct. Unlike children of color who are available for adoption in the United States, Asian internationally adopted children are viewed both as victims of their circumstances and as highly redeemable and flexible subjects who could reach their full potential with proper parenting (Ortiz and Briggs 2003; Dorow 2006a). Chinese female adoptees often are portrayed by parents as being "baggage free," desirably different, and savable (Dorow 2006a, 360); in contrast, one Chinese adoptive parent Dorow interviewed saw African Americans as lacking pride in their "disintegrating community." Dorow notes that the woman who expressed this view drew upon the "culture of poverty, model minority, and globalized humanist discourses." In other words, the "desire for Chinese children proceeds simultaneously via the 'different, but not too different' construction of Asianness and the 'too different' construction of blackness" (370).

As a group, Asian adoptees are viewed as innately intelligent and fairly trouble free to raise. The fact that most adoptees from China are female reinforces the latter image. As discussed in the previous chapter, stereotypes about Chinese girls portray them as both desirable and docile, malleable and intelligent. Most important, they are unburdened by problems associated with fetal alcohol syndrome, crack addiction, institutional neglect, and other problems often attributed to domestically adopted (usually minority) or other foreign adopted (e.g., Russian) children (Dorow 2006a; Ortiz and Briggs 2003). The model minority myth, which touts the success of Asian immigrants due to their good behavior, academic achievement, and work ethic, has also played a role for some in the desirability of Asian adoptees.

The desirability but also the malleability of Asian adoptees, particularly female ones, and the impact that this may have on them as they grow older, was clearly illustrated in the documentary *Adopted the Movie* (2008). This poignant film by Barb Lee addresses not only the desirability of Asian adoptees but also the affective labor they perform (Eng 2010), and in the case of the older, Korean adoptee, the pain that she suffered fulfilling this role while growing up Asian in a white family that did not fully acknowledge her origins or her racial minority status. In weaving back and forth between two unfolding narratives, the film opens up a space for inquiry and dialogue that intersects with many of the issues in my study regarding both the potential and the limitations offered by current adoption practices.

The film depicts the Trainers, a white couple from Nashua, New Hampshire, who are moving forward with adopting a little girl from China after dealing with infertility, and the Feros, who adopted their now thirty-two-year-old daughter, Jen, from Korea when she was a toddler. For the Trainer family we see the pain of infertility, their anxiety during the adoption process, their joy at finally meeting their daughter in China, the anguish at seeing the child's foster mother cry for her foster daughter, and the fulfillment of finally becoming a family as their daughter, Roma, makes a smooth adjustment to her new home. We see Jennifer Fero's desperate attempts to repair her relationship to her dying mother, who has always seen her as just one of the family but has not acknowledged her as an Asian woman. Jen is a high achiever both academically and in her career, but she remains needy and insecure in her relationship with her family. She articulately expresses the pain she has felt as an adoptee who is always overcompensating and demanding attention in order to feel she is part of the family. Raised during a time when it was thought that love would conquer all, her parents did not fully address issues of adoption, her developing identity as a Korean/Asian American, or her identity as an Asian women. She admits both to having internalized the racism of the majority society and to having conflicted relationships with other Asians and Asian Americans with whom she feels she has little in common. Jen bravely (and some might say rather undiplomatically) confronts her parents by challenging them to go outside their comfort zones by spending time in Asian American neighborhoods and discussing Jen's birth mother. But her parents are both baffled and defensive, as they feel that they did their best in raising her, and they remain largely unable to respond to her requests.

On one level, one may wonder what, if anything, Jennifer's parents could have done to preempt some of the issues she has wrestled with—the pain of knowing she had been relinquished by her birth parents, her struggle to feel like a part of her adoptive family, and her attention-seeking behaviors and constant need for validation that resulted from this insecurity. One also wonders which of Jen's struggles can be explained in terms of broader, structural issues associated with international, interracial adoption at the historical juncture in which she was raised, and which may be due to more individual variation. Her story is moving and tragic, but it leaves hope for the future as she tries to move forward.

By juxtaposing the Trainers' story of adoption with Jen Fero's, the filmmaker Barb Lee raises some important questions, though she does not claim to have the answers to all of them. Will this new generation of adoptive parents be able to preempt some of the issues experienced by earlier generations of adoptees?

The Trainers are adopting at a time that is very different from when the Feros adopted thirty years ago. Now, "diversity" is celebrated, and transracial, international adoptive families are not uncommon. The election of Barack Obama as president signaled (prematurely) to many that we are in a postracial society. The Trainers and their fellow adoptive families try to prepare themselves to the fullest extent possible for issues associated with adoption and with raising a child of color, by reading and gathering resources and supplies to ready themselves for meeting their child. We see them trying to expose her to a "diverse" group of friends and showing her a Chinese children's video. Roma seems like a very happy, well-adjusted toddler.

Adopted the Movie is just one of many representations of transnational adoption, but in its comparative focus on Korean and Chinese adoption, it highlights a contrast that continues to operate around adoption from these two countries. Korean adoption is often unfairly portrayed as representing color-blind adoption practices, whereas parents who adopt from China like to view themselves as progressive in their approaches to the racial and cultural difference of their children. What the movie does not and perhaps cannot address is how the stories of Roma and the thousands of other children adopted from China will unfold. The film is accompanied by a companion DVD titled *We Can Do Better* in which both adult transracial adoptees and adoption experts are interviewed. The filmmakers made the companion DVD to provide viewers with resources and tools for raising their adopted children, perhaps helping to alleviate the anxieties about how best to raise their children that many adoptive families may feel after watching *Adopted the Movie*. The filmmakers' hope is to open up space for discussion; indeed, most of the experts interviewed stressed the importance of maintaining an open dialogue with children about various adoption- and identity-related issues.

New possibilities exist for today's adoptive parents, but no matter how prepared they may be, it will certainly not be possible for them (or any parent, for that matter) to preempt all potential problems or issues their children may face. They have been made acutely aware that they need to acknowledge the racial and cultural origins of their child, as well as the adoption-related issues of attachment, bonding, and abandonment that may arise. While most have tried to equip themselves with the resources necessary to address these issues, many are unsure of whether they are doing "the right thing."

Speaking from her own experience, adoptive parent and author Cheri Register (2005) reminds us that parents need to go "beyond good intentions" because these alone do not guarantee that salient issues will be addressed. The argument has been made that parents are responsible for ensuring that in adopting a child of color, they prepare that child to navigate the inequalities of the U.S. racial climate. For white adoptive parents, this involves recognizing their privileges as white individuals, as well as the fact that these privileges do not necessarily extend to their minority children. It involves educating themselves about the various forms of racism and discrimination in U.S. society, including the ways they are masked in stereotypes, even ones that appear to be positive such as the model minority. It necessitates that parents become aware of how being color-blind in itself can have serious consequences if it results in parents not being able to recognize or understand incidents in which their children may be treated differently because of their color. But it is unclear to what extent these parents, despite their best intentions, will be able to step outside of their own experiences to achieve these understandings. As is evidenced in *Adopted the Movie*, today's adoptive parents appear to be doing their best to gather resources and preempt the painful identity issues faced by earlier generations of adoptees from Asia, but the dialogue has just begun.

Background to Korean Adoption

A basic groundwork needs to be laid for this, as for all dialogues. In this section, I briefly address the broader context that frames both the

Trainers' and the Feros' stories. Barb Lee is not the only one who jux-
taposes the experiences of Korean and Chinese adoptees, and certainly
comparing the circumstances of only these two groups represents just
part of the much broader picture of transnational, interracial adoption. However, though adoption from both countries continues today,
many Korean adoptees have now reached adulthood and have become
vocal advocates for adoptee rights and issues. Today's adoptive parents
now have access to resources and perspectives of adult adoptees that
to varying degrees shape their own parenting approaches. To further
understand this dynamic between various parts of the adoption community, it is also necessary to more fully understand both Korean and
Chinese adoption as representing two different flows of adoption from
Asia that began during two very different historical periods and were
framed by very different discourses regarding family, assimilation, and
adoption. Transnational adoption needs to be understood within a
global context, the product of dire circumstances such as war, natural
disaster, or political upheaval that resulted in children being orphaned
or in their birth parents being forced to relinquish them. It must also be
understood in relation to sets of policies and socioeconomic inequalities that result in these children being adopted outside their home
countries, nearly always by more prosperous families in Europe and
North America (Marre and Briggs 2009; Ceniza Choy 2013). The varying motivations of parents for adopting children are complex, as are the
prevailing practices that governed the ways that adoptees were viewed
in relation to their families and to society as a whole—whether as children rescued from an oppressive government, as examples of a new
color-blind multiculturalism, or something else. Numerous studies exist
on both Korean and Chinese adoption, so here I will only summarize
some of the key points.

Korean adoption began following the Korean War in 1955 when
Christian missionary Harry Holt brought orphaned Korean children to
the United States and placed them with adoptive families (Bergquist et
al. 2007; T. Kim 2009). It is estimated that 200,000 children have been
adopted internationally from Korea thus far. Holt International Children's Services, a Christian organization, was the first to facilitate international adoptions from Korea. Many of the first adoptive parents, like
those of Deann Borshay Liem, a well-known Asian American filmmaker

who was adopted from Korea at age eight, adopted not because of infertility but for altruistic reasons. Like her family, most adoptive families were white, already had biological children, and lived in areas where there were few other Koreans or Korean adoptees. As Deann details in her film *First Person Plural*, the Borshays had been sponsoring her and then adopted her to rescue her from life as an orphan in Korea. They did not know that she still had a family in Korea, and that her mother had temporarily relinquished her because she was unable to care for her. Like other Korean adoptees of her generation, such as Jennifer Fero, discussed earlier, Deann was raised during a time when assimilation was the dominant model, and as though she were no different racially from the rest of her family.

Korean adoption proved to be an embarrassment for the South Korean government when it hosted the Olympics in 1988, as it faced international criticism for being a developed nation that could not care for its own children. Tobias Hubinette (2006), who was adopted from Korea by Swedish parents, refers to Korean adoption as a form of forced diaspora. Adult Korean adoptees have been engaging in their own forms of activism and advocacy, in Korea, the United States, and other international locations, vocalizing the needs and rights of international, transracial adoptees (E. Kim 2010; T. Kim 2009; Trenka, Oparah, and Shin 2006). Some are extremely critical of the system that allowed them to be taken from their place of birth, often without the consent of their birth families and resulting in the erasure of their identities (Trenka, Oparah, and Shin 2006; Borshay Liem 2000). They have also been vocal about how they believe new generations of transnational, transracial adoptees should be raised, with access to resources on adoption, racism, and their countries of origin, as well as opportunities to network with other adoptees and Asian Americans. As discussed earlier, many newer adoptive parents, including those with children from China, are listening to these critiques. But it is all too easy for parents of Korean adoptees of earlier generations to become a "straw man" (Dorow, personal communication, 2012) for current generations of adoptive parents. Amy Traver, in her study of consumption practices of adoptive parents, notes that mothers who adopt from China often "use these objects to signal that they are not only good mothers, but that they are better mothers than an earlier cohort of similar women: the white American mothers who ignored issues of ethno-cultural/ethno-racial difference in their adoption of Korean children during the 1960s and 1970s" (2007, 215).

Chinese Adoption

In 1979, China implemented its one-child policy, which restricted Chinese families, with some exceptions, to a single offspring. Initially, the majority of children in Chinese orphanages, called social welfare homes, were healthy baby girls who had been relinquished anonymously in violation of Chinese law. Between 1999 and 2013, a total of 71,632 children were adopted from China to the United States (Bureau of Consular Affairs, U.S. Department of State 2014), primarily by white Americans. China is one of the primary destinations for Americans who adopt internationally because of its well-developed official apparatus for processing international adoptions and the allowances it has made for older and, in the past, for single adoptive parents. The majority of adoptive parents are white, middle-class, heterosexual couples who adopt in their thirties and forties, making these adoptions not only international but also transracial.

The focus on adoptee cultural identities stands in marked contrast to the secrecy surrounding adoptee origins in the past, to adoption workers' attempts to physically match adopted children to parents in domestic adoptions, and to the assimilationist rhetoric that used to mark transracial adoption. It accompanies a new openness to transnational, transracial adoption and an often color-blind philosophy, where the celebration of cultural diversity is viewed as the arena for overcoming entrenched racial boundaries (Frankenberg 1993; Lowe 1996).

However, what marks parents who adopt children from China as a group is the conscientiousness with which they go about teaching their children about China and Chinese culture. Many of the adoptive parents I interviewed saw education about China and Chinese culture as an obligation to their child because they removed the child from his or her birth culture before he or she was old enough to give consent.[10] Though these characteristics are not necessarily generalizable to the Chinese adoptive parent population as a whole, this framing of the importance of birth culture was a common thread in many of my interviews. Parents believe they have an obligation to teach their children about their birth culture, in part because children may seek out this information at a later age, but also to give them the necessary tools if they want to return to China at some point to search for their roots. Many parents go a step further and view Chinese cultural knowledge and pride as a potential defense against racism.[11]

Like most parents, the adoptive parents I interviewed consciously created social and cultural environments for their children through making choices about the schools they attended, the neighborhoods in which they lived, the activities in which they participated, and the friends with whom they associated. Parents strategically employed resources about China and Chinese culture, proactively creating Chinese identities for their children in response to potential discrimination and identity issues they may face, related both to being adopted and to being Chinese in America. Having engaged adult Korean and Chinese adoptees through panels, articles, and discussion boards, parents hoped to learn from their experiences and take action to preempt possible problems their children may face in adolescence or adult life regarding issues of loss, abandonment, and lack of exposure to their birth culture (Freundlich and Lieberthal 2000). Information from adoption experts on international and interracial adoption given to them by the adoption agency, found in magazines for adoptive parents, or available through Internet chat rooms or newsletters emphasized the importance of introducing adopted children to their birth cultures (Volkman 2005).

The public nature of international adoption from China for white adoptive families makes their practice of Chinese culture in some ways an involuntary performance to help establish their legitimacy not only as adoptive parents but also as adoptive parents of children of color. Interracial adoption results in the breakdown of the public-private barrier that protects most families from public scrutiny, marking them visibly as an adoptive family (Jacobson 2008). The questions that follow, including the clichéd but unfortunately not uncommon supermarket query "How much did she cost?," are provoked by the phenotypical "difference" (or Chineseness) of their child. One St. Louis parent I interviewed, Renee, related the unsolicited comments that she and her children received when she went to her polling place to vote:

This one older man says, "Are those your kids?" And I said, "Yes, those are my children," and he goes, "Well, where did you get them?" and I said, "Well . . ." He said, "Is she is from China?" and I said, "Yes she is." . . . He said, "Well, where did he come from?" He kept going on and on. I thought, just let me vote here. He said, "Well, she is just so cute. Somebody in my family just got through adopting one."

This invasion of privacy compels adoptive parents to respond by turning Chineseness into a positive marker of difference, something of which the child should be proud, and parents have certainly made efforts in this regard. But white adoptive parents may find themselves challenged with reworking their family identities to include a child of color, as they strive to combine elements of Chineseness into white ethnic and religious lives without placing too much emphasis on this difference. And as discussed in chapter 4, Asian American parents face these challenges in ways that are both similar and different.

3

Beginnings

The Adoption Trip

In late May 2002, I accompanied a group of adoptive parents on their two-week trip to China as they received their children and processed the adoption paperwork.[1] I had arranged to go on the trip with the director of the China program of their St. Louis–based adoption agency, with the understanding that I would pay for my own expenses and write a report for the agency on how it could improve the adoption experience for parents. Some countries, such as Korea, do not require parents to travel there to meet their adoptive children; others, such as Russia, require multiple trips during which parents have an opportunity to meet the child but not immediately bring him or her home.[2] Once they receive their referral, parents who adopt from China are required to travel to the child's home province, where they meet the child for the first time, and then travel with the child for the remainder of their time in China (almost two weeks) before receiving their final paperwork from the U.S. consulate in Guangzhou and returning home to the United States. Many waiting parents have likened the process of creating and filing their dossiers and waiting for their referral to pregnancy, and some joked that they were "pregnant" for a very long time. Continuing with this analogy, the trip to China may be seen as akin to the birthing process. However, as opposed to the labor of pregnancy, which takes place in a private, sterile environment, the process of becoming a parent to a child from China happens on the opposite side of the world, in a time zone that is twelve hours different from eastern standard time in the United States, and in a place marked by activity and chaos, not by sterility. Furthermore, it is a very public process, in the sense that most parents travel with other adoptive parents as a group, in which they negotiate the bureaucracy of the Chinese government paperwork process and, for many, have their first experience being a visible "minority."

The trip represents a liminal experience for parents, a rite of passage (Van Gennep 1961) that transforms them into adoptive parents and multicultural families by bringing them to another place and testing their experiential boundaries. Like many rites of passage, the liminal phase is marked by uncertainty, stress, and transition outside of their normal, everyday circumstances. I describe how this ritualized comfort zone is created and how parents sometimes venture outside of it, whether willingly or not. For adoptive families, China remains powerful, both as a symbolic representation of the racial and cultural origins of children and as the culmination of the adoption process. The trip to China also reflects and reinforces the dichotomy between Asian and white, foreign and domestic, that permeates the Orientalist worldviews with which most white adoptive parents have been raised. These themes may later emerge in how adopted children are viewed, in sometimes contradictory ways, as both exotic and as undifferentiated parts of the family. Thus, the China trip provides an important context for the shaping of parents' understandings of the relationship between race, culture, and adoption.

I also illustrate how as an anthropologist I mediated parents' experiences while in China and afterward through the process of interviewing and interacting with them. Using "full-bodied ethnography" (Markowitz 2006), I interweave my own presence as a researcher into my analysis of identity construction to gain further insight into the subjective processes by which Chineseness is experienced, mediated, and produced in an interactive, dialogic fashion. Though I was not a central part of parents' China experience, I did play a role in mediating their experiences in and understanding of China. I accompanied parents as they received their children, dined in restaurants, visited various tourist spots, shopped, and received their children's visa at the American consulate in Guangzhou. I helped parents take photographs, filmed Mary receiving her child from the orphanage officials, translated during visits to hotel doctors, and helped order food at restaurants. I became part of the record of their China experience, appearing in some parents' candid photos and also in group photos (at parents' invitation). I later took photos of parents, for example, as they posed with their children in front of the U.S. consulate seal in Guangzhou, which I later duplicated and mailed to them, and in this way helped create some of the content of their China record. I translated the comments of local people, migrants to Wuhan from the countryside, who had gathered around one couple and their daughter, explaining to the bystanders that she would be brought to the United States. I relayed comments and questions that people that parents encountered on the street made about the baby ("Is the baby a boy or a girl? How old? The shape of her ears shows that she is a lucky baby. Wherever she is, she will be lucky, and her new parents are lucky too").[3]

Tourist/Parents in a Liminal Phase

On one level, adoptive parents traveled through China as tourists; on another, they were there to do the important work of becoming parents to their adopted children, caring for them, completing paperwork, and documenting their origins and the process of coming together as a family for the first time. They experienced China in a manner framed by their own preconceptions, desires, and anxieties and mediated by the Chinese guides and adoption agency coordinators, as well as the broader dynamics of the travel group. As Sara Dorow (2006b), who has observed adoption travel groups as both a facilitator and a researcher, notes, the convergence of multiple players in the transfer of the child from orphanage to adoptive parents and from China to the United States stirs up numerous questions and ambiguities. Adoptive parents are understandably anxious as they enter this unsettled terrain, which represents not only the birthplace of their child (and possibly the location of her birth parents) but also her location of relinquishment. For many parents who had no previous exposure to China, the conceptions they do have were filtered through the Orientalist lens through which most Americans (including the Chinese Americans I studied previously) view China, as well as through their imagination, longing, and desire for a child who is far away but about whom they know little. Language and cultural barriers experienced during the China trip exacerbated conceptions about the foreignness of China and Chinese people, yet the availability of familiar Western goods and comforts, and the clear cachet that knowledge of English and white racial status carried, reinforced the dominance of Western culture in the Chinese setting.

Like the Chinese American participants of the In Search of Roots program I studied previously (Louie 2003, 2004), adoptive parents encounter China in very specific ways, through a travel experience that is structured and mediated for the specific purpose of facilitating the adoption process and providing parents an opportunity to learn about their child's birthplace. They experience China from within their mobile comfort zone, using what I call the "privilege of mobility" that their middle-class, first world, cosmopolitan status affords them. The China experience takes place within the safe realm of "baby hotels," tour buses, and civil affairs offices and provides access to comfortable beds, English-speaking guides, and familiar foods. Of course, parents wished to have this structure and certainly did not desire any form of adventure tourism because they were already dealing with enough uncertainty around the adoption of their child. But the journey is not (nor should it be) wholly predetermined. Parents sometimes stepped out of their comfort zones, through encounters with curious locals who asked questions about their babies and sometimes touched them, or on orphanage visits, where I was told that a baby's foster mother ran after the minivan in an effort to get one last look at her foster child.

From the beginning, the China experience was a complex mixture of tourism and business. Group members stayed in first-class Chinese hotels that most locals did not frequent and were shepherded around by local Chinese guides. Tours involved a mind-boggling combination of visits to tourist sites, shopping, and the emotion-laden work of meeting adopted children for the first time. Parents had been charged with the responsibility of capturing, memorializing, and honoring the birthplaces of their children, having been told by adoption experts and fellow parents the importance of establishing a base from which to build their child's identity. Thus, underlying the excitement of being a tourist in China and seeing these famous sights was a larger sense of mission, and the anxiety and urgency of documenting these experiences and places for their children on film and through the purchase of souvenirs. It was important for parents not only to record the actual places that were significant to their children's backgrounds but also to capture their own and their children's presence in these places and document the experience of meeting their children. These images of the adoption trip later become an important part of the child's history, as well as the history of her newly formed family unit.

Buying souvenirs captured the dual purpose of their trip as both tourists and parents. Parents shopped throughout the adoption trip, from their first day on the Great Wall to their final days in Guangzhou. In addition to buying souvenirs for friends and relatives, parents were creating a material record as a basis for their daughters' future identities and connections to China. Some parents bought pearl necklaces for their daughters' sixteenth birthdays or wedding days. One family bought Chinese dresses (Mandarin: *qi pao*; Cantonese: *cheong sam*) in every available size, to last their daughter for the next ten years. Others bought gifts to give to their children on future "Gotcha Days," sometimes also called "Adoption Day." In addition, they purchased Chinese decorations for their homes, particularly items from their daughter's hometowns. These experiences were later used to create connections to and "memories" of China as they narrated identities for their children, selecting significant events, objects, people, and places and using them as launching points for discussions of adoptee identity.

Where Does the Anthropologist Fit In?

Given the serious purpose of their travel to China, the group's dynamics were defined by a public-private duality. While they spent time together during group outings to tourist destinations, on shopping trips, and on other official business, they also had opportunities to retreat to their hotel rooms to rest, reflect, and prepare for what lay ahead. No anthropologist is able to observe all of her informants' actions, particularly as field sites and the questions emerging from them get larger and more complex. As a "guest" of the group, I tried to be very careful about respecting the privacy of my fellow travelers and also to be as helpful as possible.

I quickly learned that it was going to be very difficult to interview parents during the trip without also being too pushy and invading their privacy. I made the conscious decision to respect parents' privacy and to try to not drastically change their experiences by asking intrusive questions during this very private and important time in their lives. Once the subgroup I accompanied received their children, a personable group of baby girls ranging from nine to sixteen months, parents were not consciously thinking very much about how to teach them about China and Chinese culture or about being interviewed by an anthropologist. They were much more concerned about bonding with their babies and helping them through their grieving process of being separated from their foster parents. They worried about figuring out the babies' personalities, tastes, and developmental stage; sorting out what they liked to eat and drink, how to get them to sleep, how to bathe them; and making sure they were healthy. On top of that, they worried about navigating the bureaucracy, documenting the places their children were from, and buying souvenirs. Despite this, they were both actively and passively absorbing and experiencing "Chinese culture." Of course, mainland Chinese culture at the turn of the twenty-first century was a complex and multifaceted mixture of prerevolutionary, communist, and post-Mao elements, in some ways surprisingly capitalist and in others still unexpectedly socialist (Zhang and Ong 2008).

The Adoption Trip: Step by Step

Traveling to China

Most members of the travel group had found each other in line at the Air China check-in counter at the San Francisco airport. Among the group members were a thirty-five-year-old couple from St. Louis with a biological son and a daughter from China; the Parkers, a couple in their early thirties from Tennessee; and Mary, a thirty-nine-year-old single woman from outside of St. Louis. Some married couples traveled together, leaving older children, if they had any, at home with friends or relatives. One man traveled with his mother, and one single woman traveled with her sister. One couple brought their three-year-old daughter, who had been adopted from China. Families were from around the United States, including St. Louis, Tennessee, New York, and Iowa. All of the approximately fifteen families were from white, middle-class backgrounds.

I had been concerned about how I would be seen as a researcher accompanying the group during a very personal and private time. The agency's travel coordinator had circulated a letter explaining my background, and parents who wished to participate later signed consent forms in China. In the letter, I provided my affiliation, academic credentials, and a description of my research on Chinese adoption. Despite this formal introduction, however, the process of getting to know the group and finding my role within it was gradual.

The waiting parents had gotten to know one another as they grabbed a meal at an airport taqueria and then settled into the airport waiting room.[4] To my relief, I found the group members to be welcoming, and by the time we reached the boarding gate, I had also become the subject of their observations. One outgoing mother, Beth, who had adopted a daughter from Guangdong Province a few years earlier and was returning with her husband to adopt another child, showed everyone a picture of their daughter and began talking about how people from Guangdong "look different" because they have "rounder eyes." Using me as a convenient example, she explained to the other parents present that, like most white people, I have a double eyelid, which has the effect of making my eyes look bigger, but many Chinese people do not.[5] People had not heard about this before and checked out my eyelids, joking that soon the tables would be turned and I would be observing them. Though I admittedly felt uncomfortable having my physical features at the center of attention, I realized that, as they noted, I would soon be observing them, so I joined in the laughter. I also thought about how eyelids were a big issue in the Asian community and to some extent the Asian American community, and that it was good that the parents were learning about this distinction. However, I did not have time to go into an explanation about the politics surrounding the prevalence of controversial "double eyelid" cosmetic surgeries that were popular among some Asians and Asian Americans.

The plane ride was long but uneventful. We arrived at the Beijing airport, passed through customs, and waited while the guide and adoption coordinator rounded up everyone in the waiting room. Outside, we met Greg, our local guide, and he led us to the hotel-bound bus with his red flag. The energetic China-based adoption coordinator, Susan, greeted the families on the bus. She assured them that she would help them achieve their goals here in China. Along the way Greg described the population of Beijing, its history, and its local features, such as poplar trees. He discussed the various ring roads and other plans to build the city's infrastructure for the Olympics Games in 2008. After we checked into our rooms, many of the couples, both exhausted and excited, congregated downstairs on their way to Carrefour, a French hypermarket, which some parents likened to a "super Walmart,"[6] to get snacks such as Bugles and Pringles.

The tour as a whole represented an unsettled, intense phase for parents. People commented that it was amazing how they could be in such a different place after just one plane ride. Many parents had not been to China before, and some had not traveled abroad. One father mentioned that another parent had told him that you "wake up a tourist and go to bed a parent." However, the transformation was far from immediate. Parents had arrived with their luggage filled with baby clothes, diapers, baby blankets and burp cloths with their child's names embroidered on them, baby bottles, and gifts for officials, but they would have to wait a couple more days before meeting their children.

The next day, the jet-lagged group toured the Forbidden City. Our large group, trailing our local guide,[7] who was holding up a flag, had been an easy target for vendors. While some parents practiced saying *bu yao* (don't want), others purchased some small items, such as hats from the Beijing 2008 Olympics. People snapped pictures, took videos, and tried to stay cool in the ninety-degree heat. During the walk through the vast, crowded complex, I had a chance to chat with some parents. Though they had not yet met their children, they were grappling with the dual roles of being a tourist and a parent. One adoptive mother, Mary, told a story about a mother who had focused so much on information about China that she forgot to read books on child rearing. The Browns, from New York, shared that they already had five boys and one girl at home who were excited about their new sister. Beth said she felt she could enjoy her visit to Beijing because she had already been through the adoption process once and did not feel as anxious this time. Tina was overwhelmed with emotion and stared to cry in Tiananmen Square. She said she could not believe she was finally in China, ready to adopt her daughter. She apologized for being so emotional, as others comforted her.

After lunch and a trip to a Friendship Store,[8] the bus took us to the Great Wall. I accompanied some parents as they climbed to a high point on the wall to take pictures, while others stayed closer to the bottom and shopped for souvenirs. On the way to the Great Wall, Susan, the adoption agency coordinator, had given me some time to talk to the parents about my research. Most seemed interested, and many asked questions such as whether my research results would be available to them.

Preparing for the Big Day

On the bus on the way back to the hotel, Susan gave some advice to the nervous parents. She said that parents should prepare questions before they meet the baby. They will have a chance to ask the orphanage officials about the foster parents face-to-face. They will then give their $3,000 donation to the orphanage. She also explained how to distribute the gifts to the orphanage workers. The main gift should go to the orphanage, and one gift should go to the orphanage director, another to the registrar, and another to the notary. For children in foster care, one or two big gifts should go to the foster parents. Parents asked which babies were in foster care and were told that most of those from Guizhou were in foster care, which often indicated that the children had been given extra attention in preparation for their adoptions, but also that they might have bonded with their foster parents.

For many Americans, the idea of providing mandatory gifts may have seemed strange, particularly the provision of personal gifts for officials in the context of the adoption of a child. While most of the parents on the trip seemed to accept this as a Chinese "custom" and as a necessary part of the adoption process, the practice does disrupt common understandings regarding the separation of personal gain from business transactions. Dorow notes that these practices may also "help legitimate the exchange of the child" and alleviate concerns that the child is a commodity. She views the cycle of gift giving, including the $3,000 cash donation to the orphanage, as a "gift" that represents a form of reciprocity that turns the relationship with Chinese officials and caregivers into one of mutual exchange, rather than the purchase of children, adding that parents also give token gifts to foster parents or orphanage workers, and the child is sometime given a "parting gift of a jade amulet or other token of good wishes that connects them to the child, and the child to China, while simultaneously sanctioning her departure" (Dorow 2006b, 140).

Gift giving was just one of many concerns that adoptive parents had, as indicated by the questions they asked on the bus. Susan asked Beth, who had adopted previously, to come to the front of the bus to give some advice to the parents. Beth confidently relayed the following information to the anxious busload of parents, who listened attentively: "Have your gifts ready and know where they are when you arrive. Getting the kids is an emotional time. One parent can use a camera and the other the recorder. Write down questions beforehand—you won't remember at the time." She had some questions ready that were preprinted in Chinese, including "How long has she been in the orphanage?" "Where was she found?" "Was there a note with her?" and "What is her schedule?"

Beth also said to use the infant formula purchased in China because it doesn't upset the babies' stomachs. She said not to take the babies' clothes off in public—it is considered offensive—and advised not to be surprised if people come into the hotel room because the baby is crying. Susan elaborated for the parents that in China it is not uncommon for people to touch other people's babies. Some babies who have been in foster care might initially cry and refuse food, but they will be better after one to two days. They can sense if the parents are nervous. She then taught the parents the following Chinese words to "kill time" as we returned to our hotel on the bus:

1. *nu-er* (daughter)
2. *bu ku* (don't cry)
3. *wo ai ni* (I love you)
4. *a yi* (auntie)
5. *nai nai* (grandmother)
6. *bao bao* (precious baby)
7. *ba ba* (father)
8. *ma ma* (mother)

She joked that she would now test the parents, saying that if they failed, they won't get the babies tomorrow. The parents laughed nervously.

Indeed, during this first day in Beijing, the anticipation of receiving their children within the next twenty-four to forty-eight hours was overwhelming, making parents both excited and nervous. I later heard parents ask additional questions of one another and of Susan. Would their child go to them and make eye contact initially, they wondered? What questions should they ask of the orphanage workers about the child's background and habits? How could they make sure to capture the moment they receive their children on film, and also relish the moment itself? Would the paperwork go smoothly? The questions that parents

asked about the adoption process symbolized both the gulf that separated them from the children they would soon meet and the anxieties
they felt about meeting their children for the first time. Parents knew
very little about the children they would soon adopt. They had only
a name, a photo, the child's orphanage name and location, and basic
health information. Yet the children, the youngest of whom were already
nine months old, already had pasts—connections to caregivers, food
preferences, and for the older children, possibly Chinese language com-
prehension. While some adoptive parents had studied Chinese, the majority of the parents on this trip spoke little, if any. The vocabulary that
Susan taught them was very specific to the circumstances of adoption—
including the word for "daughter," rather than "son," the word for "auntie," which is often used to refer to the child's orphanage caretakers, and
the words for "mother," "father," and "I love you," communicating the
fact that these were her new parents.

Becoming a (Different Kind of) Family

After returning to the hotel for a rest, I went to dinner with two of the
younger couples in the group. As we sat around the table waiting for
our food, both couples discussed their adoption stories. The Joneses
had been interested in adopting from either China or Korea, but in the
end they ruled out Korea. They speculated that perhaps other people
preferred an adoption from Korea because Korean agencies escorted
the children to the United States, instead requiring parents to travel.
However, they said that they would have wanted to travel regardless,
perhaps alluding to cosmopolitan sensibilities, and adding that China
also seemed more interesting as a place to visit.[9] They joked that they
had thought they knew a lot about China before they started the adoption process, but now that they were actually in China, they realized this
might not be true.

The Joneses asked the Parkers whether they had considered adopting
a white child from Russia, and the Parkers said that they had not because
they didn't want to have the option of not telling her she was adopted.
They had heard that some parents who adopt same-race children have
hidden the fact of adoption from their child. Both couples talked about
how many Russian children had problems because of fetal alcohol syn-

drome, critiquing those who wanted to adopt them because they were white. The Joneses commented that they were so generically white—she said she looks like an Iowa farm girl—that people often would meet them and then not remember them later. In fact, they mentioned that Mary had mixed them up with the Parkers earlier. Both couples joked that because they were "so white," meaning so generically American, that perhaps having a daughter from China would give them a chance to be more interesting culturally. Though shared in jest, this viewpoint reflects broader understandings of race and culture in the United States—that white Americans do not have a culture of their own, and that Chinese and Chinese Americans possess a richer and deeper form of culture that could be taken on by the whole family. However, they seemed very conscious of their whiteness and were both willing and eager to embrace the diversity, cosmopolitanism, and multiculturalism that their new family would represent. Both couples subscribed to the magazine *Adoptive Families* and other resources on adoption, and they did not necessarily hold rigid ideas about what it would mean to raise their children as Chinese adoptees. Earlier the Parkers had told me they would like to teach their child a language, but perhaps Spanish, and not necessarily Chinese.

As a group, the Chinese adoptive parents with whom I spoke emphasized their willingness to take on the challenge of transracial adoption, and the responsibility of teaching their child about her birth culture. Hearing adoptive parents talk about their views on issues of racial and cultural socialization, I often wondered how my presence as a Chinese American anthropologist might have affected what they talked about and emphasized. Certainly, they would not want to appear culturally insensitive or unaware to someone they knew was not only Chinese American but also studying issues related to cultural socialization. However, parents had already learned about the importance of these issues from adoption agency workers and from the reading they had done on Chinese and other forms of transracial adoption.

The subject of the child's racial difference periodically came up. One adoptive grandmother talked with another parent about the attitudes in their respective families about minorities. Her ex-husband's parents had negative attitudes about her son adopting a Chinese baby. Another adoptive father noted that people often asked him why he had to go to all the way to China to adopt. He felt that they considered China to be an enemy of the United States. So while, in many respects, Chinese Americans and by extension Chinese adoptees are desired by parents seeking to adopt them, these parents also had to defend their actions to others, including family members, for whom China and Chinese people (even Chinese babies) represented the foreign and unknown. Also, while they may deny racism in their own attitudes, it is important to understand that their ideas about the difference and foreignness of children from China are heavily tied into historically rooted beliefs about the racial difference of Asia and Asians.[10]

After dinner, we retired to our hotel rooms. The next day, the larger group split into three subgroups to travel to receive their children in the cities of Wuhan, Guizhou, and Shanghai. I moved on to Wuhan with five adoptive families (three married couples and two single women). I sat next to Mary on the plane, a pleasant and easygoing woman from St. Louis who was traveling by herself until her sister could join her. She worked in the adoption field for a Christian adoption agency; her job involved supporting domestic unwed mothers who wished to relinquish their children, and then placing these children with adoptive families. For the first two months in her own adoption process, she had read about Chinese adoption, mentioning a number of popular resource books for adoptive parents by title. She told me that she was not sure how much she would teach her daughter about Chinese culture, joking that she might be the exception in my study because she had decorated her daughter's room with antique toys.

Mary showed me a picture of her daughter, referring to the child by her Chinese name. She said her father was so excited about the adoption that he took a picture of his mechanic's Asian American daughter and put it on the fridge, hoping his granddaughter would look like her. While this anecdote was touching, and her father probably had only the best of intentions, I wondered: If she had been adopting a white baby, would he have put up a photo of a white child he knew?

After we landed in Wuhan, we met our local guide, Roxanne, a slender, mild-mannered woman who had worked with many adoption groups in the past. She introduced us to the city of Wuhan, which had a population of 13 million, noting that the location was equidistant from many major cities in China, and that its nicknames were the Furnace

City and also the Nine-Headed Bird. She also informed the parents that they would receive their babies the next morning at ten o'clock at the Civil Affairs Office, where they would also need to complete some paperwork. She said she was sure they were excited to get the babies.

Many parents noted to me that they had not yet experienced "culture shock." Beijing was more modern than they had expected. They had seen a lot of English on signs in the hotels, stores, and outside on the street (because China has just entered the World Trade Organization). The rooms had modern conveniences such as hairdryers, air conditioners, and televisions. Most service people spoke at least a few words of English, and menus were bilingual. The hotel was also equipped with amenities for adopting families such as cribs in the rooms and high chairs in the restaurant. In the restaurant, there were two groups of French people who had adopted toddlers.

Meeting the Babies

At nine o'clock the next morning, we all met in the lobby, the parents ready with diaper bags, cameras, and their lists of questions. Everyone seemed fairly calm, which belied the excitement and nervousness they were feeling. On the bus, Roxanne gave the parents some advice. She said she knew they were excited to meet their babies, but that they should be prepared for some things. The babies are used to Chinese faces and many would cry, she noted, but she promised that the babies would get used to them after a while. "We think crying is good for babies' lungs," she said, in an effort to comfort parents about the emotions they would see their child experiencing. Everyone was still chatting when the bus pulled up to the building that housed the Civil Affairs Office, but then they fell silent for a moment. One parent said she had not realized the trip would be so quick. They wondered whether the babies were there yet. We entered the tall, modern structure with a marble interior and went up to the second floor. Everyone's ears perked up as we listened to babies crying in one room. To our disappointment, Roxanne checked and found out that they were not the babies for our group.

The anxious group ascended to the third floor and walked down a hallway. They could see some orphanage workers, both men and women, in the hallway holding the babies—their babies. Only one or two babies were crying; the rest seemed fairly calm. I was helping Mary film and asked if she recognized her daughter. She pointed her out, in the arms of a man trying to calm her by pacing the room. I began to film the room and the rest of the parents; they also were excitedly pointing out their children, whom they recognized from the referral pictures they must have looked at hundreds of times in anticipation of their adoption trip. We were told to sit down while the civil affairs officer spoke to the parents, though it was difficult for the parents to contain their excitement and anticipation, knowing that they would soon hold their children in their arms. I sat next to Mary in the second row of a large conference hall with many rows of wooden seats and tables. The officer, a serious-looking woman in her forties, discussed the paperwork the parents needed to fill out and also offered some advice that was similar to Roxanne's. The babies were not used to non-Chinese faces, and they may cry, she said. Your baby may not be used to air-conditioning, so please don't make it too cool in your room. Her advice reflected the dramatic nature of the children's transition from their modest origins to the first world conditions in which they would be living. The officer added that parents could ask questions of the orphanage directors after they got their babies. The whole time, the parents appeared to find it difficult to concentrate on her words because the babies were in the back of the room, and the parents kept turning around to look at them.

Soon it was time to present the children. The two orphanage directors were introduced, and the babies they were holding were presented first. The male director was holding Mary's daughter. I filmed Mary as she received her. Mary commented, nervously and repeatedly, about how upset the baby was. The baby was whimpering a bit but eventually fell asleep. We were brought to the back of the room, and the assistant coordinator translated as Mary asked the orphanage director some questions. Mary had prepared an extensive list of questions and made sure to ask them all, while also making sure I was getting everything on tape. She inquired whether the baby slept alone, whether she has been with her foster parents last night, what she ate and when, and what type of music she liked to listen to.

I went around to the other parents to see how they were doing. One couple was trying to mix formula for the first time. Their daughter appeared very relaxed in her mother's arms. Her father kept patting her and playing with her. The Parkers' baby was alert and playing with the paper that the parents' questions were written on. They told me she had already said "mama." The Grangers allowed their three-year-old daughter to hold her new sister. Her father had her sit down on a step and steadied the baby as the girl held her.

After a while the officials rushed us out of the room because another group was coming in. On our way out, we saw these parents downstairs with their empty strollers. As we returned to the hotel, Mary remarked that her group had walked out of the hotel with empty arms and returned with full arms. I reflected on how many adoptions seemed to be taking place. Within the space of one to two hours, three different groups had received their children, who were carried out in the arms of their new parents. Roxanne had told me in an interview that approximately 5,000 babies had been adopted internationally from Hubei Province the previous year (2001) from the twenty to thirty orphanages in that province. She herself had helped almost a hundred families over the past three or so years.

Upon their return to the hotel, parents retreated to their rooms to further bond with their babies. The bonding process was clearly a very anxiety-provoking one for parents, many of whom had read about reactive attachment disorder and other attachment issues. While much of the bonding took place in the privacy of their hotel rooms, they were forced to alternate between these private spaces and shared, public spaces such as the restaurants where they ate their meals or the numerous group outings to process paperwork or go sightseeing.

More Paperwork . . .

At eight thirty the next morning, we met in the lobby to go to the registry and notary at the Civil Affairs Office. The bus ride seemed to take much longer this time, perhaps because of the traffic and the restless babies. We were ushered into the same room as the previous day. The registrar was there, as well as orphanage directors. Parents were called one by one, bringing their bags of gifts, paperwork, and cash donations to the table. The registrar and orphanage official were on one side of the table, and the parents, babies, and translator on the other. Mary was called up first. The officials took her daughter's footprint and Mary's fingerprints and accepted the orphanage donation. Mary said that they asked questions similar to those she had already answered for the adoption agency home study: Why did you want to adopt from China? Do you have any children of your own? (She corrected them, asking, "Do you mean biological?") Do you promise to never abandon her? She was then given a very nice photo album from the orphanage. On the cover it said in English, "My Cute and Lovely Baby." Inside was a poem written in Chinese:

> bao bao di yi nian (precious first year)
> bao bao de sheng ri (precious birthday)
> bao bao ming zi (precious name) (her daughter's Chinese name was
>   written here)

The next section of the album listed the child's place of birth and provided some information in English about Hanchuan city, where the orphanage was located:

Hanchuan city lies in the central region of rich and beautiful Jianghan plain, it just borders on provincial city, Wuhan. With the area of 12 mu [1 mu = approximately one-sixth of an acre] and the total construction area of 4500 square meters, the social welfare institution of Hanchuan city is a [sic] institution owned by the state, which is set up by the Hanchuan municipal government in the people's Government in the year of 1980. It specially takes care of the old men and women and orphans. Our aim is to service for the adoption program.

Below, in English, were the words "Best wishes for Baby." At the end of the book were photographs with captions; some of these were general pictures of the orphanage grounds (the gate, the dining room, the infant room, outdoor scenery) and others were of Mary's daughter from January through May of that year. Later, on the bus, another parent commented to Mary that having the photo book made him feel more comfortable about his daughter's life for the past five months—knowing that she had been well taken care of.

The photo book given to parents about their child's orphanage marks a striking contrast to procedures during earlier years of adoption, when the conditions in most orphanages were much poorer and adoptive parents received little information about their children's circumstances prior to adoption. The content of the book clearly indicates that orphanage officials have a sense of what parents would like to know and of what might be valuable to both parents and children later to indicate the good care they received in the orphanage. The Civil Affairs Office itself, newly constructed and with pictures of adoptive families on the wall (including an older white child holding a Chinese baby, a white father lying on the ground with a Chinese baby on his back, and so forth), signified that adoption was a significant part of that office's work. In the meeting room where parents met with officials were two quotations, written by the director of the Civil Affairs Office and translated by an employee in her office, that read: "Children are our hope and the future of the world" and "Thank you for all of the love pouring on our children."

Sightseeing with Babies

Though parents had just received their children and were spending time getting to know them and their habits, the group continued its active sightseeing schedule. We would remain in Wuhan for the next few days while the babies' paperwork was being processed at the provincial level, before moving on to Guangzhou, where additional paperwork would be filled out. So, the next morning, we left at nine thirty for the Hubei Provincial Museum. The ride took half an hour, and the babies fell asleep in their parents' laps on the bus. The museum, which looked fairly new, displayed the treasures of the tomb of the Marquis Yi, a site estimated by archaeologists to be from around 433 BC, during the Warring States period. Roxanne gave us a tour of the museum, which featured a model of the tomb, artifacts such as coffins and burial items, and bronze ware. Another group of adoptive parents was there at the same time.

The following day, we visited the Yellow Crane Tower and Pavilion. Roxanne explained that the tower and pavilion symbolized peace and were also symbols of Wuhan. She told the legend of the wine shop owner who was visited by an immortal, who left behind his yellow crane. The alternative story is that the tower used to be a watchtower because Wuhan was a strategic military site. As we walked through the lane of shops, located along the narrow pavilion entrance, many of the young female workers came out of their stores to look at the babies, touching them and calling them cute (*ke-ai*); one young woman straightened a baby who was a bit slumped in her stroller. The women asked questions such as "How old is she [they used the gender-neutral pronoun *ta*]?" and "Is she a boy or a girl?" The group got many stares as we passed though the maze of shops and also in the pavilion itself.

At the gift shop, Mary was happy to find a red and gold padded outfit like the one her daughter had been wearing in her referral picture. She told me she had purchased a two-sided drum toy earlier at the hotel. The Parkers bought a pot made with clay from the Yixing region of China, with a dragon on it. They also bought a *qi pao* (Chinese dress) and a fan painted with the image of the Yellow Crane Tower with their daughter's Chinese and English names on it. They thought it was special because the artist created it as they watched.

Later, back at the hotel in Wuhan, I asked a kiosk worker what adoptive parents liked to buy. He said they like to purchase items that represent (*dai biao*) China. They believe that China is an old culture and differs from the United States, so they buy traditional things such as Chinese dresses and dolls depicting the colorful costumes of Chinese national minorities as souvenirs (*ji nian*) of China. Similarly, Roxanne had noted that parents like to buy Chinese music, Chinese flutes, bells from the Wuhan museum, jade, chops (carved stamps of names, usually with Chinese characters), paintings, and books about Hubei Province.

Finalizing Paperwork, and on to Guangzhou

On our final day in Wuhan, we went to the Civil Affairs Office once more to finalize the paperwork. We were told to sit in a room that seemed set up especially for adoption, decorated with the photographs and sayings mentioned earlier. Most people sat on the wooden benches under one of the signs. Soon, a female official from the registrar's office came in. With Roxanne translating, the official said she was here to present the completed paperwork showing that the adoptions had been approved by Chinese law, and that she had also included the office's business card. The office would be happy if parents sent back photos of their children, but they didn't have to. She congratulated the parents and began presenting the paperwork to them one by one, including the babies' Chinese passports. The passport stated the child's gender and Chinese name and included the baby's referral picture. As parents were called by their babies' names, they went up and shook hands with the official while others snapped pictures and clapped. They were also given a certificate of donation to the orphanage (a souvenir) and some other receipts for the money they had paid. As we filed out, the official touched each of the babies.

The group flew to Guangzhou the next day for the final part of the adoption trip. Here, the three groups that had traveled to Wuhan, Shanghai, and Guizhou would be reunited, and parents were excited to see members of the other travel groups, share their experiences, and meet the other babies. Most of the families stayed on the twelfth floor of the famous White Swan Hotel, located on Shamian Island, with all of the amenities befitting a five-star hotel—valet service, elevator attendants on each floor, fancy shops, and so forth. The hotel and its grounds, including the now-famous red sofa on which babies are propped for group photos, have become an important element of adoptive family lore, in part because they represent the final leg of the adoption trip. Shamian Island, famous as a defense point during the Opium Wars, is a former colonial outpost for the French and British in China that retains many European features, including broad walkways and Western churches. During the 2002 trip, the American consulate was located within walking distance of the White Swan Hotel, but it has since moved to another part of Guangzhou.[11] Once on the island, most parents settled in to wait for the consulate appointment, which would give them the necessary paperwork to travel back to the United States with their children. The shopped the streets surrounding the hotel, which were lined with stores catering to adoptive parents. Parents bought stone etchings of their children made on the spot by artists who sat outside shop entrances, chiseling portraits into black stone. They purchased chops with characters such as "family" on them. In one case, parents purchased a chop with a lotus design after I reminded them that the lotus was the official flower of their daughter's city of origin. Families also purchased Chinese-style outfits to bring their children home in and fun items such as children's shoes that make a squeaking sound with each step.

Together with Mary, I visited some families from the other groups, excited to meet their daughters. The Guizhou group raved about their tours of scenic waterfalls and Miao and Buyi minority villages in the area in which they stayed. The Buyi villagers had performed for them, after which items for sale appeared out of nowhere. A couple of parents told me that people in Guizhou said that their daughters looked like local minorities. The Joneses were told that their daughter looked Buyi, and they made sure to buy some dolls for her at the Buyi village. Dorow (2006b, 233) notes that some adoptive parents in her study also speculated on the possible mixed-race or minority origins of their children. Similarly, in the documentary *Somewhere Between*, Fang "Jenni" Lee, a fifteen-year-old Chinese adoptee, is shown purchasing and dressing up in the ethnic clothing of a local minority group and using her fluent Chinese language skills to ask locals whether she looked like she could be from that group.

Chinese government policies designating groups as official minorities, providing them some special rights, and encouraging the expression of their cultural distinctiveness have reinforced a form of "internal orientalism" (Schein 2000) that has produced the romanticized, performative modes of presenting culture that adoptive parents had witnessed. In this sense, parents' romanticized ideals surrounding the possible minority origins of their children may have reflected historically rooted Orientalist power structures that continued to play into the position of Chinese minorities more broadly.

A little before four o'clock the following day, I walked with the parents to the American consulate, a large concrete building just a hundred or so yards from the hotel. We filed through a security gate, where our passports and backpacks were checked. There was a nearly full lane for stroller parking on the left. Parents and babies were crowded into a room, which buzzed with excitement and anticipation. Our group members were called one by one, and the parents went up to a window where their babies' Chinese passports were returned to them with U.S. visa stamps. These documents would allow parents to bring their babies back to the United States with them. Then, an American official came out to swear them in. He indicated that this was the end of the adoption process and answered the most commonly asked question: When will my child become a U.S. citizen? He explained that this would happen once they legally enter the United States, through the immigrant line. The official papers will then be sent to the parents. He then congratulated them on completing the process, and everyone clapped, while the babies looked confused and some parents had tears in their eyes. Later, the group had dinner and took a group photo at a local tourist attraction—the largest restaurant in China. The agency coordinators gave each baby a CD of children's songs, and a parent sang a song about waiting for a child far away. The parents returned to the hotel to prepare for the long flight home with their children.

Mediating China

While in Guangzhou, I had an interesting talk with the Parkers regarding China's one-child policy. I had framed the intention of the policy in a positive light (but with negative consequences in its application) in the sense that it addressed China's population issues. The Parkers said they had always thought of it in negative terms because of its impact on female babies (abortion, infanticide, adoption) and the future gender imbalance it may cause. Indeed, this issue has been a theme in the popular media, including Lisa Ling's documentary *China's Lost Girls* (2005).

We also talked about the poverty we had witnessed in China. I noted that some parents had mentioned that they were glad to leave Wuhan because it was poor. The Parkers said that other than on the street perpendicular to the hotel, where we had seen people squatting in small shacks along the roadside, Wuhan did not appear especially poor because it was a big city. I explained that the people we had seen were probably migrant workers from the countryside who had come to the city illegally (i.e., without an urban residency permit [*hukou*]) to work for low wages (Zhang 2002).

These conversations encapsulate some of the complex and contradictory issues that factor into how parents understand what they see and hear in China, and also how this experience is mediated for them by adoption workers. On the one hand, parents are aware that it is a combination of poverty and Chinese government policies that lead birth parents to relinquish their children. On the other hand, when they travel to China, they witness the nation's rapid development and modernization, juxtaposed with continued poverty. They also are reminded of China's rich cultural heritage through their visits to local tourist sites. Together, these images provide a contradictory and incomplete picture of contemporary Chinese society that tells parents both that they are removing their children from dire conditions and that China is rapidly modernizing (for all of the loaded meanings of this term). Most adoptive parents want to portray Chinese society and culture in a positive light for their children, as a means to establish pride in their heritage, and to some extent to control or tame the negative portrayals of China that circulate in the Western media. There are many available resources to educate parents and their children about the complex blend of policy, history, and culture that contribute to infant abandonment in China, including Ying Ying Fry and Terry Fry's children's book *Kids Like Me in China* (2001), which discusses the impact of the one-child policy on rural Chinese families and the situation of children in social welfare institutions in China, and Sara Dorow and Stephen Wunrow's *When You Were Born in China* (1997). Political scientist Kay Johnson's (2004) work dispels some of the predominant myths about the one-child policy and abandonment of female infants, asserting that birth parents usually do not relinquish firstborn daughters and that the stricter enforcement of China's one-child policy in the countryside and the lack of social security provided by the Chinese government motivate many poor rural Chinese families to try to have a boy.

In China, adoption facilitators play a key role in mediating parents' experiences of China and Chinese culture. As Sara Dorow observes, "Chineseness is reproduced and performed around the body of the child through the labor of facilitators—and not just for the consumption of adoptive parents who expect to learn about 'beautiful China' but also for facilitators themselves and for local Chinese who witness the exchange" (2006b, 136).

My interviews with adoption facilitators and guides further indicate that the messages relayed through this process can also reflect conflicted ideas about China held by facilitators, who may struggle with presenting information to parents that might bring them outside of their comfort zone exemplified by Dorow's "beautiful China" idea. There exists a tension between providing parents with a positive view of China and also making them aware of the history and conditions leading to poverty and adoption. It is here that the boundaries of the parents' security bubble are sometimes flexed.

I asked Roxanne, our Wuhan guide and facilitator, about how tours for adoptive parents differed from those for regular tourists. Roxanne said that she gives the same general information about the city to both adoptive parents and other tourists, but that adoptive parents stay in the city longer to take care of paperwork and move at a slower speed because of the babies. She noted that "their hearts are open, and they are ready to accept Chinese culture" and that they seem very interested when she tells them about Chinese culture. She mentioned an example of some adoptive parents who later took their older daughter back to her orphanage, noting the parents' intense interest in learning about their daughter's circumstances before she became part of their family.

It was clear from talking with Roxanne that her contact with adoptive parents has also made her concerned about how they viewed China. While she hoped that the children adopted from China would see themselves as Chinese Americans, she also wanted them to know that China has a long history and a beautiful culture. She wanted them to respect China—even though it is poor, most people work hard. At this point, tears welled up in her eyes, and she apologized for becoming emotional. Although she respected adoptive parents and the care they provided for their children, she also seemed ashamed of the poverty and other circumstances that led to these children being available for adoption in the first place, and of how this reflected China's poverty and underdevelopment. She felt good about her work facilitating adoptions, but it seemed that she had also been impacted by the sheer numbers of infants leaving China who might grow up without an understanding of the complex circumstances in their birth country.

Similar issues regarding the complex circumstances leading to infant abandonment in China had arisen when I interviewed Susan, the main China-based coordinator for the adoption agency. I interviewed Susan in my room at the White Swan Hotel and later had an opportunity to spend time with her informally over lunch. I asked her whether she thought that the American adoptive parents with whom she worked seemed to understand why Chinese families relinquish their babies. She estimated that many families, perhaps 80 percent, do not fully understand the complexities of the Chinese "social system and social life" that lead to children being abandoned, as well as the changes in China that are leading to improved conditions for many. She explains to adoptive parents that the one-child policy became problematic because the government does not provide insurance or social security for its older citizens. Sons are a form of insurance, because a daughter must move to her husband's home. She explains to parents that the goal of Deng Xiaoping's policy was to make the cities rich first, and now in the countryside there are both rich and poor villages. She would like adoptive parents to understand that there is a "lack of balance" in China now, and that 80 percent of the people are still poor. If she could, she would like to take parents to the countryside to show them the conditions there. However, she also told me, parents are often surprised when they arrive in Beijing and see how developed it is, like any modern city. She said that the Beijing office of the adoption agency with which she is affiliated is creating a web page, which will eventually address the social and cultural aspects of adoption from China.

The facilitators also mediate understandings of Chinese adoption for the local Chinese with whom they interact. In her work with adoptive parents, Roxanne has had an opportunity to interact with locals who are curious about adoption. She said that some people thought that adoption was a positive thing and that the babies were lucky to escape orphanage conditions; others feel that it reflects negatively on the Chinese government and fear that the babies will be used for their organs. She shows them pictures of children with their adoptive families and tells them the parents will raise and educate them. She also noted that in the city, people are increasingly open to having daughters, mentioning a common saying that to have a son is for reputation (*ming qi*) but to have a daughter is lucky (*fu qi*).

Conclusion

The trip to China provides much of the raw material for parents' constructions of their children's identities as they grow older, in relation to both adoption and racial/ethnic identity issues. It enables them to engage in what many of them view as a form of cosmopolitan travel in which they are exposing themselves to new cultural experiences. However, as described throughout this chapter, their experiences are highly mediated and serve to reinforce their preexisting ideas about Chinese cultural difference and about differences between the developed world and the developing world. Of course, all organized travel experiences are mediated (Kelner 2010; Louie 2004), and ideas about the relative development of China and the first world are long-standing and persistent, driving new generations of Chinese students to venture abroad to study (V. Fong 2011). However, just as the conceptions of Chinese students may shift as they spend time abroad, one may hope that adoptive parents' ideas about China may open up as a result of the time they spent there.

Adoptive parents' experiences in China were mediated by numerous sources. Parents dealt with Chinese government officials, to whom they had to promise never to abandon their child and to teach the child about Chinese culture. Their adoption agency distributed materials on adoption and China prior to travel. And local tour guides and agency workers introduced the cities we visited, briefed parents on what to expect, guided parents to the Civil Affairs Office to receive their children and process paperwork, and took the group to local temples and museums.

However, as illustrated throughout this chapter, adoptive parents experienced China in a manner that is more broadly indicative of encounters between U.S. and other first world citizens and third world destinations, and in ways that allowed them to continue to experience and mold their versions of Chinese culture from afar after they returned home. Anthropologists, among others, serve as mediators of these constructions. As middle-class Americans, adoptive parents' relatively privileged position affords them a degree of capital, mobility, and access to resources to assemble their own versions of "culture" to insert within the so-called U.S. melting pot. Adoptive parents do not possess the mobility of groups commonly thought of as transnational (such as Hong Kong Chinese "astronauts" [Ong 1999]), whose access to capital gives them the flexibility and mobility to spread their family members across multiple locations as a business strategy. However, parents can flexibly learn about, collect, and even create their own versions of "Chinese" culture using "Chinese" ideas, goods, and personal connections available through transnational flows that permit everyday Americans access to "global" resources. In the context of twenty-first-century racial and cultural politics, identities are negotiated across national borders in relation to local, national, and transnational influences (Appadurai 1991; Hall 1990; Schein 1997). In particular, most adoptive parents and their children have the means to create linkages with fellow adoptive families and various resources related to adoption and Chinese culture, even China itself, which will allow them to continue to actively create and negotiate the content of their identities, though within limits. This privilege of mobility, for example, will allow them, if they wish, to return to China on homeland tours created specifically for Chinese adoptees and their families.

But it is also important to recognize that the set of images and understandings that parents receive in China become memorialized and renarrated in the form of the memory books they create for their children and adoption stories that they tell them. They do not necessarily remain static, as both parents' and children's understandings of these images may change over time and with new information, for example, from a homeland tour. When infused with the imagination and memory, they can take on new significance, as evidenced by an interview I conducted with a fourteen-year-old who had visited her hometown in China with her parents while on a trip to adopt her younger brother. She told me she'd had a weird feeling of déjà vu, noticing little things that seemed familiar. Before going to China, she'd had a dream in which she was in a park with metal dragons. She could see herself there as a baby in a sling. She was not sure if this image came from actual memories from when she was a baby, from looking at the pictures in her photo book, or just from the dream world created by her imagination.

4

Asian American Adoptive Parents

Freedom and Flexibility

They overdo it. They send them to the Chinese schools, and when you see them you say, my god, we don't even dress like that . . . where do you get that stuff? My husband is like poking me . . . they're all in that garb, and I'm like, I'm sorry, they should not be wearing hats with pigtails . . . remember *Bonanza*? It's a negative connotation for us when we see that growing up and all of the racism we went through in the sixties. We go to a party, and my girls are wearing party dresses. . . . I think [white parents] are trying to compensate, but I think they overcompensate. I don't think they know, and they are trying to compensate, . . . Do the kids run around saying I'm Chinese? I don't think your whole identity has to be about being Chinese. Your identity is whoever you are, you just happen to be Chinese.
—Judy, Chinese American adoptive mother, regarding white adoptive parents

I can be flippant about it, but the truth is, I get to be authentic, just because of my genetic makeup and what my face looks like, I cannot help but be authentically Chinese. . . . I can do anything I want, I don't have to eat *jook* [Chinese rice porridge] or anything. . . . I haven't earned it. . . . [It's] just the chance of where I came from, the biology. . . . You can't judge what other people are doing to pass on culture and to create culture for their children.
—Desiree, Chinese American adoptive mother, in discussion with other adoptive parents

As these quotes from Chinese American adoptive parents indicate, white parents' constructions of Chinese culture have been subject to a number of critiques, relating to the racist and Orientalist implications of these practices, as noted by Judy, the first mother quoted here, or the questions of cultural authenticity, as discussed by Desiree, the second mother. Desiree admits that as a Chinese American, she maintains the right to do "anything I want" and deem it an "authentic" Chinese practice, just because of her racial background. She concludes that it is therefore difficult to pass judgment on the authenticity of the cultural practices of others. At a later point in the conversation, she notes that while she thinks the practice of wearing Chinese dresses at adoptive family Chinese holiday celebrations is odd and not something that most Chinese Americans she knows do, she (ironically, she observes) ended up finding a nice white *cheong-sam* in China to use for her daughter's baptism.[1] In this sense, the comments from both of these mothers lead to an interesting observation: Chinese American adoptive parents possess flexibility in the ways that they create and practice (or do not practice) Chinese or Chinese American culture. Their inherent "authenticity" as Chinese Americans permits them to be, in Desiree's words, "whoever you are"; as Judy indicates, she just "happen[s] to be Chinese." However, Chineseness is always to some degree "performed" (Jackson 2001), even if the authenticity of this performance may be rooted in ideas of authenticity based on racial origins.

The Case for Comparison

In the introduction, I presented three questions that frame this research, regarding the conceptions of China and Chinese culture that inform both white and Asian American adoptive parents' effectiveness in addressing racial and cultural identity issues for adoptees, and how these meanings of Chineseness are renegotiated over time as they are practiced within daily lives. In this chapter, I focus on these issues for the Asian American adoptive parents I interviewed.

As will be discussed in the following chapter, white parents construct Chinese identities in various ways, ranging from the more superficial, celebratory approaches that are often criticized, to more nuanced approaches that reflect the multiple meanings and contexts within which

Chinese identities play out. Asian American parents, most of whom have personally struggled with issues of cultural and racial identity and cultural authenticity, also conceive of Chinese identity issues in a variety of ways. What might not be as obvious is that, like white parents, Asian American adoptive parents also take culture "out of context" as they negotiate flexible, contemporary "Chinese" (American) identities in the context of U.S. multiculturalism and racial politics. But while white parents may be viewed as both absorbing their children's racial identities and taking liberties with Chinese culture, Asian American adoptive parents' experimentations with Chinese culture may be perceived as part of a natural process of culture change over time. Of course, Chinese or Chinese American symbols carry a different significance when they are employed by whites rather than by Asian Americans because of the histories of Orientalism and white domination to which these symbols are tied. However, it is important to remember that as products of the West, Asian Americans may also hold Orientalist ideas about Asia and Asians. This was certainly true for the American-born Chinese Americans I studied in my previous work. Because they had grown up in the Cold War era, much of what they knew about China was filtered through U.S. media and propaganda about the region (Louie 2004).

Asian American adoptive parents possess a "privilege of authenticity" regarding Asian and Asian American cultural practices. All Chinese Americans, including adoptees, whether raised by white parents or Asian American parents, must negotiate what it means to be "Chinese" within the shifting politics of race and culture in the United States. Issues of cultural authenticity are thus closely tied to questions of cultural change—by what processes are new cultural forms produced, and how do the uneven power relations and histories that define the relationships between whites and Asian Americans factor into these productions? How do attempts at self-fashioning and building cultural capital present possibilities for the construction of alternative identities?

For this discussion, it is important to consider how we should conceptualize culture itself and the process by which it changes. Anthropological conceptions of culture view it not as a form of high culture that some people possess more of and other possess less of (as in manners, knowledge about the opera, etc.) but rather as a lens through which we see and understand our everyday lives. Culture can be seen as a set of beliefs, morals, and practices that guide our daily interactions with others in our community (Tylor [1871] 1920), but it has also been described as a "web of meaning" (Geertz 1973). Such conceptions of culture are important because they go against folk conceptions that identify only certain, often more visible and performative practices as constituting culture. When I ask my university students whether or not they have culture, many claim that they do not because they do not identify strongly with a particular set of ethnic traditions. Similarly, both white and Asian American adoptive parents I interviewed thought of culture as being composed of family traditions passed down from generation to generation. This shaped how they envisioned what Chinese culture looked like and how they imagined it being incorporated into their own families. The idea that culture consisted of traditions to some degree existed in tension with the idea that culture could be newly invented or modified. Thus, even those Chinese cultural practices that adoptive parents consciously implemented in an effort to honor the Chinese background of their children were framed as traditional practices that just happened to be new to their family. This did not stop parents from taking some degree of license in inventing new, hybrid traditions around adoption and Chinese culture, such as Gotcha Day. White parents are able to exercise ethnic options (Waters 1990) in picking and choosing elements of symbolic identities. But at least when it came to Asian culture, Asian American parents enjoyed a "privilege of authenticity" that enabled them to flexibly interpret both new and old practices as representing Asian or Chinese traditions for their family.

However, it is important not to think of these processes for white and Asian American parents as equivalent. Growing up as racial minorities in the United States, most Asian Americans will be more cognizant of the broader contexts of power in which meanings of Chineseness circulate. In contrast, white adoptive parents will have had less firsthand contact with China or Chinese culture. Even those white parents who have lived in China or in Chinese American communities will not have had direct exposure to racism and discrimination, though, as I discuss in the next chapter, many begin to experience these things through their children. Thus, while both groups may engage in the self-fashioning of Chinese identities in the context of their own families, their processes differ.

Although some adoptive parents may not make efforts to connect to China or Chinese people, most of these parents would not have agreed to take part in a study conducted by a Chinese American anthropologist. Most adoptive parents I interviewed in both St. Louis and the Bay Area sought some degree of contact with and acceptance from the local Chinese American community. They had been encouraged by social workers and other adoption experts to make connections to Chinese Americans so as to expose their children to Chinese culture and to provide role models for them in combating racism (NABSW 1972; Steinberg and Hall 2000). However, in acting on this advice, many parents make assumptions about the ways that Chinese Americans practice Chinese culture. Many parents I interviewed assumed that the Chinese American community approached Chinese culture in organic and authentic ways. What is interesting here is that though many white adoptive parents are guided by these assumptions about Chinese Americans, the assumptions may not be true.

White adoptive parents may draw upon the Chinese American community to ease their fears that they are unwittingly passing on "inauthentic" versions of Chinese culture to their children, in contrast to the "authentic," legitimate forms of Chinese culture that they imagine Chinese Americans practice at home. Many white interviewees expressed insecurity regarding the accuracy of their use and interpretations of Chinese culture. At a Parents' Night Out gathering in St. Louis, one adoptive mother asked me and the Taiwanese American adviser to Families with Children from China to tell her what was written in Chinese on her pant legs. She joked that she feared the words said "stupid American" and was therefore hesitant to wear them around "Chinese" people. Her trepidation reflects broader insecurities about her ability as a non-Chinese adoptive parent to accurately and competently provide her child with the resources for her to function as a Chinese person, who may not fit easily into either the white or the Chinese American community because of her upbringing. In a separate interview, this mother noted:

> What I worry about with an adopted child who is raised, you know, her being raised in a Caucasian family, is she'll never quite fit into the Caucasian community but she'll never quite fit into the Chinese American community because she is not bilingual and she wasn't raised that way.

But as we've gotten to know people in the Chinese community, at least in St. Louis, they are so open, they seem very open.

Her comment also reflects certain, not uncommon assumptions about the "Chinese community" itself—that it is a discrete community, that it is bilingual, and that its members would be literate enough to read the characters on her pant legs. However, the Chinese American community is diverse in terms of class, generation, language ability, and numerous other factors. Perhaps ironically, many Chinese Americans whom adoptive parents imagine practice authentic Chinese culture may approach issues of Chinese culture and roots in ways that are not entirely dissimilar from the approaches of white adoptive parents in terms of their flexible interpretation of Chinese culture.

Sara Dorow, who interviewed both white and Chinese American adoptive parents for her research, found that Chinese American adoptive parents distinguished their own practices from those of white adoptive parents, even though there was some overlap in their approaches. She found that Chinese American parents worried about the authenticity of the Chinese culture that white parents were teaching their children; they also acknowledged that there may be many ways to practice Chinese culture, and that as Chinese Americans, "whatever way one did it was right in the context of a particular family history and a shared, racialized history of immigration and settlement" (Dorow 2006b, 230). She notes that these parents also realized that having a strong sense of Chinese identity was not a total solution for the broader issues of belonging faced by Chinese Americans in the United States.

A Model Family?

How can we begin to unpack the complexities of Asian American identity production in the context of adoption? As I asked in the introduction, what combination of self-exploration, family tradition, and invention serves to create Chinese American culture, and what does this say about the construction of cultures more broadly? While Chinese American adoptive parents are often assumed to possess a naturalized form of Chinese cultural authenticity, which will allow them to easily pass on "Chinese culture" to their children adopted from China, upon closer examination, what may appear to be an example of a "model" Chinese American family reveals the complexity of Chinese and Asian American identities. I turn to Asian American scholar Lisa Lowe's (1996) model of Asian American cultural change to provide an analysis of these processes.

In late November 2006, I interviewed Chinese American adoptive parents Joe and Betty in their San Francisco home. I had arrived later than planned after having gotten caught in the traffic leading from Oakland to the Bay Bridge. I had brought along my husband and son (then three) to help me navigate, and they had planned to play at a local park while I conducted the interview, but once my son saw the children and toys in Joe and Betty's spacious home, he did not want to leave. Betty kindly invited him to come in and play, and I began the interview. At one point, Betty took the opportunity to introduce her son to me, and he greeted me in Cantonese. Joe and Betty spoke Cantonese to one another at home prior to adopting their two children, and they continued to do so. In addition, they sent their children to a bilingual Cantonese-English preschool and had a Mandarin-speaking nanny come in six days per week for five hours per day to care for the children and speak Mandarin to them. As a result, both children, a son adopted from Taiwan and a daughter adopted from China, were fluent in Cantonese and Mandarin Chinese. The parents planned to take their children to China in the summer to immerse them in the language—to create a "platform" for them—and also considered sending them to a Mandarin immersion school.

Betty was also involved in international business and used Chinese in her work. She thought that knowledge of Chinese would be a valuable skill for her children to acquire. Though she did not use the expression "cultural capital," it was clear that she viewed Chinese language fluency not only as representing a form of cultural heritage but also as a valuable skill for the future in an international business context. Noting that their children "live and breathe Chinese culture," she cited as examples the fact that they say "good morning" in Chinese every day, make a point of eating together as a family, and regularly eat rice, a Chinese food. They see their grandparents every weekend and also celebrate holidays with them, including Ching Ming (Mandarin: *Qingming*), the grave-sweeping festival, during which they clean their ancestors' graves with wet wipes.

She emphasized that they also celebrate American holidays. In fact, Joe had not been able to participate in the entire interview because he needed to periodically attend to the turkey he was cooking for a belated Thanksgiving meal the family was going to take to Joe's parents' house. I had asked him to follow up with me via e-mail regarding a question I had asked Betty regarding the impact of race and racism on their children's lives. Joe sent this reply the following week:

> Betty and I will try to raise our children to become "complete" persons. "Complete" meaning being functional, having awareness, confidence and inner drive, caring and empathy for others, and knowing oneself. Issues of Race/Racism are real and will undoubtably [*sic*] affect them in the future. I hope they will be able to develop a critical understanding how race/racism affects them and others in society, and still be open and fair with others. Unfortunately, I believe just telling them that they [are] just as good as everyone else in society will not be enough. Being Asian-Americans, Betty and I will expose them to Chinese culture without even trying—especially now since some of the older generation in the family are still with us. I think that this will be important for them in the future when they get older and try to define for themselves what it means to be Asian in America.

Joe's answer is not representative of all Chinese American or Asian American parents, nor is his perspective on race and identity necessarily unique to these groups. However, his words highlight a number of important issues. Joe's e-mail indicates that he understands that his children's Asian American identities will develop not only in relation to the cultural knowledge that he and Betty share with them but also in response to their positions as racial minorities in the United States. While he observes that race and racism will "undoubtably [*sic*] affect" his children, his closing statement discusses helping his children "define for themselves what it means to be Asian in America." In addition, he indicates that knowledge about Chinese culture will enable his children to achieve this.[2] His use of the broader racialized term "Asian" rather than the more ethnically specific term "Chinese" is significant in the sense that it indicates his understanding of "Asian American" as both a racialized and a politicized category. Though the term has Orientalist origins, having been employed to lump together everyone from that geographic region for the purposes of enacting discriminatory legislation, since the late 1960s, it has also been used as a basis from which those placed in this category have engaged in civil rights activism.

Also significant is his assertion that his children will define these identities "for themselves." Rather than viewing their identities as solely tied to their birth origins in Taiwan and China, he sees their identities as continuing to develop within the context of the United States, as part of a process over which they can exercise some agency. Interestingly, in his statement about passing on Chinese culture to their children "without even trying," he also refers to Chinese culture in a somewhat essentialized manner, as a naturalized phenomenon transmitted from generation to generation. It was also clear that he and Betty were "trying" and that they viewed the building of Chineseness as a form of cultural capital as a necessary and strategic matter. They had the resources—financial, social, and cultural—to provide opportunities for their children to learn both Mandarin and Cantonese. While they viewed their family's practice of Chinese and Chinese American culture as being rooted in specific practices and traditions in a naturalized sense, this coexisted with an awareness of the racialization of Chinese Americans in an Asian American context.

Joe's words illustrate some of cultural studies scholar Lisa Lowe's observations on the production of Asian American identities that she outlines in her classic essay "Heterogeneity, Hybridity, Multiplicity" (2003). In this work Lowe emphasizes both the diversity and the dynamism that characterize Asian American identities, and the contradictory "desire for a cultural identity represented by a fixed profile of traits" (2003, 136) that focuses on the idea of persistent, inherited forms of Asian American cultural and racial identity.

As a forty-seven-year-old second-generation Chinese American who grew up in San Francisco's Chinatown, Joe had likely been exposed to some of the racism and discrimination for which he wishes to prepare his children, as well as some of the social movements through which Asian Americans have struggled to negotiate identities as Asian minorities in the United States. While Joe was tending to the turkey, Betty mentioned that Joe's family had immigrated to the United States in the 1950s, when discrimination against Asians was more widespread.

Joe's father had initially come to the United States in 1917 as a laborer and had served in the U.S. military. He later returned to Hong Kong to marry Joe's mother, who grew up in a rural area. Betty implied that, as a result, Joe's values were more "Chinese" than her own. Betty was a first-generation immigrant from Macao, and generation is often assumed to correlate with the strength of cultural values, so I asked for clarification. She explained that Joe's family and others of their generation were more rooted in the traditional Chinese culture they had brought with them in the 1950s, and she thought they had retained these values. In contrast, she thought Hong Kong (and Macao) culture had continued to change. As an example, she cited the fact that in Hong Kong, there are many new and varied types of mooncakes, small, decorated cakes filled with lotus seed paste, duck eggs, nuts, or other fillings and eaten during the Mid-Autumn Festival, in contrast to the more limited and traditional selection available in San Francisco. She implied that these Chinese cultures of origin in Hong Kong and Macao continued to change and innovate, and perhaps become less traditional over time, in contrast to the Chinese American culture of San Francisco Chinatown, which remained more traditional.

Betty's observation illustrates how Asian Americans themselves employ assumptions about cultural authenticity, and about how culture is passed from generation to generation. In one sense, Betty's thoughts on generation and Chinese cultural values echo Lowe's (1996) discussion of the common perception that Asian Americans are viewed as originating from a pure mother culture, with immigrant generations struggling to continue this culture and subsequent generations feeling the pressure to assimilate into American culture. In another sense, however, her ideas about her own more recent immigrant culture being less traditional disrupt some of these assumptions and illustrate the "heterogeneity, hybridity, and multiplicity" that Lowe argues in fact define Asian American identities. In emphasizing "heterogeneity," Lowe calls attention to the variability within the racialized category "Asian American," in terms of place of origin, generation, class, and gender. "Hybridity" speaks to the "histories of uneven and unsynthetic power relations" that define some members of the Asian American community. "Multiplicity" refers to the manner in which "social relations are determined by several different axes of power" (Lowe 2003, 138). These concepts can together be used to rethink the prevalent idea that Asian Americans are "ho-mogenous" (139). In Betty's example, the varied histories of Hong Kong and Macao culture, as Chinese societies that had been subject to British and Portuguese colonialism and the transnational trading cultures that developed around them, had produced a form of Chinese culture that in her mind was less traditional than the rural Chinese values that had been transported to the United States generations ago by Joe's family.

Lowe's conceptualization of Asian American identities provides a starting point from which to discuss the construction of Chinese adoptee identities within the context of Asian American adoptive families, and possibly may be extrapolated to discuss adoptive families more broadly. There are multiple notions of culture at work within Asian American cultural production—specifically, ideas of Asian American culture as something both inherited and continually produced anew. Building upon these points, Lowe emphasizes culture as a means through which individuals can invent and assert identities as "American," resolving re-lationships to the fragmented past, as well as carving out relationships to the future (1996, 2–3) and creating new, hybrid identities (82). Rather than being fixed and inherited, they are "constituted in relation to his-torical and material differences" (Lowe 2003, 136). In other words, Asian American cultural production is marked by a dialectical process char-acterized both by the production of identities in resistance to existing hegemonies and power structures, and by the continued negotiation of these identities in relation to historically rooted inequalities that con-tinually resurface in new forms.

But while Lowe's model is useful for understanding the relationship between material conditions, resistance, and identity in Asian American cultural production, it may also be limited in its application to the Asian American population more broadly. Lowe views Asian American iden-tity as a political project involving the formation of resistance cultures. However, the Asian American movement has largely been restricted to a group of select academics and activists (Omatsu 1994). Many who may be included within this pan-ethnic category that encompasses peoples of Asian descent from a variety of backgrounds may not even identify as Asian American but rather as Hmong (American), Japanese (Ameri-can), Chinese (American), or Vietnamese (American), or perhaps even as Toisanese (Chinese), Shanghainese (Chinese), or Fujianese (Chinese).

How can this model of cultural change be applied to the everyday negotiations that characterize the lives of Asian Americans who are not central to politicized movements that are based on a shared political consciousness and goals?

In my research interviews with Asian American adoptive parents in the Bay Area, I observed that, like Joe, many Asian American adoptive parents were actively involved in negotiating their identities as Chinese or Asian American. However, to varying degrees they viewed Asian American identity as a political project and acknowledged the "historical and material differences" that shaped it. Like the adopted teens I discuss in chapter 7, they too carved out their own spheres of Chineseness consisting of customized combinations of family traditions and new innovations. They also to varying degrees acknowledged the impact of race on their and their children's lives and employed a variety of strategies in response.

So where does this leave us? Examining the complexity that characterizes what appears to be a model of an "authentic" Chinese American adoptive family that retains language ability and cultural practices allows us to view their process of Chinese American identity construction as emerging from the continuity of family traditions that, though in some ways inherited from previous generations, are also the product of hybridized histories. It also allows us to see how even families who may appear to be "traditional" in their celebration of Chinese holidays, associations with other Chinese, and retention of the Chinese language are also continually self-fashioning (Zhang and Ong 2008) their Chineseness as both a form of racialized identity and a form of cultural capital. Joe and Betty's actions remind us of the role that parents play in preemptively crafting identities for their children. It is likely that whether Joe and Betty adopted children or had biological children, they would have raised them with similar attention to building their Chinese cultural capital.

This example reveals some of the limitations of Lowe's model of Asian American identity production and activism. The following discussion of various Asian American adoptive parent identities allows for the further exploration of how these processes might be changing within the broader context of contemporary politics of race, culture, and adoption.

Varied Approaches

Again building on the questions about the production and negotiation of Chineseness I laid out in the introduction and presented again at the beginning of this chapter, this section explores how Asian American adoptive parents explored their own Asianness or Chineseness throughout their life course, and how they conceptualized Chinese culture and adjusted and negotiated its content in the context of adoption and parenthood. I hope to demystify the assumptions held by many white parents about Chinese American and Asian American parents by profiling how the latter approach issues of cultural and racial identity. I end this chapter with a discussion of how Asian American adoptive parents continue to understand and negotiate Chineseness in the context of a multicultural and racialized society. These parents employ a variety of techniques to expose their children to Chinese culture, adjusting and negotiating the content of "Chinese culture" as their children grow older. However, unlike white parents, they draw upon their own knowledge and upon their networks of family and friends to expose their children to Chinese culture, in addition to in some cases further exploring Chineseness on their own. For some, attitudes toward their own Chineseness have changed over their life course, particularly after adopting a child from China. But while some of my interviewees took the opportunity to learn more about China and Chinese culture upon adopting a child from China, others appeared to not make any special efforts to incorporate additional exposure to Chinese culture into their children's lives. Instead, they were more likely than their white counterparts to identify daily practices and values, rather than material culture or holiday celebrations, as being central to their conceptions of Chinese culture. They saw celebrating the occasional Chinese holiday and, more important, showing respect for elders, insisting on paying the bill at a restaurant, and cleaning the house before Chinese New Year, as ingrained aspects of Chinese culture that they had experienced and that they were incorporating into their children's lives. They flexibly defined or redefined these practices as "Chinese," often portraying them as essentialized Chinese cultural values, even though their white counterparts might be seen as taking liberties in their interpretations of Chinese culture if they did the same.

Like Dorow (2006b), I also observed that while some Asian American adoptive parents critiqued the practices of white adoptive parents, as a group they were not overly concerned with defining correct and incorrect ways to practice Chinese culture for themselves. Perhaps this was because as Chinese Americans, they were already familiar with the range of practices that could define Chinese culture, as well as how such practices can vary over time, across generations, and by location. As a group, Asian American parents viewed the relationship between Chinese and Chinese American culture in a more fluid manner than white parents, having grown up in households that often mixed languages and creatively modified "traditional" cultural practices. More important, the fact that parents and children were seen as racially matching gave Asian American adoptive parents the flexibility to practice Chinese culture without concerns over issues of cultural authenticity.[3] Their life experiences led them to understand cultural change and authenticity in ways that differed from mainstream American perceptions. One Chinese American adoptive father, Daniel, observed that many white families viewed Chinese American culture as a less authentic, or Americanized, version of Chinese culture. He saw Chinese American culture as its own entity, a "self-made" cultural production that is connected to living as minorities in the United States. However, he noted that many white adoptive parents judged Chinese American culture to be a less authentic version of Chinese culture:

> I was on the board of FCC way back (96 to 97) and at the time I remember they were very interested in Chinese culture but not in Chinese American culture. And I brought that up a few times. I don't think they ever really understood. They thought that Chinese American culture was Chinese culture that has been sort of Americanized. I don't think they ever understood that.

I asked him how he would define Chinese American culture, and he responded:

> It's kind of self-made. You have influence from the media, peer groups around you, your parents, and you kind of make something on your own. Whoever writes, whoever makes movies, . . . they have kind of built

something together that other people follow along. . . . It's probably more American than it is Chinese. . . . It's like an adaptation. I think it's very misunderstood.

Daniel thought that because parents had gone to China to get their children, they thought of them as Chinese, but he emphasized that the children will grow up as Chinese Americans and will have to deal with the issues that stem from living as minorities in the United States. In the U.S. context, they will not be viewed as or be able to live as "Chinese from China." His validation of Chinese American culture as a legitimate and not necessarily less authentic form of Chinese culture was also connected to an acknowledgment that their experience as racial minorities makes most Asian Americans more cognizant of racial hierarchies and inequalities.

A number of Asian American adoptive parents observed that their child was more Chinese than they were because the child was a first-generation immigrant and they were second or third generation. A child born in China had important connections to China in the form of orphanage or foster family ties and a birth mother. While parents clearly recognized that being born in China did not automatically give their children knowledge about Chinese language and culture, the idea of their child being "closer to China" remained powerful. For many Chinese Americans, China is a foreign and mysterious place with which many might not readily identify (Louie 2003, 2004). For those who grew up during the Cold War, China represented an oppressive society, and many Chinese Americans absorbed the stereotypes and propaganda that predominated at the time. These Cold War images have given way to a newer and more complex set of images and stereotypes, including China as a new economic superpower. When these Chinese Americans travel to China, many for the first time, they must grapple with anxieties and expectations that have been formed through their own imaginings of China as shaped through the lens of mainstream U.S. portrayals of China and Chinese people. The American-born Chinese Americans I studied previously reacted in various ways to these encounters with China, with some further exploring their Chinese "roots" and others feeling out of place in China and revalidating their identities as Americans. Similarly, while some Asian American adoptive parents used their children's connections to China to (re)connect with China, others acknowledged the connections but did not necessarily act upon them. However, shifting attitudes toward China in the United States and toward knowledge of Chinese language and culture as forms of cultural capital in a cosmopolitan world may make connecting to China more desirable for Chinese Americans than it was in the Cold War era.

I begin with a brief overview of the diversity of backgrounds that characterized the Asian American adoptive parents I interviewed. As a group, they possessed varying forms of knowledge about Chinese culture and defined its content in different ways, depending on generation, exposure to others in the Chinese American community, and their own processes of exploring Chinese culture. They also came upon this knowledge in different ways, some having practiced certain customs and spoken Chinese while growing up, and others discovering Buddhism, learning Chinese, and investigating other aspects of Chinese, Chinese American, and Asian American cultures later in life. Many hailed from the Bay Area itself; others came from Hawaii or directly from Hong Kong or China. They ranged from first-generation immigrants like Joe and Betty, who spoke fluent Chinese, to second- and third-generation immigrants, who spoke little Chinese at all. While some were married to other Chinese Americans, their partners were sometimes of a different generation. Others were married to non-Chinese or were not married at all. They also shared with their white counterparts concerns regarding how to address issues related to both adoption and Chinese heritage. All were solidly middle or upper middle class, with professions such as computer programmer, international financier, lawyer, and dietician. Most of their children were female, though Joe and Betty had adopted their older son from Taiwan, and another mother had a son from China. All the Asian American adoptive parents I interviewed talked openly with their children about their adoptions.

Adopting from China

Like the white parents I interviewed, Asian American parents adopted for a variety of reasons, primarily infertility or wanting to start a family as a single mother. Some had adopted in their thirties, but most had adopted in their forties, with one mother having adopted in her early fifties. Most had chosen China for the same reasons white parents had: though the laws have been modified over the years regarding the minimum and maximum ages of adoptive parents, adoption by single parents, and other restrictions, the Chinese government's system was generally conducive to adoptions by "older" parents. It was also previously a viable option for single parents.

Unlike white adoptive parents, however, the Asian American parents I interviewed, most of whom were of Chinese American heritage, had a familial connection to China. I interviewed Lucy, a youthful-looking, petite woman in her late thirties with a two-year-old daughter from China, at her home in a newer housing development in the East Bay. She had taken time off from work, and her daughter and husband were not at home. She and her Chinese American husband had decided to adopt after learning that she could not safely give birth because of a health condition. When I asked why they decided to adopt from China, she said that, for them, China seemed like a natural choice. She and her husband are both of Chinese descent, China had a well-functioning adoption system in place, and they had heard that children adopted from China were healthy, having been relinquished primarily because they were girls. Most of the other Chinese American parents with whom I spoke shared similar reasons for choosing to adopt from China—citing a combination of family heritage and the efficiency and reliability of the Chinese adoption system. However, while it might seem logical that Asian American parents would want to adopt an Asian child, Keiko, a Japanese American mother, told me that she felt she was the victim of "reverse discrimination" when she began looking into domestic adoption in the Bay Area in the late 1980s and was told by several agencies that they did not have any Asian babies. When she replied that she did not necessarily want an Asian baby, she was told that usually the babies and the parents were required to be of the same race.

While Keiko did not necessarily want a white baby, it is also rare for parents of color to adopt white babies, even internationally. The companion DVD to *Adopted the Movie* includes a section with interviews of African American adoptive parents who adopted their daughter from Sweden, and Asian American parents who adopted their son from Israel. At the end of the section, it is revealed that the families had been portrayed by actors. The filmmakers could not find any actual examples of people of color adopting white children, whether domestically or internationally, illustrating that international adoption flows were primarily unidirectional—from poorer to richer nations, and of nonwhite children into white or same-race homes.

Gender was also an issue for Asian American parents considering adoption from China, though sometimes in a different way than it might have been for white adoptive parents. The chances of receiving a female baby from China were quite high, as over 97 percent of adoptees from China are female. Lucy had been nervous telling her husband's parents about their adoption plans because she had thought they were old-fashioned and therefore would have wanted a male grandchild. Unaware that Lucy's health problems prevented her from safely carrying a biological child, her in-laws had thought Lucy and their son were going to announce a pregnancy when they said they had news to share. Upon hearing of the plan to adopt from China, Lucy's in-laws initially did ask if it would be possible to adopt a boy, but in the end they were very happy that she was not going to endanger her health by trying to have a biological child.

As this example illustrates, while for younger generations of Chinese Americans, adoption may have seemed like a viable option for starting a family, the parents I interviewed often worried about how their own parents would react. Various forms of adoption have existed traditionally in China, including the adoption of male heirs, either related or unrelated, for lineage continuity (Watson 1975). However, attitudes toward these adoptions have also been complex, and adoptees were often accorded low social status. Lucy remembers that she and her husband were worried that his father, who is the oldest male in his family, would be less concerned about having a genetic grandchild than having a male heir. After they brought their oldest daughter home, they waited a week before inviting his parents over to meet her. However, to Lucy's relief, her father-in-law has treated their daughter the same as all of his other grandchildren. Indeed, Lucy had been touched when he told them to make sure to keep the finding ad that the orphanage had placed in the Chinese newspaper. Their adoption agency had given them a copy, and her father-in-law had noted that the ad stipulated that the child would be made available for adoption after ninety days. He wanted to ensure that they retained this proof that their daughter was indeed theirs to adopt.

Joe and Betty had also experienced initial resistance from Betty's father regarding their plans to adopt. Betty was not sure why her parents had opposed the adoption, but she assumed it was related to their disappointment in her not being able to conceive a biological child and also "the idea that you are picking up someone else's garbage." She felt that her parents had wanted to protect her from the unknown. However, when she showed her father her son's picture prior to adopting him, he "fell in love" with him. Three months later, Betty and Joe brought home their nine-month-old son, and he is now an accepted part of the family.

Judy told me that she had wanted to adopt a girl from China since she was five years old, even though her own mother had said many disapproving things about Judy's father having been adopted from within his extended family. Judy felt that she had received very negative messages about adoption, and she remembers her mother using her father's adoption as an explanation for various qualities of his that she did not like. Judy's husband had also wanted a biological child, but after trying fertility treatments for a year, they started the adoption process while Judy was still in her early thirties. They eventually adopted two girls.

Thus despite initial fear or resistance on the part of older family members, all the Asian American adoptive parents with whom I spoke found that their children were readily accepted by their grandparents.

Exploring Chineseness

Unlike Joe and Betty, the mothers portrayed in this section did not grow up knowing how to speak Chinese or regularly practicing Chinese rituals. For them, the adoption of a child from China spurred the continuation of their own explorations of Chinese culture and identity, including learning Mandarin Chinese. Others, discussed further later, decided to approach Chinese culture in the same way they would have if they had had biological children, singing the same songs, eating the same foods, and celebrating the same holidays. They also gave themselves license to modify some of these activities to suit their family's lifestyles or conform to current social norms, such as dispensing with the custom of not washing one's hair on Chinese New Year so as not to offend others. In this sense the construction of Chinese identities is always negotiated and in process. Even those parents who think they are replicating their own childhood traditions or raising their child as they would a biological child need to tap into a variety of resources and make decisions about how to practice Chineseness.

Yan is a third-generation Chinese American who feels passionately about raising her son in an atmosphere rich with Chinese and Chinese American culture. Yan's example demonstrates her negotiation of Chinese identity throughout her life course, bringing together her own interests in Chinese language and Buddhism with her parents' daily practices. This shows the flexibility with which Asian American parents craft identities for themselves and their children, but also the consciousness with which this process occurs.

When I first met Yan in 2006 in her East Bay home, she was recovering from a serious illness and spoke quietly but passionately about her adoption story, often pausing to recover from coughing fits. The second time I saw her, in 2008, she was much more robust, rolling in with her son on a tag-along bike for an FCC playgroup meeting at a local park. She later e-mailed me to invite my family over for dinner so we could chat, and so our sons could play together. We had a fun, relaxing evening as Yan and I caught up and her son showed my son his tree house and other toys.

Yan was born in 1958 in Southern California and grew up in a predominantly white suburb with her brothers. Her mother hailed from Indiana, though her family was originally from the *sze yup* (Mandarin: *si yi*), or four counties, region of Guangdong Province, an area where the majority of early Chinese immigrants to the United States originated. Her father grew up in San Francisco, and his family was also from the Pearl River delta area of Guangdong. Though Yan grew up speaking English at home, she recalls that her parents "kept the culture alive" in other ways. They would go to Chinatown weekly, and she remembers her mother disapproving of her dancing in public and commenting that "Chinese people won't like that." However, as she began to explore Chinese culture on her own as an adult, she realized that her mother's views were not representative of those of all Chinese people. She became interested in Chinese medicine in her twenties and Zen Buddhism in her thirties, realizing that these were among China's "greatest contributions to the world," despite the fact that her parents had spoken negatively about them.

Yan had been thinking about having a child since she was in her thirties but had never found the right person to settle down with. After deciding that she wanted to adopt, she realized that she would need to be self-supporting financially and could no longer afford her upscale home in the Berkeley Hills. She sold her home and moved closer to downtown Berkeley, where she renovated a home and ran it as a guesthouse. When she turned forty-four, she realized that she would need to move forward with her adoption soon, having read that Chinese adoption rules stipulated that one was not allowed to adopt someone more than forty-five years younger than oneself. At the time she was adopting (in 2003), most adoption agencies had initiated a lottery system for adoptions by single women, as the Chinese government was now using a quota system to restrict these adoptions. She finally found an agency that made an exception for people whose income exceeded a certain level, and she was able to have her name added to the list. She told me that she had requested a girl, and had a bedroom ready and painted pink, when she got a call from the agency asking if she would be willing to adopt a boy. She brought her son home at the age of thirteen months, continuing to use what she thought was his Chinese nickname. She later found out that he had never been called that name after asking a friend to call the orphanage, but the name has stuck.

It was only upon adopting from China and involving her parents in raising her son that Yan realized she had much in common with her parents and began to appreciate them further. After adopting her son, she moved to a smaller two-bedroom house in back of the guesthouse and moved her parents into the guesthouse in the front, which allows Yan and her son to see her parents daily. Yan's mother cooks healthy Chinese food for her son, and her father takes him to and from school each day while Yan is at work. She considers this care and the daily practices they engage in as a family—like eating white rice every day, knowing how to cook rice, and even appreciating the shape of the rice bowl itself—as important in transmitting culture, describing them as forms of "unspoken Chineseness."

In addition to these everyday practices that extend from her family experiences, Yan has made a conscious decision to teach herself Mandarin and to speak it with her son. She said that while "emotionally Cantonese would make more sense" because it is the language of her ancestors, she has chosen to learn Mandarin and teach it to her son to give him "bridges to others." She does not allow her son to watch television but does let him view Chinese language DVDs, including *Da Tou Erzi* (Big Head Boy) and *Sun Wukong* (The Monkey King). She sees knowledge of Mandarin as something that can change her relationships to her hairdresser and other Mandarin speakers—they are now "potential allies and friends." It gives her "a big thrill" to be able to speak Mandarin to her son. However, she has not ruled out teaching him to speak Spanish as well.

Yan told me that growing up in a predominantly white culture, she had always worried about the expectations of others. She would like her son to grow up as a "whole person, not as a displaced Chinese person." She emphasized that he will grow up as a Chinese American. Language abilities will give him bridges to others, but Chinese school is not enough. She wants him to grow up around kids of other races—to be a "citizen of the world," in the sense that Chinese language and cultural knowledge, and connections to Chinese people (including Chinese Americans) would help build a cosmopolitan identity for herself and her son. Her choice to learn Mandarin may be similar to Joe and Betty's decision to hire a Mandarin-speaking nanny to teach their children Mandarin, a much more widely spoken language, despite the fact that they speak Cantonese to one another at home.

Yan had created a particularized universe of Chinese influences for herself and her son, drawing upon both knowledge and practices of her parents and expanding on her own explorations of Chinese culture and language. In one respect, she seemed to regard Chineseness in an essentialized fashion, as embodied in simple, everyday practices, including the sensory aspects of cooking and eating rice. These could be carried out together with her parents, when they cooked or ate as a family. However, Yan also found it important to incorporate Mandarin into her son's life, which she had also learned for her own benefit so she could connect to other Chinese speakers in the community. During our 2008 visit, Yan told me that she had enrolled her son in a Chinese immersion school, where he was thriving. After we ate our turkey burgers, her son asked permission to go to his room and watch his *Monkey King* DVD. The rest of us followed to sit in his room and chat. Though the DVD was in Mandarin, he understood all of the dialogue, laughing and responding to the various scenes.

Though she is half Chinese and half white, Carol, an adoptive mother, strongly identified as a Chinese American woman, both racially and culturally. Like Yan, she seemed comfortable combining her understanding of family practices and traditions with aspects of Chinese culture she had explored on her own. I first met her at her home, high up on a steep hill in San Francisco, with a wonderful view of the city. She explained to me that she had chosen this location because her father had taught her about the importance of feng shui, though she notes that he did not specifically label those practices as such. Carol had invited me to sit down at a table so that we could have tea together and chat. On the wall above me hung a scroll with Chinese calligraphy that her father had written. She asked if I could read it, and I told her that I could not.

Carol was born in New York and had lived in Tennessee as a child and in upstate New York through her high school years. Her mother is from Kentucky, and her father is Chinese from Fujian Province. Perhaps due to her bicultural background, she seemed very reflective about the role of Chinese cultural values in her own life, particularly as they related to raising her daughter. However, she questioned which practices could actually be seen as constituting Chinese culture, given that some may not be unique to the Chinese. For example, she thought that the emphasis she placed on education (she was a lawyer) might be indicative of her Chinese cultural values. She also described herself as following some Chinese superstitions and noted that, like many Chinese people, she takes off her shoes in the house. But then she reflected: Do these things actually constitute Chinese culture? "How do you parse it out?" What about things such as showing respect for older people? Her boyfriend is Jewish, and from interacting with his elderly parents, she has observed that respect for elders is also valued in their culture.

She had started reading about adoption in the 1990s, and during a 1995 trip to China with her mother, she began to think more seriously about adopting as a single woman. She had been married previously but at the time had considered herself too young to have a child. Now she felt that her biological clock was ticking. She submitted her adoption paperwork and received her referral at the beginning of 2004, traveling a few months later to meet her daughter. Her sister-in-law who traveled with her ended up returning to China less than a year later to adopt a toddler she had met at Carol's daughter's orphanage.

Carol's questioning of the uniqueness of the content of the cultural practices she deems "Chinese" illustrates the relative flexibility that Asian Americans possess in crafting their own versions of Chinese culture. Like Yan, Carol drew upon both family influences and her own explorations of Chinese culture in deciding what she will pass on to her daughter. She would like her daughter to learn Mandarin and plans to send her to a Mandarin school, noting that by the time she is ready for school there will be a number of options available in the city. She herself took Mandarin in college. She thinks that Mandarin is an important global language, and she would eventually like to spend time in China with her daughter in a Mandarin-speaking area. She loves to travel—she thinks that it gives one a "global sense" and makes the rest of the world seem accessible—and used to take a big trip every two years before becoming a mother. She would also like to take her daughter to China for the "roots aspect." She already visited her grandfather's village after her father died, and had met family members there. She sings a song to her daughter that her father used to sing to her, and that her cousins in China also knew. However, she also recalled that some Chinese-speaking children laughed at her when she sang it.

Overall, she does not think she has to "work that hard around the Chinese thing—it will come through." In some respects, Carol's approach to Chinese culture reflects a cosmopolitan outlook, in her desire to travel abroad, her view of Mandarin as a global language, and her desire to spend time in a Mandarin-speaking area with her daughter. She also talks about having family roots in China that are in some ways accessible and in others inaccessible, illustrating the many, sometimes conflicting layers that factor into the construction of Chinese identities.

She also feels very conscious of racial issues. She thinks that as a "hapa" (biracial Asian), she has "gotten it from both sides," and says that she feels most comfortable around other women of color. However, she does not think that all the practices she shares with her daughter need to be of Chinese origin. Her father was a Christian, and her mother was an atheist. Carol practices Theravada Buddhism and would like to raise her daughter as a Buddhist, even though Theravada Buddhism is not practiced in China. She is also open to exposing her daughter to other types of religious experiences, including taking her to Chinese temples. She realizes that her daughter could end up practicing another religious tradition altogether, and it would not bother her if that happened. She is also flexible regarding traditions surrounding Chinese New Year and other holidays. She remembers celebrating Chinese New Year as a child, but her family stopped the practice when she was a teenager living in upstate New York. After she became a mother, she decided to celebrate Chinese New Year again.

Though she was somewhat flexible in her own practice of Chinese traditions, Carol also critiqued the Families with Children from China Moon Festival celebration she and her daughter had attended for its inauthenticity. She viewed the event as a gathering of (mostly) Chinese girls dressed up in Chinese dresses with their (mostly) white parents, eating Chinese food and mooncakes. She still sometimes attended FCC events, seeing them as a valuable opportunity to be with families like her own. However, she decided to create her own Moon Festival ritual for her daughter and some friends, mostly other adoptive families. They each put a candle in a shrine for the birth mother (her Theravada Buddhist shrine) and brought lanterns outside to gaze at the moon. Carol had wanted to honor the birth mothers by creating a ritual around them.

Like Yan, Carol takes comfort in drawing upon family traditions and connections, while further exploring her identity through learning Mandarin, practicing Buddhism, and making connections with other women of color. She brings these influences together in raising her daughter. The manner in which she flexibly creates new rituals such as her Moon Festival celebration out of these various sources is not entirely different from what is done by her adoptive parent peers who are not Asian American, as she did not grow up Buddhist, nor is the Moon Festival part of Theravada Buddhist tradition. However, her new ritual addresses some of the same concerns that FCC gatherings do—the importance of creating positive experiences related to Chinese culture and traditions together with other adoptive families.

Could Carol be accused of taking liberties with Chinese culture in creating her own Moon Festival ritual? While critics of white adoptive parents have been concerned primarily that their celebratory focus on Chinese culture may occur at the expense of attention to issues of race, there remains an implicit critique of the lack of authenticity of these practices. This critique is not wholly dissimilar from those that Carol and other Asian American adoptive parents made about white adoptive parents and FCC events. What differentiated Carol's invented Moon Festival tradition from the "inauthentic" FCC ones she critiqued? Did she think that the white parents were co-opting Chinese culture or practicing aspects it out of context? Perhaps she felt that her own ritual was rooted in her practice of Theravada Buddhism, something that she did not grow up with, but that she had incorporated into her life in a central way. Bringing in the element of the birth mothers may not have seemed like too much of a stretch for her.

How did her revision of tradition differ from when my elderly aunt, a cosmopolitan woman who had lived in China, Taiwan, Hong Kong, the United States, and Canada at various points in her life, lit incense and brought food offerings for her ancestral shrine on Buddhist holidays (and did the same for her Buddhist shrine on ancestor worship holidays)? Though these practices were not dictated by tradition, my aunt reasoned that since the shrines were right next to one another, it would be rude to provide an offering to one and not the other. Could we say that her improvised practice was more authentic than Carol's improvisation of her Theravada Buddhist shrine for the Moon Festival?

At issue, perhaps, are questions of cultural change: How do cultures change over time and in response to both individual innovations and broader power structures? To what extent is there flexibility within this realm to customize cultural practices to incorporate one's own interests and familial traditions? Non-Asians who take up forms of Asian culture are often viewed as appropriating it. However, for Yan and Carol, the processes of taking on forms of Chinese culture and Asian religion seem like a natural form of self-exploration, backed by their privilege of authenticity. In a sense, the white adoptive parents profiled in the next chapter can be said to engage in very similar processes of combining their own familial values, ethnic practices, and religions with Chinese cultural practices they take on. Mr. Martello, an adoptive father from St. Louis, took up tai chi and went to Chinese language school, incorporating these practices into his family's culture along with Catholicism and other family traditions. It is difficult to say if his interest in these activities was strengthened due to the fact that he adopted a child from

China, or to what extent his interest in adopting from China reflected a broader interest in Chinese people and culture. He continued with Chinese school even after his daughter stopped taking lessons, and later his wife started attending class.

Both Yan and Carol combine what they perceive to be inherited familial practices with newer practices derived from broader Asian or Asian American subcultures. But while Lowe's (1996) model implies that Asian American cultural and identity production is political or antihegemonic, their examples reveal that these forms of cultural production may not necessarily be read as responses or resistance to existing hegemonies. In contrast, these cases show that these processes are in many ways highly individualized, allowing for both the selective interpretation and practice of natal family rituals and the insertion of consciously learned practices and beliefs, such as Buddhism or Mandarin Chinese.

Do Asian Americans possess greater ownership over Asian American cultures, including the right to transform and innovate them, by virtue of the fact that they are insiders, having experienced as racial minorities the oppressive structures within which Asian American cultures have developed? If we understand the category of Asian American or Chinese American as a political or cultural one that has been produced and renegotiated over time, then should their actions be viewed as a continuation of this process on behalf of their children? How do we explain the forms of cultural innovation chosen by Yan and Carol?

It is difficult to fully explain why both women may have ended up exploring forms of Buddhism and Chinese language study. Certainly, the Bay Area provides a wealth of resources for learning about both, not just for Asian Americans but for anyone who might be interested. It is also true that Chinese language knowledge is a highly charged identity marker within the Chinese American community. However, one wonders whether this marker be renegotiated to account for descendants of immigrants who do not speak Chinese. In her book *On Not Speaking Chinese*, Ien Ang writes: "The Chinese diaspora . . . has by virtue of its sheer critical mass, global range and mythical might evinced an enormous power to operate as a magnet for anyone who can somehow be identified as 'Chinese'—no matter how remote the ancestral links" (2001, 12). However, she also questions the utility of the Chinese diaspora concept for addressing the complex relationships to Chineseness held by people such as herself. A Peranakan Chinese born in Indonesia, but also raised in Holland, she writes of often being asked whether or not she spoke Chinese, even though given her family history and the number of generations removed from China, it was unlikely that she would.[4] She thus questions "the value of diaspora identity politics, indeed the importance of Chineseness itself as the symbolic anchor of such a politics" (13), and instead wishes to leave room for the "hybrid multiplicity" (17) of Chinese/Asian experiences. On the one hand, the hybrid expressions of identity that Yan and Carol create speak to the pull and power of acquiring certain markers and expressions of Chineseness as symbolic of Chinese cultural authenticity and identity, such as that of language. Knowledge of Mandarin Chinese has become a form of cultural capital within today's globalized world, and Mandarin has become increasingly popular as a second language for many Americans, as evidenced by the explosion of bilingual immersion programs across the country run by the mainland Chinese (People's Republic of China) government's Confucius Institute and other organizations.

As in the case of the Chinese American participants of the In Search of Roots program I studied previously (Louie 2004), Chinese language proficiency was often a marker of Chinese cultural authenticity, a form of Chinese cultural capital. Those who spoke little or no Chinese often felt that this signified their lack of Chineseness more broadly, and even some who spoke quite fluently considered their Chinese inadequate. A number of participants went on to learn how to speak Chinese at various levels of fluency. Perhaps this drive to possess Chinese language fluency also fueled Yan's and Carol's desires to learn Chinese themselves and to have their children learn to speak it also. As Yan remarked, she felt that knowing Chinese would give her and her son access to a global Chinese world from which they would otherwise be disconnected, and she believes that knowledge of the language is also facilitating more connections for herself. This rationale was not wholly different from that expressed by the white parents I interviewed who were sending their children to Chinese school, whether it be a weekly or an immersion program.

Yet it should also be cautioned that Yan and Carol are certainly not representative of all Asian American adoptive parents, as the examples I discuss later reveal. Approximately half of the Asian American adoptive parents I interviewed did not emphasize Chinese language proficiency for their children. Lucy, introduced earlier, initially tried to speak to their daughter in the Cantonese baby talk she had heard her own parents use, but because Lucy does not speak Chinese fluently, she stopped doing this as her daughter grew older. Lucy would love to learn how to speak Cantonese so that she could better communicate with her in-laws. She and her husband have discussed what to do regarding Chinese language education for her daughter. They would like her to learn Cantonese, but there are few schools in their area that teach Cantonese. "What about Mandarin?" I asked. Her husband thinks that Mandarin might be a practical language to learn because it is the official language of China, but neither Lucy nor her husband speaks Mandarin.

Lucy admits that if they had a biological child, they probably would not have thought as much about Chinese cultural issues, such as whether or not to take their daughter to Chinese dance classes or teach her to speak Chinese. However, because they were in the process of adopting a second child from China, Lucy had become concerned that officials would speak to her daughter in Chinese when they traveled to China to receive her little sister. She also worried that her daughter may feel closer to China because she was born there.[5] She would therefore like to expose her to Chinese culture so that she will be able to explore it further if she wishes.

Ethnic Options

As discussed in the introduction, white ethnics have the privilege of picking and choosing aspects of their heritage to acknowledge, often in symbolic ways and during specific celebratory occasions. While there is some question regarding how ethnic options may be employed by racial minorities (Waters 1990), as discussed in the introduction, Song (2003) has noted possibilities for the strategic use of ethnic options by people of color. In the context of Chinese adoption, it is important to consider whether the "privilege of authenticity" held by Asian American adoptive parents enables them to more flexibly make parenting choices regarding Chinese culture. As indicated by my interviews with Asian American adoptive parents, described later, there is not only great flexibility and variation but also a sense of self-assurance in the ways that Asian

American adoptive parents raise their children adopted from China. This may have less to do with any specific Chinese or Asian cultural values or parenting techniques (as in Amy Chua's [2011] "Tiger Mom") than with the fact that they racially "match" their adopted children and are therefore less visible as adopted families and less subject to questions about their ability to parent their children. As discussed earlier in reference to King-O'Riain's (2006) work, ideas about the naturalized correspondence of biology (race) and culture remain powerful but also involve "race work."

White adoptive parents face a great deal of scrutiny and surveillance (Jacobson 2009), and the public nature of their status as an adoptive family, combined with the racial and cultural "difference" of their children, creates a degree of pressure for them to engage in performances of Chinese culture. In addition, as discussed in the epigraphs to this chapter, Asian American adoptive parents, just by virtue of being Asian American, may appear to possess an inherent and usually unquestioned sense of authenticity in the cultural practices they choose to enact. This privilege of authenticity may be used by Asian Americans against others' claims to Chineseness, but ironically, the processes may also occur on the part of more recent immigrants in relation to Chinese Americans. Debates about cultural authenticity within the Asian American community often play out according to class and generational background and are often indexed by the ability to read and speak the ancestral tongue. However, as the following profiles illustrate, Asian American adoptive parents are able to freely draw upon and modify practices that they have learned or relearned from family traditions, as well as incorporate new practices into their lives. More important, they are able to present them as representing Chinese (or Asian) tradition or culture, without the authenticity of these cultural practices being questioned by others. So rather than passing on family traditions inherited from previous generations, the process of cultural production for Asian American adoptive parents—for both themselves and their children—is both continuous and marked by the freedom and flexibility to innovate.

I met Desiree (quoted at the beginning of this chapter) and her daughter at a small park not far from where I had interviewed Lucy. When I arrived, Desiree was patiently waiting, while her daughter toddled around the park. The contrast between Desiree and her daughter was striking, in that Desiree was unusually tall for a Chinese American woman, and her daughter, not yet two, seemed especially tiny in comparison. The other thing that struck me about Desiree was her accent; though she had lived in Portland and the Bay Area, she retained traces of a Hawaiian accent and spoke with a distinctive style—thoughtful, articulate, and forthright.

Desiree broke down her background for me. She is primarily Cantonese (seven-eighths) but is also one-sixteenth Hawaiian and one-sixteenth English/Scottish/Irish. She noted that she could not speak Cantonese but does not seem to lament that fact, explaining that Cantonese is a tonal language and joking that she is tone-deaf. She also feels that she has other strong cultural influences, having grown up with her grandmother in Hawaii and experienced its multiculturalism. She thinks that people from Hawaii have a more integrated sense of heritage because of the multiple influences there.[6]

Desiree told me that she feels fortunate that as a Chinese American she has the flexibility to pick and choose what she likes best from her cultural heritage to pass on to her daughter. For her, this is "natural." In contrast, she thinks that non-Chinese American parents might find it stressful to decide what to expose their children to. She brings her daughter to Chinatown to introduce her to foods that are not "mainstream," like jai, a vegetarian dish served during Chinese New Year. She also likes to share details about Chinese culture with other people and to practice traditions with her daughter that she learned from her parents, like eating the giant grapefruits she used to have as a child. Her Catholic religion is very important to her, though she notes that her grandmother in Hawaii maintained her Taoist beliefs while also attending church. They no longer go to bai san (a form of ancestor worship in which one pays respect to the graves of one's ancestors by lighting incense, cleaning the grave, and making a food offering) because it has "fallen by the wayside," but if her family did follow this custom, she would pass it on to her daughter. She would like to maintain family customs so that she will "have a common vocabulary from her immigrant forebearers." She would also like her to learn hula for body awareness. She described her husband, who is half German and half Russian Jew from the Bay Area, as coming from a "wonderbread" background. He is somewhat interested in his German roots. But while Desiree speaks German because she studied in Germany, she does not plan to teach it to her daughter. She was open to having her daughter learn to speak Chinese, noting that she might consider Chinese preschool for her, saying, "If you are going to pay money to sing songs and draw pictures, it might as well be in Chinese."

Desiree would also like to expose her daughter to other adoptive families, but she does not want this to be her daughter's primary identification. She feels that white FCC parents are primarily interested in authentic Chinese culture, while she herself is third generation and practices a hybridized form of Chinese culture.

Like Desiree, Keiko has made decisions about what to expose her daughter to based on a combination of family cultural and religious traditions, the acknowledgment of her Chinese origins, and speculation about what skills will benefit her as she grows older. This is not dissimilar from the perspective of other Asian American families I interviewed, who viewed Chinese identity not as a political project or form of resistance to mainstream racial and cultural identities but as a combination of inheritance, innovation, and a tool kit for the future.

Keiko was born in a Japanese interment camp in 1943. She was one of the older women I interviewed and also one of the most talkative. I interviewed Keiko at a local college campus, where she had dropped off her daughter at an on-site elementary school. We drove over to another building to grab a bite to eat and talked outside so that we could enjoy the campus scenery. She and her husband adopted their daughter when Keiko was in her fifties, after having battled breast cancer. They kept the second character in her Chinese name, combining it with a Japanese female character. The name signifies strength and survival, and according to Keiko, her daughter loves her name, making up cheers to go along with it. Keiko has endeavored to teach her daughter about both Chinese and Japanese culture, though she admits that her family would probably not be as into China if their daughter were not from there. They sent her to a Chinese-Japanese bilingual preschool, enrolling her in the Japanese track. She had learned how to add, subtract, multiply, and divide in Japanese by the time she was six. They also joined a playgroup with other children who were adopted from China. Now that she is older, she attends Chinese language school two days per week. The family also attend a Japanese American Buddhist church, where their daughter participates in a youth program, and they volunteer at the Japan festival and take part in the autumn Moon Festival dance.

Keiko said that her daughter sometimes asks whether she can stop taking Chinese, but thus far she has continued and has made a number of good friends at the school. But she is somewhat hesitant about forcing her daughter to attend language school, as she remembers being forced to attend Japanese school and disliking it so much that she often played hooky. She noted that while many families in FCC would like their child to be fluent in Mandarin, Keiko primarily wants to give her a base in case she wishes to explore the language further in college—to be able to say her name and to understand some basic Chinese. But her primary goal is to help her daughter "be functional in America." She and her husband are older parents, and they would like to provide their daughter with the tools she will need when she grows up so that she can get along even if they are not still around.

Evelyn emphasized the language piece quite a bit more than Desiree and Keiko and saw this acquisition of knowledge as being important in a cosmopolitan, multilingual context. Her daughter, Megan, aged six, had started a demanding bilingual Chinese immersion school as a three-year-old. Evelyn surmised that if the Chinese government knows that the child will grow up in an Asian environment (i.e., with Asian parents), it will give you a nice-looking kid.

Evelyn herself is bilingual. She was born in Hong Kong and has also lived in Singapore, and she speaks Cantonese, Mandarin, and English fluently. Her husband is from the United States and identifies as Jewish. They got married at an older age and decided to adopt after having tried to have a biological child. Because she was from Hong Kong, they felt that China was a logical place to adopt from in terms of fostering her child's identity. Growing up in Singapore, she was used to a multilingual environment in which people spoke English, Chinese, and Malay. She believes that knowing other languages makes people more empathetic because they can understand other people's perspectives. She would like Megan's Mandarin to eventually go beyond a conversational level to the extent that she could read a Chinese newspaper and understand a Chinese worldview. Her aim is to provide "a jump-start and a tool set," but she does not expect her daughter to be fluent enough to be able to enroll in a Chinese university.

Megan used her Chinese on a trip back to her orphanage at age five. Like many other adoptive parents with whom I had spoken, Evelyn had read the advice of Jane Liedtke from Our Chinese Daughter's Foundation that it is better to bring adopted children back to China for a visit while they are still young. She decided to bring Megan back to China at a time that coincided with a business trip for her husband. She recalls that the experience was very positive for her daughter. They had raised funds to provide donations for the orphanage, and their guide had taken them on a shopping trip with the deputy director of her orphanage. Evelyn e-mailed me a newsletter story on their visit, which included photos of the shopping trip and of Megan posing with the donations of clothing, blankets, and other goods that were piled in a room for an official presentation to the orphanage. In return, Megan was presented with an embroidered gift and a certificate of appreciation by the orphanage director. The family was shown a book of photos compiled from the pictures that Evelyn had sent to the orphanage every year via their adoption agency. The newsletter also pictured a number of informational displays in the orphanage conference room on various charitable initiatives in which it was involved, including the U.S.-based charities Half the Sky and the Amity Foundation, which sponsored programs to aid children still living in the orphanage, including disabled older children. Other posters featured children who had come back to visit the orphanage, as well as a map indicating the various locations where children from the orphanage now lived, including Belgium, Canada, Finland, France, Holland, Norway, Spain, the United Kingdom, and the United States. This orphanage's focus on its engagement with organizations and individuals outside China is indicative of the new relationships formed by the practice of international adoption, which have greatly improved conditions at the orphanage, although some might argue at the cost of having sent many children from there abroad. But the display also indicates the orphanage's desire to continue to claim these adoptees as its own, or at least to maintain connections to them.

Evelyn noted that Megan felt very comfortable at the orphanage. She was shown to the room where she had stayed during her first six months (now an office) and to the new building where she had spent the following three months. The newsletter showed pictures of Megan posing next to empty cribs in the nursery. They later visited a preschool, where she was able to join a kindergarten class and give a kung fu demonstration for the group. Evelyn reflected that she now knows more about the people who cared for Megan while she was at the orphanage, and has empathy for those who live there, worrying about the lack of heat and electricity in the winter.

Evelyn told me that they celebrate the major Chinese holidays in their home, including Chinese New Year and the Moon Festival. They do not observe Ching Ming (grave sweeping), but they do eat *zong zi* (Chinese tamales) for the Dragon Boat Festival. They also practice Jewish traditions in the household. Her husband follows Jewish dietary rituals during Passover, and she and her daughter participate in the holiday but do not adhere to the dietary restrictions. They go to temple together, and over winter break, Megan attends Hebrew school for several weeks. However, Evelyn does not want her to attend more often than that because she is concerned about the school's ties to Israel and does not want her daughter to have any governmental or political affiliations.

"Having the Culture" and "Living the Values"

Many of the Asian America parents profiled here appeared to be treating their children much as they would if they were their biological children, in the sense that they were raising them within their Chinese American family cultures and traditions. Of course, how they actually did this varied from family to family. Desiree had noted that she considered her daughter to be fourth-generation Chinese American, indicating that Desiree was taking into consideration her daughter's familial and cultural influences, rather than her first-generation immigrant status, in thinking about how to shape her cultural background. Though she was open to sending her daughter to a Chinese preschool, she did not appear especially concerned about her gaining fluency in Chinese. She was more concerned with continuing practices that would connect her to her immigrant ancestors, including those that were not specifically "Chinese," such as hula dancing and Catholicism.

Other parents I interviewed echoed Desiree's sentiments that Asian American parents did not have to worry as much as white parents about incorporating Chinese cultural content into their children's lives. Daniel felt that as long as he continued activities that he did as a child, he was passing on Chinese American culture to his daughter. Even activities such as camping with other Chinese American families constituted part of this cultural heritage. He exposes his biological son to the same influences.

Muriel and Richard were one of the few couples I interviewed in the Bay Area, and also one of the few mixed-race couples I spoke with. Their example illustrates the power of cultural authenticity that Chinese origins confer, despite the fact that these families, like all families, take liberties as they flexibly practice and alter "traditional" Chinese practices. Muriel had responded to my request for interviews, saying that she would love to chat with me and inquiring about whether I was related to one of the people in her adoption group. I found out that my cousin, who shares my last name, had adopted his daughter on the same adoption trip and from the same orphanage from which Muriel and Richard had adopted their older daughter. Muriel, who was in her late fifties at the time of the interview, is of Chinese American descent. Her husband, Richard, is white. They have two daughters adopted from China. Like the parents described previously, they chose to celebrate some Chinese holidays such as the Moon Festival with their children but also exercised some flexibility in their practices. They said that they would have used the same approach if they had biological children. Richard commented that he and his wife were in many ways more relaxed about Chinese cultural issues than some of the white adoptive parents he has met. He noted: "There's a lot of very intense white families that really go a lot out of their way . . . that go out and learn Mandarin so they can speak to their adopted Chinese kid. I think it's kind of overdoing it. I guess it's a great thing. I figure I have Muriel, so that's my pass."

Here, Richard admits that having a Chinese American wife provides him with a "pass" to approach Chinese cultural issues with less intensity than other white adoptive parents. Dorow observed a similar phenomenon with a couple she interviewed in which the husband was Chinese American and the wife was white: "The Huangs admitted that if Victor were not Asian but white, they would probably be pushing harder to integrate Chinese culture into their daughter's life" (2006b, 234).

But if Richard was joking about having a free pass regarding Chinese culture, it seems that he does feel he has been relieved of a particular burden felt by white adoptive parents who are not sure exactly how to raise their children adopted from China with a sense of Chinese identity. His statement also implies that Chinese cultural authenticity will automatically be conferred upon his children by his Chinese American wife, though this idea counters the complex processes of improvisation and negotiation discussed in this chapter. Interestingly, Muriel does not speak Chinese to their children, and in fact cannot speak Chinese very well. As a young girl, she had begged her parents to let her attend Chinese school, but they had not wanted her to go. However, she says she does pass on other forms of Chinese American cultural knowledge to the girls, by talking with them about their grandfather and other aspects of family history. She seemed well versed in Chinese American history, discussing Maxine Hong Kingston's books and the Chinese Exclusion Act, and recalling memories of attending Chinese Benevolent Society dinners with her family. Surprisingly, she had to ask her husband for help remembering the places where their daughters were from in China. This incident illustrated that, for Muriel, the details of family history stood out to her more than other details of their children's origins, showing that there are many layers and facets of Chinese and Chinese American identity.

Muriel seemed to favor a multicultural approach, not totally unlike that of some white parents I interviewed. She liked to bring her daughters to events at the Asian Art Museum, particularly hands-on events for children such as lessons on how to make mochi, a traditional Japanese confection made of sticky rice. They participated in events to learn about other Asian cultures, including Korean and Vietnamese culture. Muriel emphasized the importance of following their children's cues regarding what paths of exploration to take. For example, their oldest daughter had become a vegetarian after reading the book *Chew on This*. She now hates Chinese food and Chinatown, so they do not go there very often. Muriel also remembers when her daughter told her, "You know, Mom, I'm a Chinese adoptee, and I know about myself, but that does not mean that I want to seek out other Chinese adoptees."

Judy, who was quoted at the beginning of this chapter, feels that having a community of Chinese American friends who share common values, such as respecting elders, feeding the children first, and sharing, is essential to raising her daughters as Chinese American. I met Judy at her East Bay home, where she invited me to come interview her and her older daughter. I was greeted at the door by a small dog, and Judy also introduced me to her pet rats.

Judy thinks that her children "live the values" when they see their parents fight over who is going to treat the other person at a restaurant. She reflects: "Because we are Chinese, [Chinese culture is] our values about right and wrong, it's all about the money. . . . It's very clear things about how we handle money and our finances. . . . It's more about teaching them to save the money and working." In this sense, she considers Chinese culture as a set of moral values, to some extent viewing them in essentialized ways, more than as a set of ritual practices. She notes that the family does not usually celebrate holidays because their parents are old, though they do have a special dinner for Chinese New Year. She and her husband have not emphasized Chinese language training for their daughters, even though she speaks Toisanese (a dialect related to Cantonese) and her husband speaks Shanghainese. The children have had some exposure to Chinese language and culture through their grandmother. Judy and her husband have also addressed adoption issues with their daughters, through reading children's literature such as *We See the Moon*. They have not done much with FCC but have gotten together with their daughter's China travel group. Judy feels that her children have ample opportunities to meet other adopted children because there are many at their public school. The school also does a good job of addressing issues of racism and homophobia.

Like Judy, Laurie, a second-generation Chinese American, views Chinese culture as being embedded in her family's everyday practices; she has chosen to interpret some practices as embodying Chinese cultural values, while de-emphasizing others that she considers old-fashioned. I initially met her at an FCC playgroup during my first research trip to the Bay Area and asked whether I could interview her during another playgroup meeting during my 2008 research trip. We decided to try to talk at the park where the playgroup was meeting. I said hello to her husband, also a second-generation Chinese American, who had brought along an Asian American–themed book, and her older daughter before we walked to a quiet spot at the other edge of the park to conduct the interview, in the hope that we would remain uninterrupted by our families. Laurie, who is slender and petite, is in her early fifties but looks younger. She had worked as an actress and as a hand model. Her older, biological, daughter was fourteen at the time, and Laurie also had an eight-year-old who was adopted from China. I asked Laurie what, if any, efforts she and her husband were making to expose their daughters to Chinese or Chinese American culture. She reflected that they have not done much in particular for her younger daughter. She just "has the culture" as a result of the family's daily practices. They regularly have family get-togethers, which exposes her to other Chinese Americans. The parents try to teach the girls about what they think are important Chinese values, including the significance of wearing red for good luck, having good table manners, and showing respect for elders. As a family, they continue to practice some Chinese customs, such as giving out red envelopes of lucky money to children on Chinese New Year, but like many Chinese Americans, they have stopped the custom of not washing their hair on that day (the words for washing hair are homonyms for washing away prosperity) because they feel that it is not practical. Laurie mentioned that they have not learned any new customs because of adopting their younger daughter, though they have tried to connect her with a Hmong woman because they suspect that their daughter might come from the related Miao ethnic minority group in China. She thought that some of the adoptive white families she has met might practice more Chinese customs than they do and have more Chinese stuff on their walls, implying that she and her family do not need to go to these lengths because they are continuing to practice their family-based traditions.

For Samantha, whom I met at an adoption agency in the South Bay after giving a talk there, adopting from China inspired her to further explore what she referred to as her "Asian roots." She noted that when she set foot in the Forbidden City during her adoption trip,

> my Asian roots started to tingle, 'cause my mother taught me that we didn't need any of that, and although culture is woven into our lives, you don't really recognize it as you are living it. It became clear to me that I needed to become more Chinese . . . learn my Chinese culture so that I could share it with my children so that they could be proud of their Chinese heritage.

As a person of Korean and Chinese descent married to a Chinese American, Samantha contrasted her own conceptions of Chinese culture, sparked in part by becoming an adoptive parent and derived from her own family background, with those created by FCC. She described FCC versions of Chinese culture as "situational" and believes that the organization fills a need for community support. She feels that the organization has good intentions, but that "it's hard to replace the day in and day out."

Samantha's renewed interest in her Chinese heritage was manifested in part by the emphasis she placed on spending time with extended family, which she contrasted with the formality of FCC activities. Samantha felt that making meals together and eating family style are important aspects of daily Chinese practices that she shared with her children. Sometimes she made ingredients for wontons and invited her in-laws over to wrap them with the children. She felt that these opportunities for different generations to interact were most valuable in passing on cultural traditions and knowledge. But she also expressed a desire for her children to learn a little Mandarin and enrolled them in a class that combines language learning with fun, age-appropriate cultural activities. While Samantha is not unique in expressing her Asian heritage in these ways, it is interesting to think about how if these practices were claimed by white adoptive parents as signifying a connection to Chinese culture, the parents would appear to be reading too much symbolic significance into them and perhaps co-opting them. But isn't all cultural representation a combination of symbolism and practice/performance? Samantha herself is engaging in the essentializing of Chinese culture and practices, as she consciously rethinks and re-creates them as part of her desire to pass them on to her children. As an Asian American parent, she is able to do this with some flexibility.

Families with Children from China

Some of the Asian American adoptive parents with whom I spoke were involved with Families with Children from China because they felt that it was important for their children to be around others who were also adopted from China. However, as observed by Beth Hall, of Pact, An Adoption Alliance, many Asian American adoptive parents she has met take issue with the version of culture promulgated by FCC:

We've had Asian parents come to us who have struggled some with FCC because the version of Chinese culture they experienced there felt co-opted and sometimes inauthentic to them, in part because the large majority of parents there are white rather than Chinese. They don't want their children to feel that this is the definition of what it means to be Chinese. On the other hand, they recognize and they want to validate their kids' connection to adoption, and there's often no place reflecting their own culture to do that.

Beth shared an incident that occurred in Los Angeles that for her illustrated the narrow conceptions of Chinese culture held by some white adoptive parents. Pact had helped the local FCC group fund a program at the Chinese American Museum that included Korean American actress Sandra Oh, as well as several Chinese American adults, with no connection to adoption, who spoke about Asian identity in America. Beth said that some of the parents had asked, "Next time could you have someone come who was born in China so that it would be more similar to our kids?" She interpreted the comment as stemming from the desire of parents who adopt internationally to associate their children with that specific faraway location, rather than with the local Chinese American or Asian American community. For them, Sandra Oh was not someone relevant to their children's lives because she was not Chinese, even though she is a famous actress and a role model for many Asian Americans. As I discuss later, recognizing that Chinese adoptees are part of a broader Asian American community that shares a history of racialized stereotypes marks a particular shift in consciousness from a focus on birthplace or homeland as the main referent for one's identity in the United States. The versions of Chinese culture that many Asian American adoptive parents critique are seen as problematic in that they focus on abstracted forms of Chinese culture that are divorced from the everyday contexts from which they originated. The Asian American adoptive parents described here valued the forms of everyday culture that they had grown up with or that demonstrated a connection, even if symbolic, to their ancestors.

Addressing Race

Attention to racial issues is thought to be natural for Asian American parents, who are assumed, like all people of color, to be attuned to these matters. In this section, I discuss how the Asian American adoptive parents I interviewed understood and addressed issues of race. As in all the interviews I conducted, I asked the Asian American parents I spoke with how they dealt with issues of both culture and race. I found a spectrum of attitudes and approaches to these issues that were most often framed within two sentiments: first, that they were lucky to live in the Bay Area where, unlike in other parts of the country, they encounter less racism; second, that in general, these issues now lead to fewer problems than when they were children, particularly as China becomes stronger.

The first idea was reflected in the individual discussions I had with Keiko, Lucy, and Laurie, who felt that their children had not been affected by racism very much thus far. Just like the white parents I discuss in the following chapters, what these parents considered to be acts of racism was subjective and often based on a definition that viewed racism as consisting of overt and discriminatory acts. They also saw the diversity of the Bay Area in which they lived as something that was likely to lessen incidents of racism. However, these assumptions do not reflect the multiple ways that racial meanings circulate within multicultural societies, affecting people in both overt and less visible ways.

Keiko recalled only one incident at a Denny's restaurant in Oregon when her daughter was five or six years old, when a waitress with her hair in curlers slapped the menu down on the table and did not take their order for a long time. When she brought them the grilled sandwiches they had ordered, the food was burned, perhaps intentionally, Keiko suspected. Keiko explained to her daughter that some people do not like Asians because of the way they look. She did not indicate that she felt the need to provide an additional explanation, and this was the only incident she could think of. Similarly, Lucy said that in the diverse Bay Area, no one thinks twice about race. When she needs to leave California for work, she notices a difference in the racial climate. She does believe that racism might become an issue for her daughter in the future, however.

Laurie, who also grew up in the Bay Area and who, like Lucy, lives in the more suburban area inland from the Berkeley Hills, thought that things had improved since an earlier time when the area's demographics were more white. Her older daughter (now fourteen) had had a racist comment directed at her when she was in the first grade, but Laurie thinks that nothing similar has happened to her younger daughter, now eight. Laurie feels fortunate that her younger daughter's class is diverse—half of her class is white, and the rest of the students are Asian or African American. Laurie and her husband have not yet talked with their younger daughter about racism, but they have raised the subject with their older daughter, explaining that "sometimes people who are not the same as you may think that they are better or talk about their skin looking different." They explained to her that she does not need to follow them or participate in a dialogue with them, and that she should tell a parent or teacher if an incident occurs. However, the assumption that a "diverse" class will reduce race-related incidents does not take into account the multiple ways that racial meanings play out in multiracial settings, particularly given the in-between racial positioning of Asian Americans.

Daniel, the Chinese American father mentioned earlier, shared a second sentiment, indicating that he thought the position of Chinese Americans is improving. He had been married to a Chinese American woman with whom he had a biological son and a daughter adopted from China. They divorced, and he later remarried a white woman who had children from a previous marriage. In his eyes, the position of Chinese people, in particular Chinese men, has come a long way from when he was growing up. He was encouraged by the fact that he now increasingly saw Chinese men with white women, something he thought signified that being Chinese was becoming "cool." He felt that in the past, Chinese women were more likely than Chinese men to marry a white person, and that Chinese women were more accepted by white society, which allowed them to escape the traditional gender roles in their own Chinese families. In contrast, he believed, the male-dominated majority society had more at stake in relegating Chinese men to subordinate positions, but perhaps this has now changed. He reflected:

When I was little, there was only Hop Sing.[7] I remember telling [my wife] how excited I was when Bruce Lee came out. This couple who just moved in here [next door], . . . where before you would only see Chinese women with white men, now I'm seeing the opposite, so I think somewhere along the way, being Chinese became cool, and I didn't know it. I thought for sure our children will marry outside their race. . . . I think before it was a push-pull thing where women were more accepted into white society, and they had more rights and were treated equally. In a Chinese family you get told what to do (my sister had to do all the laundry), and also [the United States is] a [white] male–dominated society, and they keep Chinese males in an effeminate position.

Daniel's belief that being able to marry white people was a sign of progress is in itself interesting. To him, this reflected acceptance of Chinese Americans by the majority society. However, the past, and many would argue the current, "acceptance" of Chinese women by white men as marriage partners was tied to notions about the exoticism and passivity of Asian women, ideas that were popularized in the stereotypes found in advertising, popular culture, and the media and that remain prevalent today, both in these images and in the desirability of mail-order brides from Asia. Thus, though they have been accepted, Chinese women have not necessarily been viewed as equals. And Chinese men have been hampered by a different set of stereotypes that portray them as asexual, nerdy, emotionless, and unappealing to women. In fact, the issue of Asian women dating or marrying white men has historically been a contentious one within the Asian American community, because Asian men have felt that Asian women were choosing white men over themselves. Therefore, while it is understandable that Daniel found the desirability of Asian men as spouses by white women to be a step forward, the use of these markers as signs of progress in many ways reinforces the superior status, or at least the desirability, of whites and the status associated with them.

While these parents appeared to minimize the amount of racism that their children faced, other parents were attuned to the fact that racism might be affecting their children, even in the Bay Area. Muriel contrasted her daughter's awareness of racism with that of a classmate, who is African American and Chinese in background. The friend had observed that other kids direct racial taunts at the Chinese kids at their school, of which there are not many. Muriel speculates that perhaps having grown up as African American and Chinese, the friend may be more attuned to these issues. Again, this may be due in large part to the differential racial meanings attached to Asians and blacks, which will be discussed further in the following chapter.

Betty, introduced at the beginning of this chapter, acknowledged that racism "exists and won't go away." Nevertheless, she felt that "you have to live with it, and develop skill sets so that you have leverage at different levels." However, consistent with the second theme regarding the changing position of Chinese Americans with China's growing power, she also thought that as the balance of power with China changes, her children will not face race issues in the future. She plans to equip them to be versed in different cultures so that they can bring "value . . . to the table." Unfortunately, though I did not discuss this with her, many have observed that the perceived rise of Chinese power seems to be accompanied by increasing resentment and hostility toward China and Chinese people, as evidenced by a controversial episode of Jimmy Kimmel's television show in 2014, in which one of the child panelists brought to the show to discuss how to rectify the trade imbalance with China recommended that the United States kill all the Chinese people.

As mentioned earlier, Betty is having her children learn both Cantonese and Mandarin. She has found her own Chinese language skills to be beneficial in the international business world and appears to be doing all she can to help her children develop relevant skill sets such as these. Desiree, the third-generation Chinese American from Hawaii also mentioned earlier, views her relationship to China and the effect of China's changing international position more broadly. I use Desiree's example because she effectively illustrates a distinction between being Chinese versus Chinese American or Asian American that not all adoptive parents make, while also reminding us about the continuing significance of race and racism for Asian Americans. She had visited the city of Chongqing, in Sichuan Province, China, for the first time in 1989 and remembers feeling "a real visceral connection." She recalls thinking, "This is what I grew up with. I know these people." Even though she was not visiting the region from which her grandparents had emigrated

(Guangdong Province), she felt that she had in a sense gone back to her roots. As she recalled:

> The Chongqing that I visited was still rural . . . they had pig ears on the street, rickety stone steps. I was raised by my grandparents; they were basically Chinese peasants. There was the sense that I know these people. This was the life I would have had but my great-grandfather got on a boat and went somewhere else. My other experience is that even though I feel less close to China now, I experience more of a sense of being Chinese here in America. As the population of Chinese people grows, I find that people who are Asian interact with me differently from the get-go. . . . [My] husband's colleague from Taiwan . . . I could tell that she felt comfortable saying those things to me because she assumed I was coming from the same perspective. I feel more Chinese now than when I first came in 1979 when friends would say, you're not really Chinese, you just look Chinese.

Desiree had shared this comment in a small-group conversation in the summer of 2008, when excitement was building over the Summer Olympics that were going to be held in Beijing. She had observed that there was quite a bit about China in the media lately—on PBS, in coverage by Ted Koppell, and even on the *Frontline* episode "*Young and Restless in China*" (Williams 2008), which profiled nine young Chinese people. For her, seeing these current images of China made her realize that "as China modernizes . . . the connection that I feel to it is much weaker." Now, she reflected, the population of Chongqing is 32 million, and she no longer felt a connection to this rapidly modernizing city or its people.

Desiree's comments raise important issues regarding how class and generation may play into one's identification as Chinese or Chinese American, again illustrating how "heterogeneity, hybridity, and multiplicity" define the ways that Asian Americans relate both to one another and to non-Asians. Desiree's primary connection to Chinese culture was to the rural peasant culture in which her immigrant grandparents were raised. Though she had never before been to China, during her 1989 visit to rural Chongqing, she was able to link the sights, smells, and tastes with experiences she had growing up with her grandparents. She felt that she could identify with the rural population there, despite not being able to speak the language. In contrast, the modernized Chongqing she saw on television in 2008 did not seem at all familiar. China holds great symbolic significance as a romanticized homeland for Desiree, as for many Chinese Americans, representing a link to the ancestors who departed from there. This image of China is in many ways frozen in time within the imagination, infused by longing for a connection to the past. For the In Search of Roots program interns I studied previously (Louie 2004), the disjuncture of visiting a rapidly changing Guangdong Province while searching for their ancestral roots required them to create their own ritual space within which they could make meaning out of the China trip. But rather than searching for a connection to mainland China, Desiree has shifted her focus to the United States. Whereas she used to not identify strongly as a Chinese American, recalling that when she arrived in the Bay Area in 1979, her friends commented that she looked Chinese but did not necessarily act or identify as Chinese, she now finds that she feels more comfortable with and connected to other Asian Americans. Referring to her husband's Taiwanese colleague, she speaks of how they interact on the presumption that they share the same perspective, even though the only language they share is English, and their backgrounds in terms of generation and upbringing are quite different.

While mainland China has changed rapidly since Desiree first visited in 1989, so has the population of Asian Americans in the Bay Area changed since she moved there in 1979. Though the Bay Area has historically been home to Chinese, Japanese, Filipino, and other Asian immigrant populations who came initially as laborers or farmers, since the passing of the 1965 Immigration and Naturalization Act, large numbers of Asian immigrants have come to the United States under its provisions for family reunification or for the entry of skilled workers. Southeast Asian refugee populations followed in the 1970s and 1980s. The Asian American activism that arose in the late 1960s was inspired in part by this burgeoning immigrant and refugee population, involving both the demand for heritage-based curricula in Asian American studies and a call for renewed involvement in local Asian communities. This movement was led by American-born Asian Americans who, like Desiree, felt a broader sense of kinship and comfort with other Asian Americans. This shift in Desiree's identification, of discovering "a sense of being

Chinese here in America," illustrates the flexibility of identity over time in relation to a changing political and cultural milieu. Though Desiree, like the other Asian American parents profiled earlier, had some flexibility to make her own choices in how she identified, her example illustrates the dynamic between personal exploration and the broader contexts that factor into shaping it. Her eventual choice to identify as a Chinese or Asian American, rather than to continue to try to identify with mainland China, is also significant. In claiming a Chinese American identity, she is able to move away from China as the sole source of Chinese cultural authenticity or identification. Her comment in this chapter's epigraph indicates that she no longer worries about measuring Chinese cultural authenticity in relation to mainland Chinese or any other form of Chinese culture. For her, being Chinese does not require her to speak Chinese or to carry out specific cultural practices. Rather, it is something that she can define in her own way, for herself and for her daughter, drawing upon both family traditions that have been hybridized in Hawaii and her connections to other Chinese Americans and Asian Americans.

Desiree talked about feeling a "pan-Asian connection." She remembered that after the Vincent Chin killing, which occurred in Detroit in 1982, "the lesson my friends took from that is that they don't know the difference" between different types of Asians. Vincent Chin, a young Chinese American engineer, had been at his own bachelor party at a Detroit bar when two unemployed white autoworkers who blamed Japanese automakers for their unemployment began to taunt him. They followed Chin after he left the bar and later bludgeoned him to death. They never served any time in jail. For Desiree and her friends, this act of violence and the injustice that followed heightened their awareness of the continued racism and social inequality experienced by Asian Americans. Desiree admitted that she struggles sometimes to explain to others, including her husband, the fact that racism still exists. In the same group discussion with other adoptive parents, both Asian and white, she shared:

> I think the first thing is to truly believe that that's how it is. . . . I know a lot of white people . . . husband included . . . who don't really believe the experience of racism. . . . Not that he doesn't believe but he glosses

over . . . "Maybe they're just having a bad day" . . . it frustrates me because that invalidates my experience of life. . . . [I've] had few experiences . . . but they exist . . . to validate that fact of life that this is true.

Identification as Asian American or Chinese American sets the stage for the flexible redefinition of culture and identity in the context of the United States. In attaching "Chinese" to "American," this form of iden-tification recognizes Chinese culture as something that is not tied to a romanticized notion of a homeland frozen in the past, but rather as becoming a new and different entity within these new circumstances. Experiences of racism, like the incident in which Vincent Chin was ra-cialized as Asian and identified as an enemy and scapegoat, also illus-trate the necessity of recognizing that being Asian in the United States is different than being Asian in Asia.

Adoptive parents may too closely identify their children with their Chinese origins rather than seeing them as Chinese American or Asian American and introducing them to resources and tools for dealing with the racism and discrimination that result. Many parents, even some of the Asian American parents I interviewed, seemed to think that race and racism are manifested in specific incidents in which people were singled out and discriminated against due to their skin color and their ancestral origins. Its perpetrators were assumed to be white, and actions were thought to occur between individuals or in small groups. Edward Bonilla-Silva's (2009) research on race and racism has shown that whites in the United States approach issues of race from four main perspectives, all of which deny the widespread existence of racism and fail to under-stand its underlying historical and institutional structures, thus enabling it to persist. He labels these approaches "abstract liberalism, naturaliza-tion, cultural racism, and minimization of racism" (Bonilla-Silva 2009, 26), which are all essentially forms of color blindness.

Bonilla-Silva also sheds light on why some Asian Americans might not be as attuned to racism as other minorities, arguing that the United States may be becoming a triracial society, like some Latin American countries, in which East Asian Americans and other groups currently considered to be nonwhite may occupy a middle category that is in be-tween black and white. Eileen O'Brien (2008) calls this phenomenon the "racial middle," also arguing that the racial positioning of Chinese

Americans and Asian Americans vis-à-vis other minority groups may be shifting in the early twenty-first century. This middle position is somewhat of a double-edged sword, however, as it can lead those who occupy it to believe that they are no longer subject to racism. Though they are no longer positioned at the bottom, they remain subject to perhaps more subtle and complex forms of racism. As I discuss further in the following chapter, children adopted from China may occupy a similar middle position in the eyes of mainstream culture, including those of their parents. George Yancey's (2003) work on the black/nonblack divide also supports the idea that Asians are positioned close to or possibly even as part of the white racial grouping, and in opposition to blacks.

Much has changed since Lisa Lowe crafted her model of Asian American cultural production in the 1990s, when predominant conceptions of Asian Americans were of immigrants and foreigners. Though these conceptions remain, today's Asian Americans include increasing numbers of adoptees, who are well integrated into U.S. families. As China's power and influence grow, today's Chinese Americans are seen as having skills deemed valuable and strategic by many Americans, including connections to China and knowledge of Chinese cultures and languages. In this sense, some of the choices that the Asian American and other parents I interviewed made regarding crafting specific forms of Chinese cultural knowledge for themselves and their children could be understood as attempts to build a form of Chinese or Chinese American cultural capital that operates within the context of a broader racialized U.S. society.

As new forms of color blindness, preemptive parenting, and attempts to address race and ethnicity continue on the part of adoptive parents, one can speculate that their children's experiences may be different from those of Korean adoptees of the past. But how? The examples presented in this chapter show that Asian American parents may be similar to white parents in being bound by the broader context of U.S. multiculturalism, which to some extent shapes their approaches to culture. However, both Asian American and white adoptive parents can be seen as tied in different ways to the histories and institutions that have oppressed Asian Americans in the past. Though their individual histories may not reflect this, the privileges of white adoptive parents as nonminority individuals in U.S. society have meant that they likely understand and approach what it means to be Chinese or Chinese American very differently than do Chinese Americans themselves. The ways Chinese American parents go about creating and practicing Chinese American or Asian American culture are characterized by (to varying degrees) a sense of the connection between ethnic and racial identities—of being both of Chinese descent but of also being Chinese or Asian American. The cultural elements and practices consist of everyday acts and values, some reinterpreted from familial traditions and others newly invented. More significantly, however, while some of these activities may constitute discrete events that are chosen for their "Chinese" content, most become an integral part of daily lives and part of the family culture as a whole. Conceiving of Chineseness in this way more easily lends itself to the production of new forms of Asian American culture.

5

White Parents' Constructions of Chineseness

Preemptive Parenting

Adoptive families operate within the intersection of race, culture, and adoption. As I discussed in the previous chapter, Asian American adoptive parents construct Chinese identities for their adopted children by both drawing on their own conceptions of Chinese culture, which have often evolved over the years, and also engaging in strategic and preemptive forms of parenting. But for white adoptive parents, the relationship between their children's Chineseness and their own racial, ethnic, and religious identities is not as seemingly straightforward. I thus use the word "operate" to suggest the conscious and often delicate work that white parents put into considering the various elements of their children's identities. In their attempt to acknowledge their cultural and to varying degrees their racial difference, they must also take into account issues stemming from adoption. While this is also true for Asian American adoptive parents, there is also the question of how the parents' own ethnic identities factor into the equation, as these are less easily merged with constructions of Chineseness. As Dorow notes throughout her book, many white parents were concerned about Chineseness representing "too much" difference (2006b, 212, 224, 246). So what do the representation and practice of Chineseness in the context of white middle-class family lives reveal both about white parents' attitudes toward racial and cultural difference and about the larger contexts in which they operate?

Unlike previous generations of adoptive parents, today's parents can draw upon a number of forms of support, both formal and informal, some grassroots and some highly structured and commodified, as they create new forms of family identity. They form conceptions about Chinese culture and its relationship to other elements of American life in response to a set of discourses about racial difference, familial composition, and a history of Western relations with an "Orient" that is be-coming increasingly accessible to the West. Their efforts to educate themselves about Chinese culture can only be seen in relation to the place that China has historically occupied and currently occupies in the Western imagination. As the trip to China illustrates, most white adop-tive parents cannot help but view China and Chinese culture through an Orientalist lens, a worldview that on the one hand views China and Chinese people as "Other" to the West and its civilization, and on the other remains fascinated by their exotic and sometimes mysterious na-ture (Said 1979). These ideas are rooted in a Euro-American worldview that evolved out of a long history of trade, diplomatic, and other forms of mediated cultural exchange and conquest with Asia and the Middle East. They are embedded in the everyday understandings of and rela-tionships to people and goods originating from these regions. White adoptive parents integrate this information, both consciously and un-consciously, to understand the process of adoption and of becoming an interracial family. As in the adoption trip itself, international and inter-racial adoption brings parents outside of their comfort zones, requiring white adoptive parents to address issues of culture and race in ways they have not previously had to do. For white parents in the United States who have been raised in the color-blind atmosphere of the post–civil rights era, this presents a set of interesting challenges and questions. Where do their children from China fit into their family, their com-munity, and the U.S. racial structure more broadly? In what ways can and should their Chinese origins be acknowledged, while the identity of their family as a whole is built? Like many parents, they consciously cre-ate social and cultural environments for their children through making choices about the schools they attend, the neighborhoods in which they live, the activities in which they participate, and the friends with whom they associate. As such, adoptive parents are raising their children not only as members of their own families but also as members of multiple communities and categories.[1]

Adoptive parents who strategically employ resources about China and Chinese culture for their adopted children are engaged in a type of reflexive, preemptive parenting. As middle-class, educated parents, they want to provide their children with the tools they will need to negotiate life in the United States as women, as adoptees, and as Asians or Asian

Americans. They proactively create Chinese identities for their children in response to potential discrimination and identity issues they may face, related both to being adopted and to being Chinese in America. The concern with issues of adoption is exacerbated by the fact that, for Asian children of white parents, the formation of the family through adoption is readily obvious to outsiders, who invade family privacy and "question" the validity of the family in various ways. The concern with Chinese American identity relates to both its racial and its cultural dimensions and is heightened by the perception that as non-Chinese people, white parents feel they cannot provide their children with the same exposure to Chinese culture as can be provided by Chinese parents. Many parents view cultural education and pride about China and Chinese culture as a solution to both issues, though the ways that they conceptualize Chineseness and a racial and cultural identity and the ways that they address them may not always fully get at the deeply rooted nature of these issues. Chineseness as a racial and cultural identity in the United States cannot be separated from long histories and complex sets of meanings that are entangled with those of other Americans, both white and nonwhite, and remain entrenched in many contemporary institutions and attitudes.

White adoptive parents approach their children's perceived Chineseness in ways that reflect not only their respect for and perhaps enchantment with Chinese culture but also their assumptions based on their own experiences as white ethnics that they can readily pick and choose the aspects of Chinese culture that they wish to acknowledge. However, as discussed in the introduction, it is important to question in what ways these ideas of ethnic options apply to white parents with children from China. David Eng has argued that unlike other transracially adopted children, Asian adoptees are easily "folded into the imagined community of the white heteronormative middle-class nuclear family." He further asserts that the ease with which Asian adoptees are integrated into white families results in the erasure of their "racial history" and "marks the emergence of a new politics of passing in our colorblind age" in which adoptees perform the "affective labor" of completing families. He reminds us that "we need to consider how the stereotype of the hardworking, agreeable, and passive Asian girl, ever eager to please, works to smooth over the political problems, economic disparities, and cultural differences" (Eng 2010, 110).

This chapter addresses questions initially raised in the introduction surrounding the ways that white adoptive parents proactively and pre-emptively construct Chinese racial and cultural identities for their children in relation to their own understandings of Chineseness. Though, as discussed earlier, these issues have been addressed extensively by other researchers, it is important to consider them in the context of my own ethnographic research. The question of how these constructions play out within the context of everyday lives and as they are negotiated and revised as children grow older will be the focus of the next chapters. The answers to these questions are not necessarily clear-cut. There is wide variation in parents' approaches to issues of cultural and racial identity for their children. I argue that in many cases, parents attempt to proactively pick and choose aspects of Chinese cultural identity to integrate into their children's lives to address salient issues of identity, while their understanding of and ability to change the broader racial and historical structures that continue to shape Chinese identities remain limited. Thus, the attitudes they expressed may not always reflect their actual practices. For example, while they may talk about being open to introducing their children to Asian American or in some cases other communities of color, their children's neighborhood and school demographics may not provide these opportunities.

Culture and Race within Preemptive Parenting

During my research trip to the Bay Area in 2008, I had an opportunity to interview Beth Hall, of Pact, An Adoption Alliance, in her Oakland office. I had already heard her name mentioned by a number of adoptive parents I had interviewed, and had previously read the book that she and her colleague Gail Steinberg had coauthored titled *Inside Transracial Adoption* (2000), which addresses issues related to the transracial adoption of children of color by white parents. I had had a little trouble finding the Pact office, which was not visible from the street. It was located in a building that was set back from the main street. I surmised that this more private location, despite being on a busy thoroughfare, afforded its clients a bit of privacy. Pact serves both adoptive parents and birth parents who wish to make an adoption plan for their babies. It also provides postadoption workshops and additional resources for adoptive parents, particularly around issues of transracial adoption.

An adoptive mother of two children of color, Beth has worked with adoptive families with children from various backgrounds, including domestic transracial adoptions. Her knowledge of and passion about these issues were apparent as we sat down for the interview. Before I could turn on my recorder and ask her to sign my university's human subjects research (institutional review board) form, she launched into an interesting discussion about how at the root of adoptive parents' culture-making practices are what she terms "entitlement issues," which she feels drive adoptive parents to be "hypervigilant" in making parenting decisions. After I interrupted her to have her sign the form, she continued her analysis, observing that society continually sends the message that adoption is not a completely legitimate way to form a family and that at times this anxiety underlies adoptive parents' efforts "to be better than the best parent" and "to make up for" their child's adoption. She said that, as a result, parents "struggle with big decisions" and become "super-overinvolved because there's this need again to prove their legitimacy to parent this child."

In a sense, Beth's perspective provides an explanation for what drives the preemptive parenting of white adoptive parents in particular. She noted that many adoptive parents have heard stories about adult adoptees of color who have struggled with cultural and racial identity issues as they have grown older. Beth respects the fact that groups such as FCC have arisen to "take this stuff seriously, and they are trying to impart that identity piece and good self-esteem to their children." However, she also wonders whether they sometimes "go awry" in that despite their good intentions, many groups like FCC do not feel "comfortable looking at race as an issue." She observed:

> They want to talk about culture and heritage in a way that they like that can sometimes look like white paternalism or . . . They kind of co-opt that culture as they view it rather than from people who are living it. They don't understand that they're like any group of people. . . . There is a vast diversity within the community. . . . They are trying to be responsive . . . to what the first generation of adoptees told them . . . but there are still some inherent problems.

Here, she made a number of strong statements about FCC's general approach to the identity issues of their adopted children of color, particularly what she views as FCC's avoidance of race issues. She recognizes that adoptive parents may have their children's best interests at heart and are trying to respond to what earlier generations of transracial adoptees have told them. But she acknowledges that white adoptive parents may not necessarily have the tools to effectively address some of these issues; more important, they are not accustomed to talking about race. Their children then grow up facing the contradiction of having been raised in a color-blind society, in which their parents and others have told them that race does not matter, only to realize that in the real world, race is still very real and relevant. Having known only the sheltered, white-oriented world of their parents, Beth says, these adoptees eventually realize: "I'm not at peace with my identity. . . . I don't know who I am. . . . The world won't let me be white, because the only thing I know how to be is white, because that's what my parents taught me and they told me that race doesn't matter, but the minute I walk out the door . . . I understood that race did matter because the world will not let me forget that."

Much of Pact's work involves providing adoptive parents with resources on how to begin effectively addressing the intertwined issues of racial identity and adoption. The organization offers workshops for transracial adoptive parents, in addition to ones for same-race adoptive parents, who, as Beth explains, have slightly different needs and issues. It also runs a summer camp program for transracially adopted children and groups for teens.

For me as a Chinese American anthropologist, I found talking with Beth to be an interesting experience. Beth occupies a unique position—as a white adoptive parent and adoption worker who specializes in transracial adoption issues, she was able both to articulate the anxieties and concerns that might motivate white parents to form groups such as FCC that focus on cultural identity issues for their children, and also to critique these efforts in terms of their limitations in looking at race and white privilege. Having worked with adopted children, she was also aware of the impact of being raised in households where racial issues were not addressed. She emphasized the importance of talking to kids about issues of racism to provide them with a form of "protection" so they will not be "insecure about their own antennae." In other words, by talking about issues of race and racism, adoptive parents will be teaching their children that it is important and appropriate to raise these issues; in the process, children will develop trust in their own instincts when they need to deal with issues of racism. She sees these conversations not as something that can be put off until later because parents fear them but as urgent, almost "life or death" issues. In their book *Inside Racial Adoption*, Steinberg and Hall write:

> It is critical that parents not hesitate to talk to their children about racial experiences. We don't wait for children to ask us how to cross the street, or fear that talking about the dangers of cars will scare children too much. . . . No parent would let their child learn how to cross the street without clear tools for avoiding getting hit by oncoming traffic. . . . Issues of adoption and racialization are no different. Children must be taught how to anticipate and cope with social bias. . . . Talking about and understanding racism gives a child a way to see that the racism s/he experiences is *not* about her/him; rather it's about something bigger that operates on a societal level.
>
> It's a white . . . privilege to assume that it is not a life or death issue for your child to talk about these issues. Protection comes from talking about it and normalizing it. (2013, 44)

Beth's comments led me to reflect on whether I had been doing an adequate job preparing my own son, then three, to talk about issues of race. I shared with Beth that my son did not seem to have much awareness about being Chinese or Asian, but that we had already experienced an incident at his day care in which another parent whose child was in the same classroom had mistaken me and my son for another Chinese mother (who did not look anything like me, particularly given that she was seven months pregnant) and her son. We talked about how I was not sure whether the mother had merely been inattentive or whether she had been confused because we are both Asian. We also talked about how I could raise the issue with my son at a level that a child of his age could understand.

I found it interesting that I, as a Chinese American, was receiving advice about how to talk about issues of race from a white woman. It's not that I had never dealt with racial issues, but I had not come up with specific strategies for raising these issues with my son. I do not remember my parents discussing racial issues much with me either, even when in second grade a boy in my class in a predominantly white suburb of Boston told me that his father was a policeman and could send me "back" to China, a place to which I had never been. Was it because they too had been viewed as model minorities within the context of the small towns in which they grew up in Maryland and Maine? Or had I been so upset that I don't remember what my parents told me?

My maternal grandmother had been selected as the national Mother of the Year in 1952 for her story of immigrant struggle, raising eight successful children while running a hand laundry, largely without the assistance of her husband, who passed away when my mother, the youngest, was five. In their portrayal of the creation of model U.S. citizens out of poor Asian immigrants, these model minority narratives refute the existence of structural racism and celebrate the process of assimilation. It is a narrative that many Asian Americans themselves have accepted, particularly those of the second generation who were often able to lead solidly middle-class lifestyles despite the rural peasant origins of their immigrant parents. As discussed in the previous chapter, awareness of racial issues and their complexity is not necessarily automatic for Asian Americans, particularly those who had been raised to think that racism no longer existed, or who had grown up accepting this mistreatment. I began to wonder whether it might be possible for white adoptive parents like Beth and those who attend her workshops to learn about these issues, including their own white privilege, without necessarily having experienced racism directly. It is this area of potential that I wish to explore further in my discussion of white adoptive parents.

It is important to recognize that Beth Hall is not specifically faulting the parents in FCC but is pointing out some of the overarching structures that have historically made it difficult for white people to understand and address issues of race. Within the context of contemporary color-blind approaches to racial and cultural difference, discussions of race and power can easily disappear into the celebratory and aestheticized approaches to culture that can mark even some of the performances and celebrations of racialized communities themselves. It is important to analyze this context further before turning to a discussion of the approaches used by the white adoptive parents I interviewed.

The racial positioning of Chinese adoptees within U.S. racial politics, between blacks and whites, contributes to the tendency for their "difference" to be seen as cultural rather than racial, and for these differences to be celebrated in the aestheticized ways for which FCC is often critiqued. I interviewed Renee in 2001, when her daughter Julie, who is from China, was five and her son Justin, who is from St. Louis and is African American, was four. Renee is far from typical. She is the only adoptive parent I interviewed in St. Louis or the Bay Area who had adopted an African American baby, or for that matter, who had adopted a child of color domestically. Her experiences with one black and one Asian child capture the racial dynamic that not only infuses St. Louis but also shapes the positioning of Chinese adoptees within U.S. society more broadly.

The fact that Renee and her husband were initially open to adopting a black child, even against the wishes of some of their relatives, signified that they might have had open views on race. However, Renee has also learned a great deal about racial issues through her experiences with her son, having encountered the persistent and often contradictory stereotypes that circulate around both African Americans and Asian Americans.

Renee shared some insights into the differential racialization of Chinese and African American children, based on her observations of how her two children have been treated. Renee and her husband had initially decided to go to China to adopt Julie in large part because they were told by an agency that domestic adoption, particularly at their relatively older ages, might be difficult and uncertain. In contrast, the agency told them that the system in China was efficient and reliable, and that they could possibly bring a child home by the end of the year. They completed their paperwork by September 1996 and got their referral in November. Their travel was delayed two or three times, and they did not go to China until February of the following year. They traveled to China and met Julie and brought her home when she was six months old. Renee commented that nowadays, completing the adoption process this quickly would be unheard of.

When Julie was about two, Renee decided to stop working full-time so she could prepare to adopt a second child. She and her husband were undecided as to whether to go back to China, go to Vietnam (many families have adopted boys from there), or try to adopt domestically. One day, her sister, who is a pediatrician in St. Louis, and her brother-in-law, who is an ob-gyn, told her about a little boy they had treated. He had been born to a teenage mother, and the mother had decided to relinquish him for adoption. Renee sent in her home study to see if she and her husband would be selected to adopt him, but the baby was sent to another family. Renee and her husband were extremely disappointed.

Renee began to take on part-time consulting work. Her first job was with the family court in the Division of Family Services in St. Louis, where she was to serve as a special advocate to help find adoptive homes for special needs kids, which under local law included African American children. She repeatedly heard the judge and others talk about their frustration regarding the challenges of placing these children, using the example of a baby boy who had been in foster care since birth but had not yet been adopted. Though he had been exposed to drugs in utero, he had thus far shown no signs of having adverse effects. Renee asked the social worker for more information on the boy, saying that she was interested in adopting him. Shortly before Thanksgiving of 1998, she and her husband went to the social worker's office to see pictures of the boy, and by January of the following year, they had brought Justin home to live with them.

When she first told her husband's mother that they were going to adopt the boy, showing her "an adorable little picture" of the child, "her first response was 'Oh, no you can't do this.' We were like, 'Well, we already did it. He is coming to live with us.'" In contrast, when her mother-in-law first saw Julie's picture, she had commented, "Oh, she is a cute little China doll." As Renee related this story to me, Renee added, "Which I hate." Though the term may seem like a compliment, it carries many connotations, including the objectification and exoticization of the child.

In 2000, a year before I first interviewed her, I had met Renee and her children when I joined some adoptive parents and their children to eat at a local Chinese restaurant. Renee had commented that people would call Julie a China doll but say nothing about Justin, who was younger and, as those present pointed out, also cute. When I asked her about this again during our interview, Renee said that she thinks that both skin color and gender are keys to why Justin and Julie will have different experiences growing up because transracial adoption of children from China is more socially acceptable. During the interview, she reflected:

> I think in this culture what it has to do with definitely is the color of your skin. There are people in FCC who are very open to adopting a child from another culture, from China, but there are not open to adopting a black child. To me it is like there is transracial adoption and there is black/white adoption. It's like, "Yeah, OK, Chinese that is a different race, but [their skin is] white." It is still more socially acceptable.

Later in the interview, I asked her again about her comment regarding skin color and the relative acceptability of Asian children in the United States, remarking that it sounded as though she was saying it was easier to be Asian than black in this country. She responded:

> You know, having been neither, I guess I really cannot say that. But, from my perspective, it seems like the reactions I'm getting to my children, they are more accepting of her, and especially of her being in my family than him being in my family. And to me it just seems like there is just more acceptance anyway of somebody that has light skin.

She talked about how the perceptions of Asians and blacks that she has encountered in St. Louis are very different from one another. Regarding Asians, she observed:

> Whether or not that is true, there seems to be that sort of perception. [That they] are really smart, they are different from us, but they are smart. And they are harmless. Black people aren't, they aren't smart is the perception, and I'd better lock my doors if I go downtown because there are black people down there. People I grew up with that have made comments to me, it's like, "Don't they know that I've got a black child?"

Even Renee's childhood friends from the St. Louis counties, which are predominantly white, have made derogatory comments about black people in her presence. One of her high school friends had met her at a happy hour and described telling her son to keep his football helmet on while traveling on the bus to play a team from the city of St. Louis. Renee remembers asking her friend why she gave her son this advice, and her friend responded that all the kids in the city were black. Renee retorted, "I have one of those kids." Renee knows that people will no longer see Justin as cute when he grows older—as a young black male, he will be seen as a threat. "They'll see a big black kid. You had better lock your doors. The world will look at him very differently. [Julie] will always be fairly harmless and cute and exotic."

While Renee expressed her awareness of the stereotypes surrounding Chinese girls, and acknowledged that they are also affected by racism, it was interesting that she viewed Julie's skin color as being white like her own. Perhaps she was responding to her personal experiences, which seemed to show that, in contrast to blacks, Asians were effectively racialized as honorary whites and viewed as a model minority. Although many Asians may have skin that is "lighter" than that of many African Americans, and in some cases even lighter than "white" skin, in other cases the opposite is true. Thus, it is important to understand that it is the racialized meanings that are inscribed into perceptions of different skin tones that become salient, more so than actual skin color. These meanings are inseparable from the histories of enslavement, exclusion, and absorption that have characterized the histories of Asians and blacks in the United States, as well as the changing trajectories these perceptions took as a result of shifting immigration patterns. As George Yancey (2003) argues, predictions that whites are becoming a numerical minority in the United States do not take into account that "nonblack racial minority groups" are assimilating as whites, while the gap between these groups and African Americans remains wide. Renee's experiences with her children, and indeed her own perceptions of their "difference," support Yancey's observations, as well as those of Bonilla-Silva discussed in chapter 4.

But while Renee critiqued the racial views of families who would adopt a Chinese child but not a black child, she did not seem as worried about the complex racialized discourses that may affect Chinese adoptees. Perhaps it was more difficult for her to pinpoint the more subtle ways that Asians are racialized, particularly because the predominant images of Chinese girls are often framed in a positive light. The image of Chinese adoptees as well behaved, cute, and harmless model minorities, while not necessarily accurate, may seem difficult to object to.

Renee was annoyed at her daughter being called a China doll, but this label might have seemed minor in comparison to the assumptions being made about her son.

In addition, she felt that she had support in raising her daughter in the form of FCC, which focused on cultural identity and adoption issues and provided resources not only for parents but also for the children as they grew older. She was concerned that there were no similar groups for her son. Justin usually attended FCC events, participating along with his sister. Renee showed me a picture from the Missouri Botanical Garden's Chinese Culture Days in which Justin was wearing a Chinese outfit, surrounded by Chinese girls in their Chinese outfits. What did Justin's performance of Chinese culture along with his sister say about the extent to which Chineseness is so easily practiced and performed, while blackness is not?

Renee realized that as the children grew older, it would be insufficient to merely focus on the fun aspects of culture:

> When our kids get to be adolescent or preadolescent, when we put on a Culture Day, we are going to have to do stuff dealing with those issues at their level. You know, right now they are just out making fun little snakes, and little animals and stuff like that because they are five. I am glad to know that the [FCC] group is there to evolve with them and with their needs. They sort have their own little built-in support group. They have other kids that are going to go through the same thing that they can talk to.

Renee had tried to build her own network of resources to learn more about various forms of racism. For example, she has sought out friends and neighbors who are black so that she can learn about racial profiling and other issues that even transcend class distinctions. She learned that one neighbor who is a surgeon often gets stopped for "driving while black." Renee admitted that she "can't pretend to know what it is like to be nonwhite," but she thinks that being a woman has helped her on a certain level to understand what it is like to face discrimination, unlike her husband, who has never faced barriers as a white man. While she has intentionally sought out information from African Americans regarding racism, and realizes that racism affects both her son and her daughter, though perhaps to different degrees, it seemed that she would not have become as aware of these issues if not for her experiences with Justin.

I had an opportunity to interview Renee again in the summer of 2009. Julie was now almost fourteen and had grown into a shy teenager who liked reading, drawing, and writing. Justin, now eleven, was very interested in sports and dreamed of going to the University of Missouri one day on a basketball scholarship. The family lived in a town that was not far from the city of St. Louis, having moved there shortly after I interviewed them in 2001 because of the good school system, which was attractive to them because it was relatively diverse. Renee admitted that they lived in a "cocoon" of sorts, but she also believed that "the racial thing is always in the background." Although her children have never complained to her that someone has made fun of them for being different, her boss at the time, who worked for the school district, once made a comment to her about how her daughter wanted to date a black boy, and how she had warned her daughter about how society will look at her for doing this. In Renee's mind, her boss was essentially telling her daughter not to date people like Justin, but Renee did not say anything because she did not want to anger her boss. She related another incident in which the assistant principal of their public school was out directing traffic one day when a carload of kids came by and called him a "coon." He has also been pulled over for "driving while black." Renee has warned Justin that these things may happen to him someday also.

She also told me about a recent incident. In the car on the way back home from summer school, Justin had lamented, "Everyone in my class is black. Black people aren't as smart." Renee, who had been learning about racism in the schools for her work, replied that it was untrue that black people were not as smart. She had read that the schools were not doing a good job of teaching black kids and were treating them differently. As an example, she cited a summer math program for which only the black kids received brochures. The program had been targeted toward narrowing the "achievement gap," but Justin and his black friends had called it a "racist" program. Renee complained to the organizer of the program, who was also a colleague, and got the school to change the admission criteria for the program to race-neutral standards. She also believed that many of the African American parents seemed happy to get special services for their children and therefore might be less likely to complain about the racial bias of the program. She commented to me that, unfortunately, she has stereotypical children, with her Chinese daughter enrolled in gifted classes and her African American son often struggling with his homework. Unfortunately, she said, he sees it as a given that he is not in the gifted classes.

So while Renee has done her best to preemptively address issues of race for her children, she has also realized that there are limits to what she can control. She has seen blatant examples of racism within their "cocoon," even toward adult authority figures such as her children's assistant principal. She has also seen racism emerge in more institutionalized or insidious forms, such as in the enrichment programs that target students by race, rather than by educational needs, or in the offhand remarks of her boss, who worked for a presumably progressive school district. But perhaps most powerfully, she has seen her son internalize the idea that "black people aren't as smart."

Renee's experiences reflect the broader tendency within U.S. society for the "difference" of Asians to be conceived in terms of culture, and the "difference" of blacks to be understood in terms of race (and to some extent in terms of cultural deficiency). As indicated in her comment quoted earlier, although Chinese adoption is sometimes seen as transracial, it is perhaps more often viewed as international, and as adopting from another *culture*, whereas adopting a black child from the United States is more commonly viewed as adopting from another *race* in the sense that although Asians are seen as a different race, in Renee's mind, their skin is still "white."

Though Renee and other adoptive parents did acknowledge the racial difference of their Chinese children, within the context of FCC, they were much more likely to focus on fostering identification with China and Chinese culture as a means of addressing issues of cultural and racial identity, as well as adoption more broadly. This focus on "culture keeping" (Jacobson 2008) has been written about extensively by Dorow (2006b), Jacobson (2008), Shiu (2001), Volkman (2005), and others. For Justin, Renee was left to create a support system on her own to learn about the racial issues that affect him and other African Americans. Indeed, it seemed that she had learned most of what she knew about race and racism from her experiences with her son, for whom these issues were front and center, as opposed to with her daughter, for whom race often was manifested in more subtle and complex ways. As has been widely noted by, the racial and cultural positioning of Asian Americans makes their integration into white families much more easily imagined. But what might the consequences of this erasure of race be?

Birth Cultures and the Cultural Difference of Chinese Adoptees

As evidenced by the previous example, the in-between (some would argue near-white) racial status of Asians in the United States may facilitate a focus on the cultural over the racial aspects of Chineseness (Dorow 2006a). However, this integrative approach to dealing with racial difference, which involves the folding of Chinese cultural elements into the lives of white adoptive families, may be misleading in that it treats Chineseness as a choice. Many adoptive parents have actively pursued the avenues opened up by U.S. multiculturalism to connect to, identify with, and celebrate racial and cultural diversity, but it is important to recognize that underlying these avenues are deeply rooted relations of class and racial privilege that have historically positioned white middle-class Americans in relation to nonwhites. As much of the recent adoption literature notes, children adopted from China into white American families enter U.S. society in a relatively privileged place within its race and power hierarchy. As orphans of color from a foreign country who become part of (usually) white middle-class homes, they move directly from the marginalized periphery to the center of mainstream white America. Within this context they are viewed as being remarkably flexible and redeemable, able to adapt to and thrive in their new settings (Dorow 2006a; Ortiz and Briggs 2003). What is of concern in the context of international adoption is the ease with which Asian American adoptees are assigned cultural identities to be preserved, or celebrated, and the ways that this focus on culture may occur at the expense of attention to the ways that these children are racialized within domestic U.S. politics.

As illustrated by the experiences of Renee's children, within middle-class folk understandings of cultural difference, some groups, such as Asian Americans, are viewed as possessing more, as well as better, culture than others, and their "difference" is viewed in cultural rather than racial terms (Ebron and Tsing 1995). The perceived cultural difference of Asians actually has deep historical roots, as racial hostilities against Chinese immigrants to the United States in the late 1800s were framed in popular rhetoric in terms of the immutable cultural differences of the Chinese, rather than the economic terms that underlay their tensions with white working-class laborers (Dirlik 1998). However, in a contemporary context, these views have shifted so that they are masked within the more positive model minority stereotype. This myth asserts that Asian Americans have in many ways become "honorary whites" who have overcome racial barriers and, in many cases, outperformed whites, often due to their strong "cultural" values (Zhou 2004; Tuan 1999). Their in-between status on the black-white spectrum of U.S. racial politics (Ong 1999; Zhou 2004) has the effect of displacing their difference from the realm of race into the realm of culture. While they may be seen as to some extent having "overcome racial barriers" to achieve economic and educational success, their cultural values such as a "strong work ethic" are seen as largely responsible for their rising status in education, business, music, and other life pursuits (T. Fong 2007). Other minorities, such as African Americans, are viewed as a contrasting case, as domestic minorities who are lacking in culture and are performing below white standards (T. Fong 2007).

During an interview at their home, about a forty-five-minute drive from where I was staying in St. Louis, I talked with Darrell and Stephanie, a couple in their forties, about their decision to adopt. Darrell recalled that, after accepting infertility and not being able to have biological children, he and his wife, Stephanie, began to consider adoption, first from Latin America and then from China. They had started taking Spanish language lessons and attending mass again, but in the end, their plans to adopt from Colombia fell through. Their decision to adopt children from China, Darrell admitted, was guided in part by the positive U.S. stereotypes of Chinese girls versus negative ones of South American boys:

> I remember sitting here on a sofa and weeping buckets, and she had seen something about a program in China. . . . So we got to thinking about it . . . and really I had this real racist thought going through my mind at that moment. When somebody comes to the door and a Chinese girl

opens the door that person thinks, "Oh, math major at some snooty Ivy League school," and if it is a South American boy who answers the door, they think gardener, waiter, or something like that. It was real stereotypical in my mind.

As teachers, both Darrell and Stephanie were aware of these stereotypes and, to some extent, their structural nature. Darrell even admitted that his own stereotypical ideas about South American boys were racist, and Stephanie commented that these racist stereotypes are so ingrained that in education "black boys and Hispanic boys are pretty consistently underestimated. Asian students are frequently overestimated." But they were so eager to have a baby, they thought they were prepared to deal with either of these stereotypes. They talked about how people would assume that their children were "brilliant" just because they are Asian, and how Darrell would joke, "They don't think they got it from me!" However, they said they were "comfortable with that. " Darrell cited some studies in the field of education that illustrated the positive impact of the teacher having high expectations of students:

Well, we know, having worked in education, we know that probably one of the major effective elements in somebody's education is what the teacher . . . the teacher's expectations. It really covers so much, and there [have] been a zillion studies done on that. This is something that was new when I was first an elementary ed major in the seventies. I mean, it was from the sixties that the studies were done. They become what we think they are. So if everybody thinks she is smart . . . well, OK. We'll roll with it. It is a powerful thing for them.

Darrell said his older daughter had confidence in her ability to overcome some speech issues for which she was seeing a specialist, noting that one of the biggest challenges he works on with the students in his own school is convincing them that they have the ability to overcome the difficulties they face.

Still, neither he nor Stephanie seemed as concerned about the possible drawbacks of the positive stereotypes surrounding Asian Americans mentioned earlier. When I asked whether they thought their children were aware of being minorities, Darrell replied, "They are almost treated like pets at the Montessori School over here. They were just fawned over all the time, and they had buddies, and the teachers all loved them and everything. I don't know if there was any negative connotation." Stephanie added:

> I think that people make themselves feel very good by accepting a minority child. You know, people in a school can really make themselves feel very liberal by saying, I like that kid. And you know coming up to me and saying, "I really like your daughter, she is a nice kid." It's less trouble than saving the whales, and it makes them feel really good about themselves. I can't begrudge them that.

Stephanie's comment reveals that she is aware of the liberal color-blind discourses that may compel those surrounding her minority children to treat them positively. Nevertheless, it seems that Stephanie and Darrell did not see any negative connotations of these well-meaning acts of others, nor did they express concern about the impact that being seen as "pets" will have on their children.

For white adoptive parents, understanding and integrating their children from China into the family required them to deal with issues of race and ethnicity in new ways. Though some Asian American parents made distinctions between their own family histories and the more direct ties to China of their adoptive children, they could use their own Chinese or "Asian" heritage as a launching point from which to craft Chinese identities for their children. For white adoptive parents, Chinese culture comes into play primarily as a form of birth culture that is not closely linked to, and may even be seen as working against, their own family heritage. The term "birth culture" is usually specific to adoption, conjuring up biologized notions that assume a link between ancestral origins and cultural identity. The idea of birth culture encompasses a number of powerful assumptions about the relationship between biological and geographic origins, and the "culture" and identity that the individual develops as he or she grows. Though parents may not know exactly where the child was born and later relinquished, the ways that parents imagine these locations figure centrally into how they construct adoptee identities (Volkman 2005). For adoptive parents, there exist the simultaneous pull of the child's essential Chineseness, encapsulated in her birth origins and circumstances, inscribed in her physical features and history (Dorow 2006b) and framed by a history of U.S. relations with China and the Orient, and the desire to move beyond this background in creating a new family identity. Though Chinese adoptees are viewed as easy to assimilate, their foreign origins nevertheless remain a challenge to their integration into the United States. As Dorow observes "In her move from China to the United States and as she got older, the attractive, flexible Asian child became suspiciously fixed and foreign" (2006b, 215).

The circumstances surrounding the relinquishment of the child haunt her in her transition from peasant child to orphan to adoptee (Dorow 2006b, 214, 215),[2] forming the basis of the adoption narrative that parents construct. In this sense, her identity remains tied to these places, while simultaneously these places are reimagined and reconstructed as adoptees and their parents create new relationships to them. Friendships formed through adoption travel groups among parents whose children came from the same orphanage are based on these shared origins but also represent an investment in future relationships based on this commonality. At an adoption agency reunion I attended, children's names were listed on a board by province, and some parents met and socialized on this basis. At FCC Chinese Culture Day and similar events, maps of children's hometowns are sold, and many children learn to pick out their hometown or province on a map. A number of families whom I interviewed had maintained these connections to others from their travel groups as the children grew older, holding periodic reunions. Some adoptive families have traveled back to their child's hometown or orphanage, in a sort of return to roots tour. Similar experiences are seen in the documentaries *Somewhere Between* and *Found in China*.

However, the focus on the Chinese origins of adopted children, and the tendency to "fix" children in their birthplaces (and birth cultures) that results, is in many ways at odds both with the changing nature of contemporary Chinese culture and with the construction of a new family identity. In other words, the focus on birth culture renders Chinese culture static and also separate from American lives or Chinese American culture. The irony of the term "birth culture," of course, is that culture is the flexible, changing product of the environment in which one is raised, and cultural attributes cannot be assumed solely on the basis of one's birth, biological, or ancestral origins. And despite the efforts of adoptive parents to educate themselves and their children about birth-places and birth cultures, there remains the need to create a narrative of family identity that both acknowledges the child's Chinese roots and validates the family as legitimate and complete in light of the public nature of adoption discussed earlier.

Adoptive parents may view Chinese culture as a very positive asset to which they should expose their children, and potentially as something that would differentiate them from other minorities. Thus, while on the one hand, female Chinese adoptees may be viewed as victims of their culture of origin's preference for boys, on the other hand, Chinese culture is viewed as an asset that gives them the potential to excel despite their underprivileged origins. Although this potential is to some extent locked in their unknown genetics, one wonders if the emphasis placed on Chinese birth culture and its associated positive values is not viewed as key to the maintenance of the cultural piece of adoptee upbringing and success in later life.

Popular psychologized conceptualizations of identity imply that the individual can proactively create an individual identity if he or she is given the right opportunities, makes the right choices, and employs the right resources. Rather than being the product of structural forces and group histories and processes, identity is viewed as being out there, waiting to be discovered through self-examination and exploration (Bondi 1993). In addition, this identity work becomes focused on the creation of a sense of origins that plays to the expectation, exemplified in the melting-pot idea, that people of color are rich in both roots and culture.

A long history of Orientalism (Said 1979) has made Asia and Asian things into objects of desire for Westerners, to be collected, displayed, and admired. These Orientalist conceptualizations of Asian difference channel understandings of cultural difference into the realm of aesthetic appreciation. The trip to China reinforces these tendencies in its focus on China's historical cultural splendor and the purchase of goods that represent it. The foreign origins of transnational adoptees facilitate the imagining of their difference as more cultural than racial. Publications such as *National Geographic* and other popular representations of "foreign" cultures portray other parts of the world as different in terms of culture and custom, but they rarely discuss issues of racial and power difference (Lutz and Collins 1993). This mentality allows travelers going abroad to be concerned with how to negotiate local language, customs, and currencies, while remaining less aware of the global politics that produces inequalities between first world and third world and between white and black (or brown or yellow).

Melanie, who has always admired Chinese culture, commented to me:

> I just have always thought the American culture is so boring, I know everybody has their wars, but what have we got. How boring is massacring Indians and wars, and just really nothing spectacular. And then you've got China. You've got thousands of years of history, beautiful legends, beautiful artwork, they take a lot of pride in their history, and they've kept that history still in the modern day. You still see that traditional dress in certain things that they do. You still see that. . . . They just take a lot of pride in their history. Even though you may go to one side, one part of China, and show it actually poor, but they still have something to do with the traditional stuff. Stories and legends and Chinese New Year's all have [been] brought down from a legend [for] years. I have a lot of respect for that.

Melanie's example illustrates the ways that some parents develop their initial romanticized views of China even prior to adopting their children from China through the Orientalist worldview that characterizes their early education. Though Melanie is well-intentioned, her admiration for Chinese culture—its rich history and arts tradition—reinforces notions about the exoticism of China and Chinese people. I interviewed Melanie and her husband, Frederick, at the modest home they shared with their four special needs children adopted from China. I asked Melanie how she had learned about Chinese and other Asian cultures, with which she had become fascinated. She recalled having studied Asia in school and thinking that American culture paled in comparison. She contrasted the brooms made by American pioneers to the rich arts and crafts history she had observed in China, exclaiming, "They are making different arts and crafts from hundreds and thousands of years ago. We've got not much of anything. Well, you know what I mean, nothing real . . . that is so awesome I have to buy that. You go to China and you say, 'That is so awesome I have to buy that.'" Melanie's views about the arts and crafts traditions of Chinese versus U.S. culture are clearly selective, most likely having been shaped by her early education, which may have emphasized the rustic pioneer foundation myth of the United States, on the one hand, and the Oriental splendor of Asia, on the other. The adoption trip's emphasis on Chinese history, of which the consumption of Chinese goods marketed as "traditional" was a central part, would only have served to reinforce these views.

Melanie was also straightforward about her preference for Asian children. She and Frederick joked about his brother's baby, who was born around the same time they adopted their first daughter, noting that it was "the ugliest little thing you have ever seen" and expressing (in jest) their relief that they had not been able to have biological children. Perhaps her comment was a way of dealing with the infertility she was experiencing. In addition, she said she just liked the appearance of darker-skinned babies:

> I remember when I was young, you know, you talk when you are kids . . . whatever, I thought if I ever couldn't have kids I wanted an American Indian baby. There was just something about them, I liked the darker skin tones, and I liked the look. If I couldn't go to China, I would probably go to someplace like Guatemala. It is just my personal preference. I think biracial babies are beautiful. It is just kind of a preference. It's like a preference of some people wanting certain pets. You know, they prefer a certain breed or a certain size. And that is not a good comparison, but you know what I am saying. You just can't explain it. It is just hard to explain that part of it . . . about why you would do that. I prefer darker-skinned children. But, you know, if I would have gotten a very, very milky-white-complected baby, I would have been just as happy, I don't think it would have mattered.

Although her honesty was admirable, Melanie's equation of children with specific physical characteristics with the selection of breeds of pets would be disconcerting to many. Though she said she would have been happy with a baby of any complexion, the idea that she considered the aesthetics of skin color in deciding where to adopt may seem superficial. While the fact that she would consider adopting a child of color showed that she was to some extent open-minded, she had talked primarily about foreign-born and biracial children, and it was unclear whether she understood the social implications of skin color, particularly in the context of the United States.

Melanie's husband, Frederick, characterized her understanding of China and Chinese culture as "romanticized." Melanie admitted that her view of China was more "from mythology." She described herself as a visual person, who was not "political at all." In contrast, when I asked Frederick what he thought about China while he was growing up, he said that his main impression had been formed based on his experiences with his best friend in his senior year in high school, who was from China, and whose family had been "displaced by the Communist regime." He remembers going over to the friend's house and hearing his family "rant and rave" about what was being done in China.

However, now that they have adopted from China, they do make an effort to keep up with current events there "for our kids' sake." Melanie brings her children to a culture center and rents Chinese movies for them (not just kung fu movies, she jokes). She goes into the classroom for each of her children and arranges special activities for Chinese New Year, including bringing in a Chinese dragon, reading a story, making paper lanterns, and having the children practice using chopsticks to pick up pompoms. She brings in fortune cookies, flavored gelatins, and rice cakes for the children to eat. She is gratified that her children like it when she visits their classrooms. She feels that it gives them the sense that "it must be really cool to be Chinese."

As the only Chinese children in their schools, her children have always been "popular," receiving extra attention from their teachers. Melanie admits that this attention has sometimes gone too far, such as when teachers give them too much "physical attention," touching them, holding them, and brushing their hair.

Chineseness as an Ethnic Option

Many, but not all, white families I interviewed saw themselves as having little culture of their own. Bringing Chinese culture into their homes was both a way to honor the heritage of their adopted child and a way to explore a new and exciting culture that complemented the existing family background or provided a way for a family to become "ethnic" by incorporating "Chinese" traditions, decorations, and costumes into their lives. Having culture was something that parents viewed positively in the current atmosphere of multiculturalism and globalization. Many parents with whom I spoke talked about the influences of their own cultural backgrounds on their children, whom they now considered to be part Irish, Italian, Armenian, German, or some other ethnicity, in addition to being Chinese. This easy mixing of heritages reflected the melting-pot idea. However, after adopting, the parents realized that their children could not easily merge into an ethnic American cultural identity as easily as they had originally thought. One mother, Corinne, noted that at first she thought that her daughter would become Irish American like herself and her husband, and that she and her husband have also become Chinese, meaning that they have an affinity for and awareness of Chinese culture. Still, Corrine and her husband said they have heard more insensitive comments and questions relating to adoption than to race. Or was it that they were not sure how to interpret these issues when they arose? They told me that one day their daughter came home from day care and asked if she was black. They took this question as a sign of misidentification on the part of their preschooler, and as an indication that she was still sorting out aspects of her identity. But one wonders what else this racial confusion might have signified for their daughter, or what type of learning moment regarding racialization for them as parents might have come of it.

Anthropologists have observed that in the context of U.S. multiculturalism, a pluralistic view of culture allows people to select bits and pieces of cultural influence to be blended within the context of family life. There is a tendency for cultures to be viewed as consisting of discrete elements that can be selected to enter the American melting pot (Segal and Handler 1995). This is consistent with the notion of ethnic options, as discussed in relation to white ethnics in the introduction and as illustrated by Corinne's example here. However, white parents to some extent learn about the limits of applying ethnic options to their nonwhite children as they learn more about the persistence of race as it continues to define their constructions of their children's ethnicity.

In the context of exercising their ethnic options (Waters 1990), parents I interviewed tried to selectively edit the aspects of Chinese culture to which they exposed their children, at least while they were young. The Chinese New Year activities that Melanie introduced to her children's classes were not at all unusual among adoptive parents. However, parents had somewhat limited repertoires, in large part because much of contemporary Chinese culture is not readily distinguishable from U.S. culture. People in mainland China have for some time been riding bicycles, wearing blue jeans, and even going to church and eating at McDonald's, so these practices were not readily identifiable as "Chinese" and therefore would not serve as effective symbols of Chineseness in an American context. Unlike Asian American adoptive parents who could draw from family traditions, and deem specific daily practices or cultural values as representative of their family's Chinese culture, white ethnics were more limited in the symbols they could employ to effectively represent Chineseness in the context of their everyday lives. While Yan could talk about how eating white rice in rice bowls with her Chinese American parents represented a continuity of family tradition and values, white adoptive families would be viewed as having co-opted Chinese culture and symbols if they made similar claims.

White families appeared to be more concerned with symbolizing traditional, "authentic" Chineseness, favoring objects that had Chinese writing on them or that had historical meaning, such as antiques. In addition, parents with young children are often focused on symbolic representations of Chinese culture. But while white adoptive parents were concerned about authenticity in one sense, they also were inventing practices that combined Chinese traditions with aspects of their own family lives. As Volkman (2005) notes, these included a newly created ceremony mimicking a scene they saw in a Chinese movie that involved passing a baby through a large steamed bun to commemorate his turning one month old. The adoptive parents had a bakery create a large, doughnut-shaped challah bread especially for the occasion, and the ceremony involved passing their daughter through the challah as part of her baby-naming ceremony.

In 2001, the Hurleys invited me over for dinner on the Shabbat, during which their six-year-old daughter adopted from China recited prayers in Hebrew. They discussed the complexity of their daughter's identity, commenting, "You also then throw religion into the mix, and there are just so many things that go into bringing up a child. [She] is more than a little girl from China." Their daughter is not only learning Hebrew but also takes ballet and gymnastics. Her parents also try to learn about Chinese culture, and the family attends the New Year celebration in one of the Asian enclaves in St. Louis in which Vietnamese and Hawaiian cultures are also represented. They must also consider the identity issues of their son, who was adopted from Vietnam.

Given the history of Orientalism that has defined China and Asia as distinctly different from the West, timeless and unchanging, the symbols that have come to represent China and Chinese culture are often framed in binary opposition to Western cultural elements. Chineseness is thus often represented through material objects such as chopsticks, silk outfits, and traditional crafts and foods, and encapsulated in ideas and practices such as feng shui, Chinese calligraphy, language, and so forth. Thus, while both "Chinese" and "American" elements contributed to the cultural makeup of adopted children's lives, these cultural elements were conceptualized in binary, static terms although, in reality, there were many areas of overlap between these essentialized conceptions of Chinese and American culture, particularly in the context of everyday family life.

For many parents the content of birth culture did not focus as much on abstract values and ideas as much as it was selected by parents both for its ability to be visibly implemented and to represent Chineseness to young children in the context of everyday U.S. family life. In the context of U.S. multiculturalism, "culture" was imagined in the form of "material culture"—objects that could be displayed and passed down through the generations as symbols of family cohesion—or viewed as a set of ingrained cultural practices that have been imbued with the weight of tradition (Segal and Handler 1995). Parents expressed Chinese culture through engaging in particular activities and through the display of particular items, such as those purchased on the adoption trip. Parents also collected additional items related to Chinese culture and adoption for their children's use, whether in the present or the future. As I discuss further in chapter 6, the issues surrounding the commodification of Chinese culture are complex. At the time of my research interviews, books that dealt with adoption from China more specifically, such as Sara Dorow and Stephen Wunrow's *When You Were Born in China* (1997) and Ying Ying Fry and Terry Fry's *Kids Like Me in China* (2001), were popular. Amy Tan's children's book (also a cartoon on PBS) *Sagwa the Chinese Siamese Cat* was also found in many homes. Videos such as Disney's *Mulan* and Sesame Street's *Big Bird in China* were especially popular. Parents read books and watched movies about China and adoption issues for their own education and enjoyment. These materials included books and magazines specific to adoption from China such as *Lost Daughters of China* (Evans 2008) and *A Passage to the Heart* (Klatzkin 1999), as well as books by Amy Tan. Parents purchased stones with Chinese characters engraved on them and other home decorations with Chinese themes and intermingled these items with other family heirlooms and artwork. Some children's rooms were decorated with Chinese artifacts such as stuffed panda bears, Chinese dolls, and Chinese artwork. These items were usually mixed in with pictures of kids and their soccer teams, kids' artwork, and the usual clutter of toys, stuffed animals, and clothes. In most homes I visited, items from China were distributed throughout the house rather than being contained solely in the child's room. Children did not always clearly differentiate between "Chinese" items in their rooms, and their other toys and books. When Laura was five, her mother, Jane, asked her to show me the books from China in her room. She proceeded to show me other Chinese things people had given her and then showed me everything on her dresser top, much of which was not "Chinese," including some U.S. fifty-cent coins.

Many parents developed an ongoing interest in Chinese items not only for their children but also for themselves. One mother had her friend make a swing for her with the Chinese characters *chun tian* (spring) engraved on the bottom. I was often reassured that I had located the right house for my interviews when I saw a panda flag or a doormat with a Chinese character in front of the house. These items are commonly available at stores such as World Market and Tuesday Morning. Some St. Louis families bought high-quality "authentic" antique Chinese furniture and decorations from a local China import shop. These antiques, which in the past had served as everyday Chinese furniture, took on new meanings as they were used and displayed in the homes of adoptive families as collectibles and symbols of authenticity and respect for Chinese heritage. Citing Giroux (1994), Amy Traver astutely observes the manner in which consumption is integrally associated with the expression of ethnic identities in today's economic context, linking these practices to "post-Fordist economic organization" that produces not only the consumer goods available to express ethnicity but also "the need for that consumption" (2007, 203).

Limitations

But these celebratory and material-based forms of acknowledging Chinese culture also proved to be limited in many cases as children grew older and lost interest in having their parents come into their classrooms or in attending FCC events. The St. Louis FCC group has evolved over the years as the attendance of older adoptees dwindled. For some families, busy schedules limited the amount of time that children had available to attend these events, as other extracurricular activities took precedence. The St. Louis chapter now has special activities for children aged five to eight and for teens, which cater to their specific interests.

A number of other factors also come into play in a child's identity formation, and these change over time, as illustrated in the example of Jane and her daughter, Laura. While parents deliberately and selectively researched and collected information about Chinese culture, the experience of trying to implement it within the household may further complicate the idea of Chinese culture and identity for adoptive parents. The attitudes of the child toward China also change over time and are marked by a combination of ambivalence and curiosity. They also develop and shift in tandem with the exploration of other areas of interest and identity.

Jane, a high school German teacher, was not yet married when she adopted her daughter. I interviewed Jane three times over a span of nine years. I first talked to her in 2001, when her daughter, Laura, was five years old, and caught up with her again in 2004 and 2009. During my first visit to her home, she had put on a video about the everyday lives of people in China for her daughter to watch while we talked. As discussed earlier, Laura proudly showed me her room, which contained books, decorations, and other knickknacks representing China. Jane told me that they attended FCC events together, where Laura enjoyed participating in activities and playing with the other children. Jane recalled that her daughter had been excited after seeing a performance put on by a local Chinese school about the Great Wall of China that I had also attended. She had previously seen pictures of the Great Wall, including in the video *Big Bird in China*, so she had many questions about the performance. Jane had talked with Laura about someday going back to China, and Laura had seemed excited about the idea.

I talked with Jane again in 2004, at a picnic for the single mothers group that she and a friend had organized. The group, consisting of mothers with internationally adopted children, was meeting at a park on a steamy St. Louis summer day. As the mothers gathered at a shaded spot and unloaded food onto the picnic tables, the children, mostly girls, ran around the playground. Mary, whom I had met in China in 2002 when she was adopting her daughter, had driven forty-five minutes to attend.

Sitting at the picnic tables with some of the other mothers, Jane told me that Laura, now nine, was no longer interested in participating in FCC activities or in visiting China or Germany, where Jane's family was originally from. Jane was happy that they had maintained friendships with other families with children adopted from China, and with members of their single mothers group. She also noted that Laura's primary concern at the time was not centrally related to her Chinese origins but to the fear of losing her mother, particularly given that Jane was a single, older parent. She emphasized to me that perhaps issues of children of single mothers manifested in a different way because of these additional concerns that the child might have. This echoes Dorow's observation that "single white mothers often said to me that the 'absent father' seemed to trump or compound racial difference and again wondered if 'too much' culture would unravel the fragility of these family differences" (2006b, 245).

I last interviewed Jane in the summer of 2009 in the new home where she now lived with her daughter and husband, whom she had married since I had last seen her. By this time, I had started interviewing teens, and though Laura was home, she declined to take part in the interview or even to come out of her room to say hello to me. Jane was not surprised at her daughter's reaction, noting that she felt that Laura still had a fraught relationship with her Chineseness, and that she "doesn't want to deal with it, or talk about it, or have any connection whatsoever." Not only did Laura no longer wanted to attend FCC events, but she even got mad when Jane attended Chinese culture events. I asked if Laura was unhappy about Jane talking with me, and she agreed that she probably was. Laura does not want to do anything that will single her out. Jane noted: "She doesn't identify herself as being Chinese. She's just an American, that's all she wants to hear. And if someone points something out to her . . . maybe in high school . . . if someone asks the question 'Where are you from?' she takes offense."

Laura has continued to explore other aspects of her identity. She has attended a Catholic school since the fifth grade, leaving the public school where she had been taunted for being Chinese. Despite the fact that neither Jane nor her husband is a practicing Catholic, Laura decided after a couple of years that she wanted to become Catholic. She is also interested in art and plays the piano. Jane was still not sure about how Laura feels about going to China someday. Laura recently expressed interest in going to visit a non-Chinese friend and her mother who were living there for the year. However, she mentioned it only once and did not raise the subject again. She is learning German this summer with Jane, who is a German teacher, so that she can begin with level two German in high school her freshman year. She has already been to Germany twice and enjoyed the trips. Jane believed that Laura would also sort out her relationship to her Chinese identity when she was ready: "I look at it as the same as religion. She found it herself. I think that the same thing will happen with cultural identity. I can't force it on her. I can just show her that we accept it. Give her opportunities, like a trip to China."

Jane told me about an interesting dinner conversation they had recently that had ended in Laura expressing some interest in going to China. They had been talking about whether one could tell the difference between a person of Chinese, Japanese, Vietnamese, or other Asian descent based on facial features or body shape. Jane had previously told her about the double versus single eyelid distinction among Asians, and Laura had asked again about this. The conversation had shifted to what it would feel like to be a minority, or for a minority person to be in a place where he or she was no longer a minority. Jane had shared with Laura her experience of having traveled to Mérida, Mexico, in the Yucatán Peninsula, where she had felt very out of place, "tall and pale and pasty looking." Laura had wondered what it would be like in China, where she would blend in with the general population. Jane joked that she should go ahead and buy her plane ticket before Laura changed her mind again. Laura has also recently expressed interest in Japanese anime and manga, even watching the shows in Japanese when they were not yet available in English. She has also grown to like having dark hair; whereas she used to want to have hair that matched her mother's, she now envied her friend whose hair was blacker than her own dark brown shade. Jane saw this as signifying Laura's increasing acceptance of her appearance.

But Race Still Matters

The focus on the cultural difference of Chinese adoptees serves to deflect attention from the fact that race still matters for them. As much as they become a fully integrated part of their adoptive families, within the broader racial formations of the United States, adoptees and other Asian immigrants remain involuntarily defined by their racial and cultural origins, regardless of how long they have been in the United States or whether or not they have in-depth connections to China or knowledge about Chinese culture (R. Lee 1999). They are assigned these characteristics based on "racialized" features—phenotype—and not on their actual cultural practices. Chinese Americans, whether first or fourth generation, are assumed to know Chinese, are complimented on their English as if it were their second (rather than only) language, and are thought to have continuing close ties to China, despite the fact that for many, this is far from the truth.

Adoptive parents conceptualized their children's racial and cultural difference within the context of broader social, cultural, and historical frameworks that shaped how they understood issues of culture and race—particularly what constituted racism, how it was experienced, and how to best "defend against" or change the conditions that produce racism (Shiao, Tuan, and Rienzi 2004).[3] These frameworks served to both essentialize race and racism, and mask the power relations that define the significance of "racial" differences within U.S. society. Sociologist Ruth Frankenberg observes that the key paradigms that define race in U.S. society have shifted, noting that while the discourse of essentialist racism that focuses on biologically based inequalities that has historically defined racial differences is now less prevalent, a second paradigm, that of color blindness, has arisen in response. She terms this approach "color evasiveness" and "power evasiveness" because in asserting that "we are all the same under the skin; that culturally, we are all converging;

that, materially, we have the same chances in U.S. society" (Frankenberg 1993, 14), its proponents are in many ways dismissing race as a powerful factor that shapes opportunities and perpetuates structural inequalities. The invisibility of these racial discourses, according to Frankenberg, often makes race into an absent presence (138).

Writing about the practices of white adoptive parents, anthropologist Ann Anagnost similarly notes that "the discourse of multiculturalism sets up the paradox of absorbing 'difference' into the intimate space of the familiar while also reinscribing it." This, she argues, "speaks to the practice of white, middle-class parenting more generally in exploring how race and class must always be constructed for the child, even when they go unmarked" (Anagnost 2000, 390). Just as the white women that Frankenberg studied reworked racial meanings in different variations and "deployed [them] with varying degrees of intentionality" (1993, 140), adoptive parents also engaged in reworking racial meanings that contain numerous contradictory discourses and therefore do not always play out without ambiguity.

Overall, many parents perceived the flexibility of Chinese adoptees as allowing them to overcome many of the problems commonly associated with racism against other minority groups, particularly African Americans (Dorow 2006a). In this sense, their practices do not necessarily challenge existing racial hierarchies. Indeed, some of the parents I interviewed said that despite their fears, they had seen very little racism directed against their children, but it was not always clear what deeds and acts parents deemed racist. For example, many parents were not sure how to interpret comments from both friends and strangers who viewed Chinese girls as cute and exotic or referred to their daughters as "China dolls." Some seemed to find fault more with the accuracy of the description ("my daughter is far from fragile") than with the term's racialized and gendered (sometimes sexual) connotations. Some parents seemed unaware of the forms of gendered Orientalism that their daughters would be subject to as Asian women growing up in the West. Although being called a "China doll" may seem like a compliment, the term has historically carried implications about the exotic, subservient positions of Asian women in relation to the West.

Most parents understood race and racism as consisting of discriminatory acts rather than as a structurally embedded and historically rooted system of historical inequalities. As Frankenberg observes, it is often difficult for white Americans to understand the "structural and institutional dimensions of racism" because racism has historically been framed in essentialist terms in which "particularly intentional, explicit racial discrimination remains, for most white people . . . paradigmatic of racism" (1993, 139). Furthermore, they viewed racism as something that could be overcome through education and cross-cultural sharing, in the vein of contemporary multiculturalist rhetoric. Parents understood offensive comments as stemming from the lack of open-mindedness of others. Aside from some "ignorant" comments from adults and "stupid" questions from friends and family members, most parents felt people had been supportive and positive toward their family. They viewed the formation of their families across racial and national lines as an important step in opening the minds of others. Thus, by acknowledging and celebrating their children's cultural difference, and teaching others to "appreciate" these differences, parents believed that they were preparing their children for life in a racist society. Acknowledging that their children were in sheltered environments, parents were concerned about what will happen in everyday settings such as at school when parents are no longer there to protect them. The acts of racism they worried about were imagined to come in the form of mean comments from other children about their child being adopted or being "different." Many said the issue may be not as much about race as it is about difference—"kids will make fun of those that are different."

With a history of "white flight" from the city, race relations in St. Louis continue to be defined in primarily black and white terms, with most lower-income blacks living in the city proper and most affluent whites living in the suburban "west counties." As Dorow notes, in the context of transnational Chinese adoption, "blackness emerged as a kind of 'white noise' against which Asianness became flexible in the white American imaginary" (2006a, 360). In the black and white racial climate of St. Louis, parents' narration of their adoption choices reflected this relationship. A number of parents I interviewed said that "if race hadn't been an issue," they would not have hesitated to adopt a "biracial" or black child.[4] While most who raised this issue said that they did not consider adopting a black child to be problematic, they had heard that the adoption of black children by white parents was "controversial" in the black community. But it was also clear that many perceived adopting an Asian child as different than adopting an African American child (Dorow 2006a, 364; Ortiz and Briggs 2003).[5]

Many adoptive parents I interviewed in St. Louis noted what they perceived to be a cultural and racial distance between whites and African Americans. Francine and Erik live in a town outside the city of St. Louis that is known to attract the faculty of a local private university who want both a diverse community and a good school system. They kindly invited me to their house to have pizza before I interviewed them. When Francine and her daughter Amelia, aged three, answered the door, I was struck by her naturally curly hair, which was unusual, though not unheard, of within the Chinese population. Later in the conversation, it became apparent that Amelia's curly hair was important to Francine, who saw it as a similarity between her and her daughter that helped affirm their commonality as family members, even though Amelia was not a biological child. Francine mentioned that the adoption social workers had told her about the importance of validating these similarities. Dorow (2006b, 242) similarly noted in her study that while parents encouraged their children to be proud of their physical features, they still looked for markers that identified their similarities to them as adoptive parents.

Over dinner, we discussed the diversity of Francine and Erik's neighborhood, which included families from Egypt, Nepal, and China. They showed me a picture of Amelia's last birthday party, noting that most of her friends were also Chinese adoptees whose parents Francine and Erik had met while waiting to adopt from China. They also talked about a Chinese couple in the neighborhood with whom they had become close. Francine had engaged in a cultural exchange relationship with the wife prior to adopting Amelia from China, teaching her about American culture while learning about Chinese culture from her.

After dinner, Amelia's grandparents, who lived across the street, came by to take her out for a frozen custard so that we could continue the interview. At the time of the interview in 2004, Francine was in her midthirties and worked as a speech-language pathologist in the St. Louis school system, often with autistic high school students. Erik was an architect. They had been married for six years. After trying to get pregnant for two years, they found out that they could not have biological children. They had considered domestic adoption but were not comfortable with open adoption and also feared that the children available in the United States may not have received good prenatal care, implying that they may have been the result of unplanned pregnancies. They had ruled out adopting from Russia because they had heard that Russian adoptees sometimes came with drug and alcohol problems that had begun in utero, and they felt that having a Caucasian child was not important to them. They did not consider domestic African American children because of concerns that these children may have had prenatal drug exposure, and they also felt that the "cultural differences" between African American and Caucasian culture were too great. They had both attended public schools in predominantly black districts in the St. Louis area, and both were among a handful of white kids in their classes. Based on their experiences in school, they had concluded that black and white cultures were "more on top of each other," whereas Asian culture was "more aligned" with white culture. They had also considered adopting from Guatemala, but in the end they preferred the idea of traveling to China.

Francine and Erik had tried to expose Amelia to other Asian American and adoptive families. They sought out a church parish with a significant Asian population and tried to get to know other families with international backgrounds. They have also tried to put themselves in situations where Amelia does not encounter racial prejudice. They are happy that she will attend a diverse school district, and they would like to expose her to professionals from a variety of backgrounds.

Francine and Erik's story was not atypical, in the sense that adopting from China had appealed to them because they felt that Asian culture was "more aligned" with their own white culture. In observing that African American culture was more in conflict with white culture, they were likely not considering the political and economic factors that also played into these perceived conflicts, which were not only race-based but also class-based. Thus, they viewed these differences as "cultural" rather than as emerging from class or racial distinctions that were shaped by the history of racial segregation in St. Louis.

Moreover, it was interesting that China appealed to them because of the similarities they saw between Asian culture and white culture, even though they adopted their daughter when she was just thirteen months old, before she had much exposure to Chinese culture at all. Their example illustrates Frankenberg's assertion about the ways that discussions of race have been diverted into the realm of culture within U.S. multicultural rhetoric, and the concept of Asians occupying a "racial middle" (O'Brien 2008) between white and black, as discussed earlier. Nonetheless, it seemed that Francine and Erik were making sincere efforts to expose their daughter to cultural diversity, focusing on exposure to local international and adoption communities. Like many adoptive parents, with the exception of Renee, this did not seem to extend as consciously to other domestic minority communities such as African Americans or Latinos, in large part because of their perceived cultural differences that more likely stemmed from the ways that these groups were racialized.

For many families, the differential racialization of African Americans and Asians was highlighted in what they saw as competing desires to expose their children to "diversity" while also preparing them for mainstream society. In the context of St. Louis, where African Americans constituted the largest minority group and statistically occupied lower socioeconomic positions in relation to whites, some parents worried that exposing children to "diverse" (meaning urban and predominantly black) schooling may compromise the quality of their education. The Greens had originally sent their daughter to a public school in the city of St. Louis. Half of the students in her class were black, and her mother, Deborah, was concerned because some of the teachers and teacher's aides spoke "black English." Deborah clarified that her concern was not with "black English" per se but rather that her daughter would not learn "proper English." Nevertheless, the fact that she equated "black English" with improper English made this differentiation into more of a racial and class distinction than a cultural one. The Greens were raised as Catholics, and signed their daughter up for the nearby Catholic school but later changed their minds because the classes there were not "diverse."

As these examples indicate, parents struggled to give their children access to a degree of "diversity" with which they themselves felt comfortable. This relates back to the discussion of how parents "operate" within multiple contexts to craft Chinese identities for their children. While they may be interested in exposing their children to different experiences as part of building their identities, part of this process involves regulating their children's exposure to particular types of difference. This, of course, is true of many parents, not just adoptive ones.

Beginning to See Race

Anthropologists and other social scientists have observed that the formation of racial meanings is a dynamic process through which understandings of race are continually being produced and reshaped (Frankenberg 1993; Visweswaran 1998; Omi and Winant 1994). Racial identities are formed dynamically through experiences of racism (Visweswaran 1998). After all, Asian Americans did not view themselves as part of a common racial category until they were racialized as a single group upon immigration to the United States. Similarly, adoptive families I interviewed in St. Louis understood racism through a combination of U.S. racial and ethnic discourses that they attempted to remake in their own ways. In particular, adoptive parents to differing degrees began to rework their prior views of race to see it as "a system that shapes our daily experiences and sense of self" (Frankenberg 1993, 6). Upon adopting a child of color, white adoptive parents had to deal with racial difference on a daily basis as part of their family life rather than as an abstract concept. Some parents said they learned about racism through other people's reactions to their children. In many cases they found themselves in positions where they needed to educate others who held racially rooted misconceptions.

While many narratives emphasized triumph over racism through the final acceptance of the child's difference by family members and others, this acceptance nevertheless occurred in a broader climate of racial/racist meanings, with an adopted child sometimes serving as an exception in being accepted by otherwise racist friends and relatives. It was not unusual for parents to discuss with me their openness to people from different racial backgrounds, and the ways that attitudes toward race in general were improving.

Bruce and Annette lived in a spacious home in what they stressed was a diverse area, including families from China and Taiwan in their neighborhood. They talked about how their daughter's day care was also diverse; Annette had noticed that even the toys there represented different races. The children at the day care had been outside doing water play and had brought out their baby dolls to play with—the dolls were black, white, and Asian. Bruce and Annette contrasted their current situation with the prejudices they had seen expressed both by Bruce's working-class family and by some of Annette's extended family. Still, while they told me they believed that racial prejudice was decreasing, they still sometimes needed to educate others around them.

Bruce and Annette had met through their work in mall property management. After they got married, they tried to have children but found out that Annette would likely have to undergo fertility treatments to get pregnant. Annette felt that this type of intervention went against her religious beliefs, so they decided to move ahead with the adoption process. Even though they had had some concerns about the reaction of their families to their adopting a child from China, overall they have had a positive experience. Annette remembers her six-year-old niece welcoming them at the airport upon their return from China and commenting to her mother, "I told you she would make a cute mom." This touched Annette, who had been worried that their daughter would not be accepted because she did not look like the rest of the family. However, they still worried about the reaction of Annette's brother-in-law. As a context for this concern, they explained more about their family backgrounds.

Bruce described growing up in a blue-collar family in Chicago and how his parents did not accept his changed views after he began to attend college:

> Basically this is the vernacular you hear. Oh, they're all Polacks, or I happen to be Russian. They really talk bad about the Polacks. Meaning, my elders or back when I grew up, it wasn't blacks or Negroes, it was niggers. We used to hear that phrase all the time, which I think is abhorrent now. Or the spicks, the micks, the WASPs, dagos. . . . It is dago red wine, it wasn't just the red wine, but dago red wine. . . . And so when I came back from college, my mother and I and my father would have lots of fights all the time. One time they said that "college sure changed you." They meant in a negative way. I said to them, "That is the point."

Annette said that although she also came from a blue-collar family, she did not grow up with prejudicial views, in part because she was enrolled in a desegregation program and her class at Parkway South was 40 percent black. However, her sister married a man who in Annette and Bruce's opinion is very racist. Bruce described him as "one step out of *Deliverance*," with only an elementary education. However, Annette prides herself on standing up to him. As she explained:

> My brother-in-law's father has a third-grade education. My sister all of a sudden forgets she grew up in West County. She somehow now thinks she is from St. Charles, and they hate black people. They use that other word. So I'm always on my soapbox. One night I literally stood, there was a black man that came in Old Elmer's [Bar], and they were shooting pool, and he was fine, but he was with a white girl. They were going to beat him up. I literally put my body in front of them and said, "You have to hit me, if you are going to." So, now it is like the family joke, like . . . "Oh, we can't say that around [Annette]."

The brother-in-law openly expressed his hatred of black people—in fact, when his sister bought his daughter a Magic School Bus toy, he threw out the black play figure. Bruce and Annette said they will try to build a protective shield around their adopted daughter until she is older. They believed they have good resources in the area to support her because St. Louis has both a large Asian community and a large adoption community.[6] They also noted that their brother-in-law now thinks their daughter is cute.

Overall, Bruce thinks that racial prejudice is lessening. He shared his hypothesis that it may take generations for prejudice to be eliminated, but race relations are improving. "I think the whole discrimination problem, and I'm not talking about just minority meaning blacks, I'm talking if they are Oriental persuasion,[7] if they are Spanish, it doesn't matter. I think it takes generations." Moreover, he sees himself and others as being in positions in which they are empowered to facilitate this change. He cited an incident he had experienced with his son from a previous marriage. They had been living in Des Moines, Iowa, and a new black family had moved into the neighborhood. He recalled entering the living room and seeing his son sitting next to the boy, watching television with their arms around each other, and also feeling the neighbor boy's hair with his son's and the boy's encouragement.

Annette thinks she has begun to gain insight into the various ways that racial meanings take shape through interacting with individuals who are apparently well-meaning but ignorant about their racializing practices. She has taken it upon herself to educate those individuals about their misconceptions. She recounted her efforts to teach her next-door neighbor that not all Asians look alike. Upon returning from an out-of-town adoption agency reunion, she wanted to share some cute pictures of her then two-year-old daughter with the neighbor, noting that the reunion had been a big success, with a thousand families attending. The neighbor replied, "Boy, I'll bet you really had to keep a close eye on her." When Annette asked why, the neighbor replied, "Well, they all look alike. Were you afraid you were going to lose her?" Annette recounts: "So I started going through the pictures. . . . I said do these two look like [my daughter]? I was just taking pictures randomly of two girls, so I lined them all up and I said now you tell me if these people look alike. Can you find [my daughter]?" In quizzing her neighbor on whether she could identify Annette's daughter in the pictures, Annette was confronting her on her ignorance about the variation among Chinese people, something she most likely never had to do prior to having an Asian child.

Serena shared similar experiences she had with her sister, who had said, "Oh, there's this couple that moved down the street, and they have a daughter that looks just like [your daughter]." Serena remembers thinking: "That's one sentence I hate to hear. That gets under my skin. There is no one that looks just like anybody. She's got black hair, OK. The girl you know has Asian eyes. OK, that means she looks just like [my daughter]?"

She is also trying to teach her daughter not to lump all Asian people together. She told me, "Yeah. A lot of people say that out of ignorance . . . that aren't familiar with Asians. I keep telling [my daughter] . . . she'll see somebody in a store and say, look they're Chinese. That may not be. . . . They could be Korean or Japanese."

Potential for Change?

The preceding ethnographic descriptions of constructions of Chinese culture in the context of white middle-class family lives illuminate the racial and cultural politics that define these culture-making processes and the complexity of their actual productions. The construction of Chinese culture by adoptive parents may lead to the reproduction of parental racial and class positions, but also to a limited extent their transformation, as these productions play out within the context of family lives. Is this because parents have limited understanding of and investment in enacting these new identity forms that encompass non-white racial and ethnic positions? Some of the ethnographic evidence here points out how, in thinking about ways to address the Chinese-ness of their children with family and friends as well as strangers, many white parents begin to realize that race affects both themselves and their children in ways that are not always overt. Many also questioned their focus on culture and the danger of exoticizing their children that an uncritical focus on culture might lead to. And though they might not have necessarily labeled them as racist acts, some parents also talked about incidents that happened in their everyday lives, such as igno-rant statements involving assumptions that all Asians look alike, and found themselves in positions where they were educating their friends and family about the fallacies behind this thinking. They had gained an increased understanding of racism through their daily experiences with their minority children and in the process "encounter[ed] their own racialized locations relative to domestic and transnational, Asian and black" (Dorow 2006a, 374). To some extent, this illustrates how "U.S. adoption does not necessarily reproduce but also potentially challenges the racialized structures through which children are differentially com-modified and sacralized" (374).

Within the context of daily lives, parents strove to understand and negotiate meanings attached to both race and culture. Like many other scholars who have worked on adoption (Dorow 2006b; Jacobson 2008), I found that my interviewees often addressed my questions about race by talking about culture—viewing cultural pride as a solution for the focus on the child's difference, falling back on culture as a means of ad-dressing the potential racism their children may face. This is not a sur-prise, as adoptive parents work within the broader confines of U.S. racial and multicultural politics, which celebrates culture at the expense of ad-dressing the inequalities surrounding race, and which positions Asians as a model minority foil to other minority groups. In other words, in many cases adoptive parents, like many others, did not know how to dis-tinguish between race and culture, though they were aware that some-thing called racism existed.

In seeking out resources on Chineseness, parents were also creating networks and connections to the local Chinese American community upon which they hoped their children could later draw as they began to create their own social networks. FCC members reached out to and jointly hosted events with the St. Louis chapter of the Organization of Chinese Americans (OCA), a civil rights–based group. Adoptive parents enthusiastically attended meetings such as a Parents' Night Out hosted by an FCC parent, where I led a discussion on Chinese American identities in which I introduced the concept of Orientalism, as well as the perpetual foreigner and model minority stereotypes, and talked about how these ideas affected Chinese Americans. They also searched for other connections with multicultural and multiracial families. FCC programming has also evolved to include activities for older children and numerous guest speakers on topics related to both adoption and Chinese American issues.

But despite parents' best intentions, there remained limits both in their understanding of these issues and in their ability to fully change the existing structures and institutions that create and perpetuate racial meanings and inequalities. This is due in large part to the subtle but powerful discourses of color blindness that make it difficult to see racial inequalities at work, and that instead direct parents' attention toward issues of culture in ways that often remain superficial and celebratory. It is indeed impossible for adoptive parents (or any parent, for that matter) to preemptively address all potential issues their children may face. Many say they hope to set the stage for the later exploration of issues of cultural and racial identity, though it can also be argued that they are shaping their children according to their own visions of who they should become, as is the case with most parents. The examples discussed here show that today's adoptive parents operate in a context in which the nonwhite origins of their children are seen as positive aspects of identity that should be fostered, and not wholly absorbed or erased. Or perhaps these elements are being integrated and absorbed into the family in different ways. Thus, while whiteness historically may have served as an unmarked racial identity created in contrast to nonwhite identities, the practices of these adoptive parents may signify a new type of identity formation in which whiteness is no longer necessarily created solely in opposition to nonwhites but rather through incorporating parts of a nonwhite culture into family identities (Dorow 2006a; Jacobson 2008; Traver 2007).

Bill O'Brien's Irish heritage became a basis for identifying with his daughter as a Chinese immigrant. I interviewed Bill and his wife, Sally, at their cozy home in a quiet St. Louis suburb while their daughter played nearby with her toys. After covering a number of subjects, including their loss of a biological daughter at twenty-three weeks' gestation and their decision to adopt from China, we discussed Bill's strong identification with his Irish heritage and his desire to teach his adopted daughter, Emily, aged five, about it. Bill talked about how through his identification with his Irish heritage—the history of poverty, discrimination, hard labor, and eventual upward mobility—he was able to identify with Chinese immigrants. In one sense, he is merging the histories of these two groups and fitting them both into a rags-to-riches narrative. It is good that he recognizes his daughter as a Chinese immigrant who is connected to past Chinese immigrants and their struggles by virtue of her racial background. However, there seems to be a disconnect between the understandings he expresses here and his approach to teaching Emily about both her Irish and her Chinese background. I asked about how they planned to balance exposure to the Irish (ethnic) family heritage with which Bill so strongly identified with Emily's Chinese (racial and ethnic?) heritage. Bill said that he sometimes sings his favorite Irish songs, "My Wild Irish Rose" and "Green Is My Favorite Color," to Emily while she is taking a bath. I asked whether or not they celebrated Saint Patrick's Day, and Sally replied, "We do, and we read stories about Leon the Leprechaun and stuff like that, and she is really into it, and the leprechaun comes to our house and leaves a little sock full of coins for her."

When I asked whether they considered Emily to be Irish American, Sally replied, "Yeah. And I consider myself to be Chinese American. I mean, I consider us to be a Chinese family." Bill added, "Chinese Irish American." Sally continued, "I mean, I think that is why I have an interest now in all . . . anything Chinese interests me because I feel like when we adopted Emily, we became a Chinese American Irish multicultural family."

On many levels, this integration of Chinese and Irish American traditions represents the idea of ethnic options at its best, with the seamless integration and blending of various cultures into the family culture as a whole. According to Bill, Emily has become Irish American while also retaining her Chinese heritage, and her parents have become Chinese American while also remaining strongly identified with their Irish (and, in Sally's case, English) roots. But these ethnic identities largely take the form of symbolic displays or specific activities that are deemed Irish or Chinese. This does not reflect the actual extent to which Bill might feel a sense of pride and attachment to his Irish heritage, but it does involve the separation of (symbolic) cultural from racial forms of identification. While Emily's parents may now see themselves as Chinese American and express a genuine interest in Chinese culture, they will never be identified as racially Chinese. Similarly, although Emily may identify with Irish cultural traditions, she will likely be assumed to be Chinese, both culturally and racially, by those who do not know her well. This example illustrates the limitations of white adoptive families' ability to exercise ethnic options that encompass both their own and their children's identities. Chineseness cannot be fully integrated into white family cultures, in large part because the activities and meanings that clearly signify Chineseness to an American public must be seen as separate and distinct from daily "American" family life in order to do so. Folk conceptions of the "difference" and otherness of Chinese (or Asian) cultures and people reinforce this distinction. In contrast, the Asian American families portrayed in chapter 4 have more flexibility in what they choose to label "Chinese" or "Chinese American/Asian American" practices. Most thought that if they replicated what they had done while growing up, such as camping with large groups of Chinese American relatives and friends or eating certain foods, they could be considered to be practicing Chinese culture. Many explored aspects of Chinese or Chinese American culture as adults, whether prior to or after adopting their children from China, and were able to selectively incorporate these practices into their family routines and freely interpret them as signifying "Chinese" or "Chinese American" culture.

So, while white parents may now conceive of themselves as having a new awareness of cultural and racial differences, they also find themselves in a position where the "difference" of their children needs to remain marked for it to be honored. While children are integrated into the family in other ways, significant challenges remain to incorporate both Chinese and family ethnic cultures into a form of family culture that is produced, practiced, and experienced on an everyday lived level by all family members. In contrast, Asian American adoptive parents, in part due to their increased flexibility and their racial similarities to their adopted children, are able to achieve this more easily.

As one would expect, children actively participate in the ethnic and religious activities that signify the broader family identity. But is it possible to work toward a shared family adoptee culture that incorporates both the family's interpretation of Chinese culture and practices and a broader sense of family ethnic background and identity? In the following chapter, I examine more closely these constructions of Chineseness and whiteness and what they reveal about whether these new forms of color blindness leave room for discussions of race and adoptee identities. While it appears that new forms of Chinese or Chinese American culture are being produced, one may still ask by whom, and with what results? These constructions are negotiated over time in the context of daily family lives and within the complex of religious, ethnic, and other aspects of identity that families also deem salient.

6

Negotiating Chineseness in Everyday Life

In this chapter, I turn to the ways that the productions of Chineseness as a form of cultural and racial identity play out within the context of everyday lives of adoptive parents and their children. In other words, how do these forms of Chineseness operate within the nexus of race, culture, and adoption that define adoptive families? Insufficient attention has been paid to adoptive parents' productions of Chineseness. Those of white parents are sometimes dismissed as the essentialized, decontextualized, and Orientalist creations and as co-opted versions of Chinese culture. Though it is clear that white parents' ideas about both culture and race are being filtered through these lenses, it is also important to examine these productions in more depth to further reveal the nature of white parents' racializations and Orientalism. In the previous chapter, I found that the ways that white adoptive parents understood the relationship between culture and race shaped the choices they made about exposing their children to Chinese culture activities and Chinese, Asian, or other people of color. Most had embraced a view of color-blind multiculturalism that both reveled in its representation of diversity and viewed overt racism as a thing of the past that impacted Asians to a much lesser extent than it did African Americans. But while the previous chapter discussed what both drives and constrains white parents' productions of Chinese identity, this chapter examines in more depth what adoptive parents do with their new, though often admittedly limited, knowledge about Chinese culture. I return to the issue previously raised regarding how processes of Chinese American cultural production work, and what combination of family tradition and cultural innovation characterizes the production of Chinese culture by adoptive parents. While parents may feel compelled to practice Chinese culture based on their understandings of what constitutes it, in reality their efforts are made much more complex by the everyday, lived context within which these practices are enacted. In the end, what is produced may in some ways challenge rather than reproduce the "traditional" notions of Chinese culture that some adoptive parents are attempting to create. These productions may also be complicated by the presence of other cultural and religious identities that the adoptive family emphasizes. It is also important to acknowledge the possibility that these constructions may play out in relation to the ever-changing climate of racial and multicultural politics that shape constructions of culture, and they may be renegotiated over time as children grow older and begin to express their own interests. Given how entrenched both adoptive parents and Chinese Americans, both adopted and nonadopted, are in the politics of U.S. multiculturalism, it is essential to examine in more ethnographic and comparative depth whether their enactments of Chineseness can also work to modify it, as well as the structures surrounding it.

In other words, returning to the question posed in the introduction, I consider whether there is any "work" that these productions of "Chineseness" may perform, despite their limitations, within the context of shifting patterns of U.S. multiculturalism. I divide my discussion into two main sections. The first explores how what appear to be discrete and compartmentalized conceptions of Chinese culture, as enacted through Chinese cultural activities and other forms of conscious (or self-conscious) association with Chinese people, become more complex and open-ended as they are negotiated in relation to daily family priorities, which include other forms of ethnic or religious familial identity. The conscious insertion of Chinese culture into the lives and schedules of adoptive families did not make for a seamless process. Parents struggled with both the content and the intensity with which they should implement Chinese cultural education. But through this process of negotiation, it is possible that these compartmentalized and often essentialized notions of Chinese culture may gain a certain flexibility and dynamism.

Building on this possibility, the second section reexamines the construction of adoption narratives by adoptees through the use of archived photos, souvenirs, and other material goods collected by adoptive parents, a process that is often viewed as a coercive one. While productions of Chinese identity are heavily mediated by parents who are trying to "do the right thing," it is perhaps pessimistic to think that their children will never be able to move beyond the worlds their parents have attempted to create for them. I explore the possibility that within this context there may be some room for adoptees to begin to explore these issues in their own ways.

The crucial question here is, what are the limits to adoptee identity formation within the approaches defined by today's multiculturalism? Are today's adoptees, as David Eng (2010) asserts, restricted to the "affective labor" of forming "complete" families, at the expense of having their pasts and their racial identities absorbed into those of their adoptive parents? Or do the approaches of today's adoptive parents, though still hampered in their ability to challenge contemporary multicultural discourses that celebrate culture at the expense of attention to race, leave adoptees with some tools to move beyond these limitations? Is it possible that for today's Chinese adoptees, unlike for past generations, the process of absorption remains incomplete? In other words, is there any room within these productions for the negotiation of meanings of race, identity, and difference? If so, what tensions are produced for both parents and children?

The production of new forms of Chinese culture by adoptive families occurs within a context of power relations that shape the desires, hopes, and anxieties that these cultural productions reflect. Asian American adoptive parents constructed Chineseness in ways that relied somewhat on essentialized notions of Chineseness and Chinese culture, but that also reflected new and changing relationships to Chineseness that they had explored as they grew older and became parents of children from China. Their attitudes toward their own Chineseness had evolved over the years, and perhaps even more attention was paid to their Chineseness upon adopting from China and becoming parents. Their identities as Chinese or Chinese American were not statically reproduced from generation to generation but were continuously negotiated in relation to their own changing experiences. While the "privilege of authenticity" held by Asian American adoptive parents meant that they were able to freely innovate their practice of Chinese culture without being seen as taking it out of context or needing to legitimate their actions, there were also outside influences that shaped the particular aspects of Chinese identity they chose to emphasize or develop in their children. Because of this flexibility, however, they were easily able to interpret practices that were significant to them as representing the continuity of family tradition along with folding in new practices. This dynamic is captured in Lisa Lowe's (1996) model of Asian American cultural production that accounts for the historical and material conditions that circumscribe the formation of Asian American identities, but also for the possibility of new identities that may in some ways serve as the basis for resistance against some of these long-standing power structures. Can this understanding of Asian American cultural production be applied to Chinese adoptees in the context of white adoptive families? How can the case of Chinese adoptees further add to the heterogeneity of which Lowe speaks, as well as illuminate the hegemonies that frame its expression?

As revealed by the examples in this chapter, productions of Chineseness will play out in relation to other areas of family cultural and religious identity, many of which remain tied to historically rooted forms of racism and Orientalism as well as contemporary forms of multiculturalism. As illustrated in the previous chapter, despite their best intentions, white adoptive parents produce Chineseness within a context that reflects the worldviews in which they have been raised. However, we can also gain new insights by examining how these constructions are renegotiated over time, particularly as children grow older and begin to more actively engage in their own identity formation projects. What spaces, if any, are available within this realm of improvised culture to set the stage for today's adoptees to begin to sort out their relationships to both Chineseness and whiteness?

"Culture" in the Context of U.S. Multiculturalism

To understand the complex meanings circulating around the Chineseness of Chinese adoptees, it is thus essential to understand in a broader sense how notions of culture and race have been constructed in the context of U.S. multiculturalism. Numerous observers have commented that the danger of multiculturalism is that its celebratory focus on cultural difference distracts from the power relations that make constructions of race so salient (Anagnost 2000; Dorow 2006a; Omi and Winant 1994). As Dorow notes, adoptive parents' approaches to creating cultural identities for their children reflect broader "organizing principles that more generally discipline normalized subjectivity in the United States" (2006b, 212). Summarizing Aihwa Ong's discussion of culture, she writes:

The American obsession with "culture" as the foundational issue of citizenship misrecognizes a key feature of U.S. history: so-called cultures become equated with race-based traditions because new immigrants are judged and categorized through the racialized lens of an unspoken black-white continuum. Her point is complicated in adoption by the formation of intimate relations of kinship across cultural-national borders. From one side, parents' race and class privilege conditions the flexibility of the child's citizenship; from the other, the child's abandonment and racialized body circumscribe the promise of such flexibility. (212)

Like Ong, other critics have asserted that culture, as employed both by policy makers and everyday citizens in the form of multiculturalism and discourses of pluralism, has become an inadequate shorthand for addressing more difficult and complex issues of race and inequality within broader U.S. racial and cultural politics. As Lisa Lowe observes, "Pluralism's leveling of the material, and not simply aesthetic, unevenness of racial, ethnic and immigration cultures, as well as its erasure of exclusions, effects the depoliticization of multiculturalism" (1996, 90).[1]

Constructions of "culture" are also viewed as problematic by academics and cultural critics because they are being produced not only by but also for the groups they claim to represent, in the form of packaged cultural experiences and cultural products.[2] As Dorow (2010) notes, while many of these resources aim to provide adoptees and their families with advice on navigating the racialized and gendered stereotypes that Asian adoptees often encounter, these efforts occur within a context of commodification that caters primarily to the needs and anxieties of white adoptive parents. Dorow discusses how for families who adopt from China, issues of race and gender are heavily intertwined with processes of constructing new forms of kinship as an adoptive family. Describing the various industries that have arisen to address the needs of these families, she notes that their "implicit customer[s]" are "the white mothers of Asian girls." She writes:

China Sprout sells books on and encourages discussion in its community forum on the serious issues of how to understand and deal with racism, and *Mei* magazine has featured articles on gender stereotypes of Asian

girls and racial discrimination. . . . Yet these concerted attempts to produce adoptee identity within its broader complexities and enchainments
sit alongside a world of shopping that threatens to spill over to racialized
and gendered packaging. (Dorow 2010, 79)

Dorow's analysis illustrates how multiculturalism represents a double-
edged sword. While multicultural discourses to a limited extent
encourage the discussion of various types of difference and in their
own ways attempt to open up discussions of race, they often channel
these dialogues in directions that ultimately serve to reinforce parents'
projects of identity, in this case the "kinning" (Howell 2007) of Chinese
adoptees as part of their white adoptive families. As noted by Dorow,
the multicultural industry that has arisen around Asian adoption serves
to "transform adoptive kinship across racial divides, and from another
angle, fold the exoticism of Chinese girls into domestic white kinship"
(2010, 79). This assertion is also supported by Eng's claims, discussed
earlier, that Asian adoptees are being absorbed into their white adoptive
families, aided by new forms of color blindness that operate within the
context of family and kinship. The dolls, crafts, clothing, and other goods
that these adoption-related businesses sell aim to validate the identities of Asian adoptees by representing the cultural richness and beauty
of their birth cultures, but as Dorow notes, they also serve to reinforce
existing gender and racial stereotypes about female Asian adoptees. As
the creations of white adoptive parents, or those entrepreneurs fulfilling
a market demand for Chinese cultural goods, these industries reflect
predominant, often Orientalist views about Asian culture. Some of what
is on offer is similar to the items available for purchase on the adoption
trip—Chinese dresses and decorations that are consumed and displayed
at particular moments and in particular places because they symbolically
represent Chinese culture. While many goods are of course produced
in China and are available for purchase, only certain of these serve the
purposes of adoptive families who wish to incorporate them into their
practice of "Chinese culture." Other items have been customized for the
U.S. adoption market—language-learning activities; English language
books about adoption, Chinese culture, or both; or T-shirts displaying
the words for "sister," "mother," or "father" in both English and Chinese.
Through owning and using these items, adoptive parents aim to create

positive associations with China and Chinese culture for their children in rather overt ways. This stands in contrast to previous generations of adoptees whose "difference" was not usually acknowledged in the same positive manner. However, it is important to consider the implications of this approach to cultural identity, which brings the "difference" of adoptees front and center but does not necessarily address the full nature of this difference, particularly as it connects to racial meanings.

Nonetheless, it is important to recognize that the adoptive parents I have met sometimes question or critique these approaches. At the Parents' Night Out discussion mentioned in the previous chapter, I introduced parents to the current events scrapbooks I assigned to the students in my Asian American studies classes, in which I have students collect fifteen representations of Asian Americans from newspapers, television, movies, or their own life experiences and analyze them in relation to concepts we have learned in class. Most of my students, I explained to these parents, were not Asian American but had learned about the ways that Asian Americans are stereotyped and represented in the media through completing their projects. Understanding these stereotypes, I stressed, is important because these media and popular culture representations reflect the modes through which racialized and gendered messages about Chinese adoptees circulate through society.

I showed the parents an example of one student's project that had used Pokémon and Hello Kitty, Chinese characters, and tai chi to discuss the increasing popularity of East Asian culture in the United States. Although this is not negative in and of itself, the student also used the concept of Orientalism to discuss how the popularity of these Asian goods reflects the persistence of exoticized images of Asia and Asian people. I told parents that I had noticed that popular culture from Asia had become popular among Asian Americans, perhaps as a way to express their identities as Asian in a way that connects to things that are contemporary and cool, without necessarily knowing how to speak the language or exploring one's specific ancestral origins. This prompted a parent to comment: "I've been reading up on my furniture, and chinoiseries were popular in the seventeenth and eighteenth centuries. The exotic influx from Asia is nothing new." I responded, "It's interesting because it's so trendy, but it's easy to cross the line into becoming exotic." She then reflected, "It's kind of what [the FCC adviser] talks about, all of our stuff, it's the stuff versus the content. . . . Is it really something more meaningful?" She was referring to a comment the adviser had made to her earlier about how FCC families are "too into buying stuff." I replied, "There's nothing wrong with having stuff, but you think about non-FCC families who buy that stuff, what does it represent to them? Is it conjuring up Eastern mysticism? It's nice that they think that Asia is cool, but is it cool because it's different?" In response, Stephanie, who was discussed in the previous chapter, stated: "It's this desire for something totally unknown and mysterious that makes our kids' classes receptive to a brief calligraphy or history lesson, on Chinese culture. . . . What is the Lunar New Year? It's a great deal of what we contribute."

I asked if she thought there was anything wrong with this, and she continued, "That's what I'm asking. Are we feeding voyeurism here? I don't know. I feel the more you know, the less frightening it is."

This exchange illustrated that parents were to some extent aware of critiques about their focus on consuming Chinese goods, and of the exoticism that this consumption might represent. Stephanie talked about her concern that going into their children's classes and teaching the other students about Chinese culture might be feeding their interest in the exotic. However, she believed that educating other students about these things was a means of making them less strange or "frightening." Parents viewed themselves as combating the negative images of China and Chinese culture they were concerned would be associated with their children's Chineseness; they hoped that teaching their children more about the positive aspects of Chinese culture would help remedy this. However, they were less comfortable considering the potential impact of exoticized views of Chinese culture, especially because the implications of these views were not overtly negative, and they wanted to know whether they were "doing the right thing" by focusing on Chinese culture in these ways.

Thomas, Renee's husband, asked:

I want to get your opinion on . . . I think it's important that our girls learn their culture and their heritage, but do you think that it's a mistake to . . . try to portray them as different from their classmates by wearing their clothes and wearing their hair in traditional Chinese-looking-type things? Trying to impress upon them that they're different than the other kids? I mean, I don't know if we're doing that consciously or subconsciously, but sometimes I feel that by having these Chinese days and having them wear this special garb and making them appear different, it kind of takes away from the idea that they're just like everyone else.

I said I was not in a position to judge them, particularly because I was not yet a parent. But I explained that I thought it was important that parents consider the fact that their children will be not only Chinese but also Chinese American. In addition, the stereotypes that affect Chinese Americans are often complex and not overtly negative, so it is important that parents learn how to read them and teach their children how to do this also.

What I did not have time to say was that this may be a difficult task for parents, for as Beth Hall mentions, attention to these issues needs to occur on an everyday basis, to help children develop their "antennae" for understanding these issues. This approach contrasts with the ways that most adoptive parents addressed issues of Chinese culture—as a series of specific scheduled events, classes, and family rituals that were seen as related to Chinese identity or adoption. In contrast, while Chinese Americans may also attend specific events related to Chinese culture or community, for them, being Chinese was something that affected them every day, in ways that were both subtle and overt. In the context of a racialized U.S. society, Chinese Americans *are* different, though not because they wear Chinese garb. But how can they be taught to understand the histories and inequalities that give power to these perceptions of difference? And will they be able to find ways to respond to and perhaps modify these structures within the context of a multicultural politics that renders them almost invisible?

Fitting in Chineseness

Within this context, what roles are the "Chinese" activities in which white adoptive parents involve their children intended to fill, and what place do they actually come to fill within the context of their everyday lives? Within the scheduled and compartmentalized lives of U.S. families today, Chinese cultural events may just become another activity that competes for time with playgroups, school, church or synagogue, swimming lessons, and birthday parties. As much focus and attention as parents place on constructing Chinese culture, these culture-keeping activities (Jacobson 2008) operate within the context of daily family lives. Chinese cultural activities and material culture coexist with other aspects of daily routines. Busy family schedules required many families to make discrete choices about how and when to expose their children to Chinese culture, constrained by a number of factors, including local resources and children's interests. Many of the teenagers I interviewed commented about how they were so busy with school and other activities that they no longer had time to attend Chinese-related events, except for perhaps the annual New Year dinner celebration.

Heather Jacobson observes that what she terms "culture-keeping" activities were viewed as key to developing a "well-rounded child" with a healthy identity, but these activities had to be slotted into the broader schedule that included homework, sports, and other extracurricular activities. Adoptive mothers found themselves in "time binds" as they engaged their children in various activities designed to develop their children's minds, bodies, and "self-esteem" and in "culture-keeping" activities, including "Chinese dance, language classes, or strategic play dates with other Chinese children," a schedule that Jacobson notes is "taxing" (2008, 94). As Hilary Levey Friedman notes in her book *Playing to Win* (2013), parents are raising today's children by cultivating the skills children will need to compete in what she calls the "tournament of life." Thus, after-school activities are not seen as leisurely ways to occupy children's time but as necessary training for their future. Chinese "culture keeping" must compete with these other activities and in many ways may not be seen as important to a child's future success. While some parents like Betty and Joe may view facility with Chinese language and culture as a potential resource for competing in a cosmopolitan world, other parents may see the building of other competitive skills as more valuable. What is clear is that there is limited time available, and that these various types of activities are often viewed as competing with one another for space in the family's routine. The attention that has been given to Amy Chua's (2011) "Tiger Mom" approach to parenting may appear to reinforce the importance of Chinese cultural approaches to training children for success. Upon closer examination, however, Chua does not emphasize learning about Chinese culture itself, but rather employing forms of extreme discipline combined with an emphasis on academic and musical achievement, which she essentializes as "Chinese" methods of parenting.

It is also important to remember that the significance of these culture-keeping activities themselves or of being Chinese more broadly does not remain neatly slotted into certain realms of family life. These issues of race, adoption, and identity often emerged in unpredictable ways, whether in the context of an upcoming birthday celebration, a comment made by a friend, or a question raised by the child herself. The Martellos said that their daughter had a difficult time every year during the couple of months in which they celebrated her sister's birthday, her birthday, and her Gotcha Day. The older sister is the biological child of her parents, and her parents think that this annual series of events makes their younger daughter think about her adoption. Stephanie, mentioned in the previous chapter, observed that her two daughters reacted in very different ways to the loss surrounding their birth family. Their oldest daughter started asking "very serious questions" about her birth parents at a fairly young age, while the younger daughter just "brings it up: 'Can I have toast for breakfast and where is my birth mother?'" These examples remind us of what adoptive families already well know—that these issues are multilayered and overlapping, reaching far beyond the confines of specific culture-related activities. Rather, these efforts to expose children to Chineseness can only be understood as they play out within the broader context of daily family life.

Learning Chinese

As discussed in the introduction to this book, Chinese language education is often a key issue in discussions of Chinese identity by parents of Chinese American children, whether adopted or not. The question of how important it was for their children to attend Chinese language school encapsulated many of the discussions and debates that parents had about the place of Chinese cultural education in their families' lives. Many parents viewed knowing the Chinese language as an essential marker of Chinese cultural authenticity. They felt that language facility will be important if children want to visit China in the future. Attending Chinese language school also provided an opportunity for children to socialize with other adopted and nonadopted Chinese Americans from the local community.

At the time of my interviews, there were three Chinese schools in the St. Louis area, though most adoptive families attended the one school that they considered friendlier to and more compatible with adoptive families because its programs were geared to those who were not already fluent in spoken Chinese. Based on my son's one-class experience in a Chinese school kindergarten geared toward native speakers, I could now see why adoptive parents favored this program. My son could not understand a word the teacher was saying, but other students were freely conversing in Chinese with the teacher, skillfully employing a sophisticated vocabulary that was not part of the lesson, and speaking with perfect accents. But despite the availability of these classes, these St. Louis families faced the additional challenge of not having a daily context in which their children could hear and practice their Chinese. Nevertheless, they faced pressure to expose their children to Chinese language that some of the Asian American parents I interviewed perhaps did not.

Jane, whom I discussed in the previous chapter, talked about the difficulty of deciding whether or not to send her daughter, Laura, to Chinese language school. Because Jane was a single mother and a teacher, she and her daughter were left with very little time for extracurricular activities. Most of these activities took place in the evenings, including a Chinese class for young children held at a local world cultures museum, and resulted in her daughter staying up past her seven o'clock bedtime, which they needed to stick with because she had to be awake early to get to before-school care by seven o'clock in the morning. As a language teacher, Jane understood the importance of learning another language in order to understand the culture in depth, but their schedules just did not allow time for Chinese school. But she also shared with me her fears about teaching her daughter too much about Chinese culture. I appreciated her honesty, and that she had the insight to realize that these issues may come into play on some level. She shared:

> But I should mention this to you. This is something that was just a little thing in my brain. That I guess there has been a little bit of fear that if I teach [Laura] or let her be too involved in Chinese culture and let her learn Chinese, even though as a language teacher, I know she probably

will never be fluent, but gave her that proficiency that maybe she'd want to go back and live in China and I'd lose her. As a mother, that is just a scary thing. I don't know, maybe your parents felt that too when you went back and lived there for a year. Like, would you come back again, would you meet somebody and get married and live over there? Which I guess, I don't know, it's a scary thought for me. I know you've got to give up your kids, and you've got let them fly and be free and do what they want to do, but I guess there is just that little part of me that was afraid if I let her be too much Chinese that maybe I'm going to lose her again. She is going to go and be a part of that culture, and I'm not part of that culture. I don't know . . . does that make sense?

Jane's example illustrates how decisions about Chinese cultural education cannot be made in the abstract but must be made within the context of specific family schedules, needs, and concerns. It also illustrates the tension that many families feel between encouraging their children to explore Chinese culture without threatening the "kinning" processes (Howell 2007) that constitute their own family identity. Similarly, Chinese identities continue to play out within these contexts, in response to the child's interests, in addition to numerous other factors.

Although Jane felt torn and perhaps a bit guilty about not providing her daughter an opportunity to learn Chinese, many of the second- and third-generation Asian American adoptive parents I interviewed who did not grow up with the language themselves often put learning Chinese on the back burner. Instead, they emphasized other forms of Chinese cultural knowledge, which often included shared family values and traditions. This reflects a type of ethnic option specific to Asian American parents who have Asian American children, whether adopted or not.

Serena observed that, ironically, the Taiwanese American adviser to the St. Louis FCC chapter did not think it was important for his children (now grown) to learn to speak Chinese. Adoptive parents, Serena noted, do not have the luxury to make this choice on behalf of their children. She recalled what the adviser once told her:

He came to America in the [19]50s, I believe, with his wife, and their two children are Chinese American now. He was firm, he did not want them to know the language. He was very firm about that. He wants them to be fully integrated American people. He went away from that, and now they're here. His daughter is really nice, but she says I don't know a word of Mandarin. She's OK with that because Dad is OK with that.

But Serena realized that the adviser's situation is quite different from her own, observing that due to her daughter's adoption, she feels an obligation to provide a "foundation" and "open up some doors" for her. Her daughter can later choose not to associate with China, but Serena feels that "if I don't explain anything now, I will have lost a great opportunity once childhood has passed. It's kind of hard to go back and say, 'Oh, yeah, did I ever tell you about Chinese New Year? What your birth mom and dad are celebrating right now?'"

Serena began sending her older daughter to Chinese school at the age of four because she seemed ready to start then. However, when I asked her daughter (then six), who happened to be nearby during the interview, "Do you like Chinese school? What do you think about it?," she hesitated to answer. Her mother told her it was OK to answer me, following up by asking her daughter, "What don't you like about it? What do you like about it?" Her daughter replied that she did not know. Finally, Serena asked, "Do you like the folk dancing class?" Her daughter answered, "Yes." Serena explained that every year, her daughter has said she does not want to return to Chinese school, but when she goes back, she remembers how much she likes the folk dancing class and playing with her friends at recess. She seems to be "embarrassed about being Chinese" when she is with her non-Chinese friends, but she enjoys dressing up in Chinese outfits and counting in Chinese with her Chinese friends. Serena notes, "She has these two lives. Her Caucasian friends and her Chinese adopted friends. It's kind of hard to explain."

Serena's rationale for sending her daughter to Chinese school reflected that of many other adoptive parents with whom I spoke. Her daughter's response to attending Chinese school likewise reflected the responses of other adoptees whose parents I interviewed. Chinese school differentiated these children from their non-Chinese peers and represented a substantial time commitment. Over time, many parents and their children had to renegotiate their commitment to learning Chinese. Many families made arrangements with private tutors who could adapt to the family's schedule and curricular needs.

Wang Laoshi (Teacher Wang) gives private lessons for Chinese adoptees. I had seen her and some of her students give a performance at the FCC Chinese Culture Day celebration and had admired her energy and enthusiasm. She was employed as a "native" educator through a local children's museum that focused on world cultures, and during my interview with her, she talked about the various hands-on methods she had developed to teach children about China and Chinese culture within the context of the museum. I had visited the museum with an adoptive family and had been impressed with its China exhibit, which included Chinese games, educational exercises about Chinese characters as a form of pictograph, a Chinese market, and a drugstore. These adoptive families had hired Wang Laoshi to teach a group of four- to five-year-olds about China and Chinese culture. She has taught them to count from one to ninety-nine in Chinese. She opens the class with the greeting *shang ke le*, and the students respond by standing up and greeting her. When she tells them to *ju gong*, they bow. She believes that this exercise teaches the children respect and introduces them to the way that Chinese people learn. She has taught them kinship terms such as *yeye* and *shushu* and also how to say "thank you." Wang Laoshi explained that she has adapted her teaching style to a U.S. context in other ways, taking the children on imaginary airplane rides to China and back by swinging them around and saying "*zuo feiji*" (catch a plane). She brings in food, such as apples and crackers, and uses it to teach the students how to say "*wo yao che bingan*" (I want to eat a cookie). She has taught them songs that introduce the words for eyes, ears, nose, and mouth. She rewards the children if they count to ten in Chinese. Overall, she believes that they will learn about Chinese culture through learning Chinese, in addition to learning to study hard and be "friendly." She has been impressed with how fast the children learn Chinese and thinks that this exposure will allow them to be comfortable around Chinese people (in her words, not be "repelled" by them) and also make them proud of being Chinese.

Whereas a number of parents I interviewed in the Bay Area could choose to send their children to a bilingual immersion school for their primary education, at the time of my interviews in St. Louis, this was not an option. For St. Louis families, Chinese school represented an extracurricular activity above and beyond regular school, sports, music, and so forth. Therefore, it was much more rare for me to meet families like the Martellos. When I first interviewed the Martellos in 2001, they had expressed how strongly they felt about the importance of Chinese school. They said that while FCC made parents feel comfortable about dealing with adoption issues, attending FCC events does not help the child deal with being Chinese in a non-Chinese family. They felt that language school instilled confidence in being able to claim a Chinese identity, in that if you say you're Chinese, you should know the language and the culture. Not being ashamed of who you are will help you deal with discrimination, they believed. Salvatore, the father, had begun taking lessons along with his daughter Sarah at the Chinese school, noting that it probably looked comical to see him sitting in the little desks along with the fifth graders. He had tried to stay a step ahead of Sarah so that he could help her with her homework. The other students, children of Chinese American families, have gotten used to him, so when a new teacher asked if Mr. Martello was in the wrong room, the children replied, "No, he's been with us for a few years."

In 2009, eight years after our original interview, I reinterviewed Mr. and Mrs. Martello, having seen them a couple of times at local adoption-related events in the meantime. Sarah had just graduated from high school and had also graduated from Chinese language school. Her parents let her decide how long she wanted to attend, and Sarah had chosen to remain in Chinese school through graduation. Mr. Martello had ended up taking Chinese for five years before "burning out," and Mrs. Martello had recently started to take Chinese, something she had delayed previously to be able to stay home with their older daughter (who was not from China) while Mr. Martello and Sarah attended classes. Still, when they had toured China the previous year, Sarah was not able to speak much Chinese. Mr. and Mrs. Martello were not sure whether it was because she felt self-conscious or because her school had emphasized reading and writing over oral proficiency.

Some parents did not aim for language fluency. Rachel and William Myers had not yet sent their daughter, Sabrina, to Chinese school. Rachel would like to expose Sabrina to Chinese culture, and they considered this "the right thing" to do, but it would be difficult to try to become proficient in Chinese. Rachel's reason for Sabrina attending Chinese school would be to expose her to and have her appreciate Chinese culture, without an intense time commitment. In Rachel's mind, the ideal Chinese school would be held for a total of one hour per week, providing a combination of song and dance, and language and calligraphy, without the goal of language fluency. But Chinese school takes place on Sunday, and along with attending church, it makes for a very long day. Other parents raised similar concerns about overscheduling their children.

Other families said that while it was important for them to expose their children to Chinese culture, they did not necessarily consider language to be an essential element of Chinese or Chinese American culture. This issue is paralleled in the Chinese American community, with some parents emphasizing learning to read and speak Chinese as central to Chinese identity and others emphasizing other practices to signify Chineseness.

I first interviewed the Kelly family in 2001. At that time, the Kellys had a biological son, Aaron, and a daughter, Amanda, adopted from China. They had tried to ensure that Amanda was exposed to Chinese culture by bringing her to FCC and adoption agency gatherings. Mulan was her hero, and the family had read the Chinese story and seen the Disney video. However, Amanda's mother, Terry, went back and forth about the language issue. She wondered how important language was when the majority of second-, third-, and fourth-generation Chinese Americans did not speak Chinese. She had decided that if they did try language school, it would be OK if they did not continue. Their primary concern was whether they would be able to help Amanda with the homework. Amanda had expressed an interest in learning Chinese, but her parents felt that she could still learn the language later by going to China if she wished. They did not think this would be her only chance. Chinese language school is a big commitment—four hours on a Sunday afternoon.

A further concern for the Kellys is that their son Aaron is not Chinese, and they also have Irish and American cultural influences in the family. Paul, the father, is from Ireland and has retained his Irish citizenship. He felt strongly that all his children should learn about Irish culture and politics. He went to great lengths to obtain Irish citizenship for Amanda when she was first adopted, and she had already visited Ireland with her father (he went back every year, and the whole family went every other year). He also wanted his children to learn about China and Chinese politics. The family displayed three flags—Irish, Chinese, and American—in their home.

In fact, Paul says that he is not in favor of Chinese language school. In Ireland, he had to learn the Irish language, which very few people actually spoke, and those who did would not speak to him and his classmates because they had the wrong accent. Though Amanda would never be mistaken for an "American American," Paul felt that whether she likes it or not, she will be American, though not to the exclusion of honoring her Chinese heritage. Knowing the Chinese language may help her feel her proud of her heritage, but it may also make her feel more marginalized. Paul does not want being Chinese to be Amanda's entire identity, and so they are trying to create an identity for her without too great an attachment to China only. Paul commented, "You'd better have more of an identity than the little piece of ground where you were born." He observed that some Chinese adopted from China may become "more Chinese than the Chinese."

When I interviewed the Kelly family eight years later, in 2009, having seen them a few times in the intervening years since the initial interview, Amanda had two younger siblings from China. None of them had attended Chinese school.

Other parents had similar questions about the extent to which they should emphasize Chinese language and culture in their homes. Learning about and "practicing" Chinese culture takes time and energy, and there were many factors to take into account. Like the Kelly family, many families had children of different birth cultures. Some children adopted from China had siblings to whom their parents had given birth; others had siblings from Romania, Vietnam, or other countries. Renee, discussed earlier, who has a daughter adopted from China and an African American son from St. Louis, asked, "Where do we stop?" When they adopted Justin, her husband half jokingly said that they had to draw a line in terms of celebrating their children's cultural heritages. They were not going to do Kwanza too! Because no organization like FCC exists for adoptive parents of African American children, Renee is not sure how to go about creating the same type of cultural support for Justin as she has for Julie. For example, she knows about Juneteenth, but do people actually celebrate it? Of course, this may relate to the perceived inaccessibility of black culture due to its entrenchment in racialized meanings.[3] But as discussed in the previous chapter, Renee does give attention to issues of race and racism related to African Americans She also collects African masks for Justin to have when he grows up.

Some parents have taken an international, cosmopolitan approach, wanting their children to learn about all world cultures, not just China. Sharon helped to organize an international festival at her daughter's elementary school, drawing upon diverse community resources. Melody, her daughter, talks about how she is from China, her father is from Australia, and her mother from Oklahoma.

These examples illustrate how the initial intentions of adoptive parents to expose their children to Chinese culture may over time require some renegotiation. The question of Chinese language education is a loaded one, which also speaks to questions about how parents view the purpose of learning Chinese (To achieve fluency? To be comfortable around other Chinese people? Just to have some exposure?) and how time spent on this is negotiated in relation to other family activities that are deemed important in reproducing parental and familial identities more generally.

Chinese cultural activities compete with other aspects of adoptive family identities—particularly ethnicity—and the daily work that goes into supporting these aspects of identity. These examples illustrate that holes and ambiguities might open up in attempts to construct Chinese culture as adoptive families live their daily lives, particularly given that implementing Chinese identity complicates the reproduction of parental ethnic, racial, and religious identities, even as parents would like to think that they remain very open to incorporating Chineseness into their lives.

Within this context, is Chineseness merely folded into daily life (or sometimes put to the side) as just another competing activity? I have illustrated the ways that Asian American parents incorporated their own family values and priorities into their constructions of Chineseness. How is this similar or different for white parents? And can these processes occur even in the context of white adoptive families? As shown in the previous chapter, despite their best efforts to become aware of issues facing their minority children, white parents may inadvertently perpetuate them. The following examples show the ways that children can begin to construct identities from the materials made available to them.

Carla

As the previous sections illustrate, parents struggled to help their children develop aspects of their family's ethnic identities that they deemed important to making their child into well-rounded individuals. But though deliberate attempts to integrate Chineseness into the daily lives of adoptive families take on what appear to be specific and compartmentalized forms—outings to special events, learning Chinese language, displaying Chinese objects, viewing adoption photo albums from China, and collecting Chinese dolls—in practice, these abstract conceptualizations and superficial representations of events and practices may yield to more complex or ambiguous and unsettled meanings. This is particularly true if we examine how the children themselves understand and react to the various influences in their lives. This two-part ethnographic vignette illustrates this fluidity. I spoke with Marcia and her nine-year-old daughter, Carla, who at the time of the first interview (2001) was one of the older adoptees in the area. Because Carla was old enough to understand that I had come to talk about Chinese adoption and was curious about my conversation with her mother, Marcia suggested that she be present throughout the interview. As Marcia openly discussed their adoption story, Carla put in her two cents when she felt like doing so. What became evident was that there were multiple layers to the daily production and performance of Chinese culture in their household, and that the meanings as understood by the children as recipients of these Chinese cultural productions were subject to interpretation and negotiation.

Vignette: Part I

As I entered the Redmond family's house, I was struck by the abundance of Chinese- and Asian-themed items. These included two antique tables, one that was quite ornate, with two drawers set into each side (Carla said she liked the table because you could hide things in the drawers). There was also a Tibetan cabinet. Items had been purchased at various places—I recognized the doormat with the *ping* character on it from Cost Plus. Displayed downstairs were a two-sided abacus with other Chinese characters down the middle, as well as some baskets bought at the store Tuesday Morning, numerous paintings, paper napkins with Chinese characters and designs, and a large stone or ceramic bowl with characters on it. Upstairs, a chair had been reupholstered with a fabric displaying Chinese characters. Carla asked her mother to show me her room last. Upon entering the room, one was greeted by a large pile of stuffed animals, mostly pandas, displayed on an antique bed. According to the proprietor of the local Chinese antique store from which it was purchased, the bed was called a "nap bed." It was topped by a custom-made futon, covered with fabric with Chinese characters on it; Carla's two bedspreads were made of a similar fabric. There were also some small Chinese-looking storage cabinets in the room, a pile of Chinese-themed pillows on one bed, and a wall calendar featuring the same breed of dog as the family's white lap dog.

Taken alone, this vignette appears to be a textbook example reinforcing stereotypical images of white adoptive parents' well-intentioned efforts to honor their Chinese daughter's heritage and to integrate it into her daily life. The home impressively displayed more "Chinese" items than most mainland Chinese and Chinese American homes I have visited. This could be interpreted in a number of ways: as a proud declaration of Carla's heritage, a sophisticated sense of decoration expressing a taste for Chinese items, or (more cynically) an "artificially Chinese" environment created by white parents for their adopted child. However, as will be discussed in the second part of this vignette, while in many respects Carla and her family have engaged in Chinese cultural activities that are somewhat stereotypical and fairly representative of those of other adoptive families who emphasize bicultural socialization, there are additional layers of meaning both on and below the surface. To some extent, representing Chinese culture to children in the context of everyday life requires a symbolic approach, focusing on ritual celebrations and the collection and display of material objects. Therefore, what may appear to be superficial and symbolic efforts at incorporating Chineseness into their lives is part of a larger process of negotiating its meanings, as these household items and Chinese cultural activities serve as a basis for an ongoing dialogue about Chineseness and identity.

Vignette: Part II

Carla said she must attend Chinese school until the twelfth grade. When I asked her if she liked Chinese school, she said she likes the chocolate cake that her teacher brought, which was provided as a reward for her students. Because she is interested in art, she says she also likes the art class. Carla then said, "Mom, I have a question for you. . . . If [my French dog] could speak, would you send her to French school?" Marcia replied that indeed she would.

Carla participates in the lion dance at Chinese school, which she says she likes because sometimes you get money in the form of red envelopes. Sometimes she plays the cymbals, but eventually she'd like to be the back of the lion; she would have gotten to do this already, she said, if an older girl had not come along.

Marcia noted that while some adoptive families go to Chinese restaurants, they haven't done that as often. Carla used to cry out of frustration when she couldn't use chopsticks at a Chinese restaurant. Marcia said that young men on the staff would come over and offer to help. I asked Carla why she thought she should know how to use chopsticks. Was it because the kids she saw eating with chopsticks at the restaurant were younger or because she was Chinese? She answered, "The first one."

Marcia said that it is up to Carla whether she wears Chinese dresses at special events. Marcia goes into Carla's class for Chinese New Year celebrations but usually brings in a video because she is concerned that she might inadvertently perpetuate some stereotypes if she were to do the presentation herself. Carla's (older) nephew, the son of her much older brother, who is the biological child of her parents, wore his Chinese outfit to school too.

Carla told me that she does not like her Chinese name, Yu Rong. Her mother explained that the character *Yu* is for the region Carla is from. It is difficult to write, but Carla also does not like how it sounds like "you wrong."

Carla goes to a private school, and next year she will be learning Spanish. When her mother said that it's important to know another language, Carla asked, "What about English or Latin?" and then playfully said, "[The dog] wants to talk about her background."

One may surmise that Carla was responding as a typical tween jokester and may have felt a bit self-conscious about our conversation's focus on her Chineseness. But several important points are also evident from her responses: (1) Some "Chinese" activities, such as going to Chinese restaurants, do not always have the intended effect of boosting Chinese cultural pride; (2) children such as Carla playfully, and perhaps irreverently, create their own alternative meanings around China adoption activities and narratives, which are often understood within a larger schema of childhood interests and priorities (such as pets, friends, and chocolate cake); and (3) parents must respond flexibly and engage in dialogues with their children around Chinese identity and adoption issues.

As Carla's comments show, children view their parents' well-intentioned efforts to construct Chinese cultural identities for them in multiple ways. While some may be too young to differentiate the Chinese parts of their world from other aspects of their lives, it is clear that they may begin to bring their own meanings to issues of adoption and efforts to expose them to Chinese culture. Even issues as emotionally laden as birth mothers may take on different meanings in the minds of children. When they were younger, Renee's children competed with each other over how many mothers they have. Julia was jealous that Justin had three mothers (a birth mother, a foster mother, and Renee), but she had only two (a birth mother and Renee). Volkman (2005, 103) similarly recounts the story of a child who took pride in having six mothers: her birth mother, foster mother, adoptive mother, mother's sister, and two different close family friends.

I interviewed Carla again in the summer of 2009 at her home, along with her mother. The family still had their dog, though Carla told me that they had found out she was not actually French. Carla had grown into a poised, athletic young woman of sixteen. She still displayed the feisty personality she had when she was nine. I asked whether she had continued attending Chinese school, and she told me she had stopped in the third grade because she was too busy with other school activities, including cross-country and club soccer. She "hated taking Chinese language class" because she did not like the teachers and was "not good at it." She recalled, "They expected you to memorize everything." She was now studying Latin and loved the subject. Chinese was now being offered at her school, but it did not fit into her schedule because it would conflict with her Advanced Placement classes. She noted that, ironically, both her non-Chinese nephew and her boyfriend were taking Chinese.

Carla recalled having Asian American friends during her freshman year at her private school, including some who were adopted, and a girl who was part Chinese and part Korean. She admits getting into what she called the "Asian thing" that year. She explained that Asian people seemed to seek out other Asian people at her school. One of her friends often talked about being "Asian," and through her, Carla became interested in Korean music. Carla received Asian gifts from her Asian friends on her birthdays, and she wore panda T-shirts. She said she "was proud to represent" and that it was fun to be Asian, though she noted with hindsight that maybe she set herself up for being teased for being Asian. She also recalled hating being asked "Are you Chinese or Japanese?" and found it annoying that her Asian friends only wanted to learn Japanese and listen to Korean music.

Carla has also experienced some negative incidents related to being Asian and adopted. She recalled that one of her teachers had asked the class during roll call one day, "Would you save a fly ball or a baby?" Another student had commented, referring to the baby, "If it was Chinese we shouldn't save it because there are so many." For Carla, this "hit close to home." She retorted by hitting the other student with her Latin book so hard that the book broke. The student apologized afterward, realizing what he had said and what it meant to Carla.

Carla also recalled being "pissed," along with another of her Asian American friends, that the Asian culture club was run by an "African American [girl] and a white Jewish boy." I asked what the club members did. "Eat food," she said. I wondered why non-Asians were involved in the club leadership, and Carla cynically replied that the girl was involved because she needed something on her record for her college application.

Carla recalled accusing her mother of pushing her to attend when she didn't want to go to Chinese school. She used to say to her mother, "You care more about this than I do." Or "Just because I'm Chinese, why do I have to learn Chinese? If I was Mexican, would I have to go to Spanish school?" (Her mother replied, "Yes.") Carla would also protest that her parents had not made her brother, who is not Chinese, learn a foreign language, though he did end up studying Mandarin as an undergraduate at Yale.

I asked Carla how she felt about the fact that her mother had encouraged Chinese cultural activities. Carla said that now, looking back, she's glad she did. She is also glad that she has other friends who were adopted from China. Because everyone is so busy, she hasn't seen them in a while, but she would like to get together with them. Carla remembers bonding with one adoptee friend around their mutual dislike of Chinese tutoring, but she also remembers how much she liked a Chinese watercolor class she took with two of her other friends. Marcia noted that they had all originally come from the same orphanage in Jiangsu Province and had been adopted within the span of a few years through a St. Louis adoption agency. However, based on Carla's comments, the bonds relating to their experiences with Chinese cultural education seemed more salient.

Recalling the number of Asian decorations I had seen in their house, I asked Carla what she thought about growing up with them. She replied that this was just how she grew up—with that stuff around. She didn't think about it. She knew her house was Asian themed, and she herself chose a red, black, and gold Asian theme for her room. She still likes her room but mused that if she redecorated it one day, it would be fun to have some friends come over and do a splatter paint pattern.

Like Carla, other teenage Chinese adoptees who are "coming of age" and beginning to express their identities in a number of ways may shed some light on the complexity of adoptee identities. While some claim that they are "unique," others do not see themselves as different at all. The *New York Times* (Clemetson 2006) profiled a thirteen-year-old who held her bat mitzvah on Chinese New Year, had yin-yang yarmulkes for her guests, and in her speech seamlessly connected her history of adoption with the Jewish tradition of taking in strangers. Another young woman chose her college based on the presence of Asian American student groups on campus and also expresses herself through classical music, punk rock, and Japanese anime, even though "everyone would expect" her to be interested in China.

Recontextualizing Cultural Symbols and Artifacts

Carla's story provides a sense of how meanings of Chineseness are continually reworked over time as children grow older. I discuss more interviews with teens in the next chapter. In this section, I go into further depth regarding how the production of Chinese cultural identity works within the broader context of adoptive family lives. White adoptive parents have been criticized for the ways they decontextualize Chinese culture, focus on the consumption of goods, and create "coercive" adoption and identity narratives on behalf of the child. Here, I describe some examples of how adopted children construct Chineseness that illustrate that there is some potential for them to craft identities that frame both adoption and Chineseness in nuanced yet open-ended ways. Understandings and representations of Chinese culture may continue to take on new meanings as children's own understandings of and relationships to China and Chinese culture change over time. As adoptive parents and particularly their children continue to draw upon resources about China and Chinese culture, and to form new social networks related to these issues, what may appear to be static, essentialized representations of Chinese culture and superficial cultural celebrations may take on new meanings in the context of family life.

Adoption researchers have examined the ways that the lifebooks and videos that parents produced from the materials they collected in China are later used to create "memories" and identities for their adopted children (Dorow 2006b, 172, 212). Volkman (2005) describes adoptive parents who activate the archive of experiences and artifacts in China for their children by going on homeland tours and searching for potential birth siblings. Many attempt to verify those linkages with DNA tests.[4] Dorow asserts that parents craft and actively incorporate histories based on these archives as a way to "connect past and present,"[5] but she notes that these records are far from neutral:

Life books—which most often exhibit written and photographic evidence of the parents' journey to China to adopt, information on the child gathered before and during the journey, the child's development and transformation after returning home—strive to chronicle and approximate the life of the adopted child, by way of adoptive parents' rendition of historical

traces. It is parents who most expressly strive to create that "unique platform" for identity formation. . . . the fact is that the origin stories vary in
the truths they convey and the kinds of information they deem important.
The narration of Chinese origins can reinscribe desires for exclusive kinship and managed foreignness through what they both include and omit.
I have encountered, for example, a number of families who do not remember their child's Chinese name, let alone the town she is from. (2006b, 173)

As reflected in the earlier quote by Jane, she has tried to encourage
her daughter's connections to China despite the girl's resistance and her
own fears that these connections might threaten their bond. The se-
lectiveness of adoption lifebooks and the origin stories they tell reflect
parents' desire for their children to have a sense of their own past that
is positively framed, affirming their family identity, and that provides a
framework for the discussion of children's questions about their relinquishment and adoption. The problem, as Dorow notes, is that these
narratives reflect the parents' anxieties and their visions of the identities
they think their children should have, rather than ones expressed by the
children themselves. Similarly, in her article "Scenes of Misrecognition,"
Ann Anagnost (2000, 409) quotes an essay by Judith Williamson that
describes the family photo album as creating a "coercive," selectively edited narrative.

As part of my research, I asked families to share their memory books
with me. While it was certainly true that in creating these books, parents
intended to tell a specific and sometimes romanticized story about how
they came to be a family, I also saw evidence that the books can serve as
a catalyst for additional conversations as children grow older. The underlying question is whether these archives can become active—and interactive—as they are accessed by adopted children over time. Although
parents (usually mothers) may be compelled to produce these narratives
out of the anxieties that accompany the process of connecting the child
with her past and affirming her as part of the family, once we accept that
these documents are selective representations of the adoption experience, it becomes important to ask how they are used within the broader
context of family lives. To what extent are their meanings fixed, and to
what extent are they subject to reinterpretation, particularly by adoptees
themselves? In the following section, I explore the ways that adoptees

employ these materials in the process of exploring and creating identities as adoptees and Chinese Americans.

I discuss some of the ways that adoptees created meaning around Chineseness and adoption, both through customized creations such as memory books and souvenir collections and through the more general consumption of material objects representing China, Chinese culture, or adoption. I consider how these objects can become part of ongoing dialogues and narratives of family identity, Chineseness, and adoption. Though they may have originated as part of the "coercive" narratives created by parents, these artifacts also potentially took on new meanings as they were employed in various ways over time. If the concern is with the ways that adoptive parents are taking culture out of context, it is important to consider that cultures no longer have (and perhaps have never had) discrete contexts. Rather, it is more appropriate to think of a cultural bricolage in which decontextualized cultural symbols have come to play a central role in identity formations. Given that culture has become the key vehicle for the expression and discussion of difference in the context of twenty-first-century U.S. multiculturalism, the question becomes whether it can be effectively employed within these constraints as a lens through which to understand and address the many issues surrounding "Chineseness" as both a racial and a cultural identity in the context of adoption and family. To what extent do these seemingly decontextualized cultural symbols have the potential to be recontextualized into new narratives as identities are explored and asserted? What role might the consumption and display of cultural symbols play in identity construction? This analysis of course must be balanced with an awareness that these cultural symbols do not completely shed the historical contexts of inequality in which they were originally produced, and in fact can relay different meanings depending on how they are used and who is using them.

As families outside the mold, adoptive parents attempted to creatively produce their own family histories and narratives to provide their children with a sense of a past that also served to connect them to the present as a member of their adoptive family. They accomplished this in part through the production of videos and memory books, using materials collected in China as a base. Many parents purchased scrapbooking supplies from various companies, which sometimes included archival-quality materials along with ideas for how to organize the scrapbook. Online guides also provided suggestions for topics and content to include in the scrapbooks. During the course of my fieldwork, many parents I interviewed in St. Louis showed me the lifebooks and videos they had made to document their children's histories, beginning with the trip to China and continuing until the present. Parents had saved artifacts from the trip in these books, from plane and train ticket stubs to plastic slippers from their Chinese hotel rooms, to the split pants that the baby wore when she came to them from the orphanage. Often when children were present during the interviews, they would watch the videos and view the photo books as parents showed them to me, making periodic comments. Many children looked at the videos and lifebooks regularly, and they often knew the story by heart, just as they had learned other stories, both fictional and nonfictional, that their parents had read to them. When Melody was six years old, I visited her house and viewed her pictures. She pointed to a picture of herself as a five-month-old infant with her parents on the train in China and said, "This is when we drank Chinese Coca-Cola." Though at the time she had been too young to have actually tasted it, the story of receiving a can of Coke as part of their boxed breakfast had become part of their family lore. When they returned to China for a visit when Melody was ten, she brought home a Coke bottle with Chinese characters and displayed it in the living room. In addition to artwork and souvenirs that parents bought on their trip to China and other items symbolizing Chineseness they had purchased in the United States, parents often kept these memory books and videos of the adoption journey in their living rooms, where they could be easily accessed.

When I reinterviewed her in 2004, Mary Kelly showed me the books she had made for her two daughters from China. I commented that my own childhood had not been nearly as well documented, and she and her husband agreed. I asked if their oldest son, Mark, who was not adopted, also had a memory book. They replied that he had four! The book for their younger daughter contained the usual pictures of temples, street scenes, and other adoptive families. It also included touching pictures of Mark, who was then eight, asleep with the baby on his stomach, and being mobbed by people at a local park. His parents had decided that he would travel to China with his mother to adopt his youngest sister. In a sense, the memory book was as much for the child who was adopted as it was a document for the rest of the family who had not traveled to China. It took on special significance for Mark because it documented not only his trip to China but also the special experiences of bonding with his sister.

Particularly when they were young, children frequently looked at these memory books, and most knew the stories by heart. Sometimes these narratives were reinforced by stories told at bedtime. Parents told me that their children loved to hear about how much their parents wanted them, how hard it was to wait to go to get them, and how excited the parents were to go to China. But they seemed to especially enjoy hearing parents tell the more negative details that kids love in all stories, about how "you cried for a whole day when we first got you" or how "you threw up on us all the way home on the plane ride." These narratives were often revisited as children grow older; for some adoptees, they provided a narrative framework for structuring and interpreting return trips to China, even if the narratives remained "fictions" or fantasies on some level.

Thirteen-year-old Stacey Brenner showed me the pictures her parents had taken in 1995 when they went to China to bring her home. Along with her mother, she had visited China in 2005, four years prior to our 2009 interview, on a China Ties tour for returning Chinese adoptees. She explained that she liked to compare the 900 new digital pictures they took, many of which she showed me on her iPod, with the ones her parents had taken back in 1995 when they traveled to get her. As we spoke, she took out the old pictures of her foster parents and the orphanage and compared them with the new ones from the more recent trip. The original pictures were kept neatly organized in a box in the family's living room, which she brought over to show me. I could see that she had looked at the photos many times and had been familiar with them before her own trip to China. She then proudly showed me a book of pictures from the summer 2005 trip that her parents had made and presented to her as a surprise that Christmas. The book contained some photos from the original trip but mostly incorporated photos from the recent trip. On the front of her book is a picture of her hugging the director of the Hong Kong charity that sponsored the orphanage from which she was adopted. Stacey asked her mother, Rosene, to tell me what the director had said to Stacey during their recent visit. Rosene recalled that the director said, "I want you to know that you were loved from the very beginning. You will always be loved." But then Stacey actually corrected her mother's wording—she herself had remembered exactly what the director had said.

Stacey then showed me a special scrapbook that one of her best friends made her for her thirteenth birthday. Her friend had been adopted at the same time from the same orphanage and had traveled with Stacey on the 2005 China Ties trip. Their families lived about fifteen minutes apart in the St. Louis counties, and both girls had younger siblings who had been adopted from Vietnam. The book contained pictures from when they were infants being adopted in China, through their childhood years, including their China Ties trip and the heritage trip their families had recently taken together to Vietnam for their younger siblings. Stacey said that her friend had told her that the pictures in the book she created proved that they had been friends their entire lives. Her friend had also left blank pages in the album for future adventures together. Stacey planned to make a similar book for her friend for her thirteenth birthday.

This example illustrates the ways that artifacts become the basis for the ongoing life experiences that are key to the negotiation of identities and relationships with both family and friends. Rather than being fixed and coercive, they can be employed by adoptees themselves within the context of meaningful friendships and new experiences that are part and parcel of the ongoing process of identity construction. The elements of adoption narratives that adoptees can access are far from a complete rendering of an adoptee's history. However, they can to some extent be disassembled and reassembled by adoptees to create their own narratives. The availability of digital media such as digital cameras, computer photo management systems, programs for creating one's own videos and slideshows, and iPods and other portable means of sharing these productions has facilitated the creation of new types of photo albums and memory books, allowing people to view, share, reuse, and recontextualize photos in new ways. In the past, when photos were negative based, they were less convenient to duplicate, share, or self-publish in a custom album. Now Stacey can show photos on her iPod but also access them to make the album for her friend.

Mary, whom I had first met in China on her 2002 adoption trip, told me that she had purchased a China adoption workbook for her seven-year-old daughter, Marissa, on her Gotcha Day, and that her daughter had completed it in three days on her own, working very hard on it as soon as she got up in the morning. When I was conducting research in St. Louis in 2009, Mary had invited my family over to her house for dinner. I had last seen her in 2004, when she had invited me and my husband to her home. Marissa was three at the time and had taken an immediate liking to my husband. Mary explained that Marissa paid attention to most men, perhaps because she did not have a father (Mary has since gotten married, and Marissa now has a father and siblings). Marissa had grown into an active young girl, as she promptly demonstrated by scaling the doorway between the kitchen and dining room. In fact, perhaps in an effort to help her daughter burn off some energy, Mary kept an inflatable bounce house in the basement, which entertained Marissa and my son while Mary and I chatted.

An adoption professional who worked at a domestic agency that supported unwed mothers who wanted to make an adoption plan for their babies, Mary was acutely aware of adoption-related issues, including questions about birth parents and issues of transracial adoption. After our pizza dinner, Mary asked Marissa if she could show me her China adoption workbook, and Marissa and I sat down together in a large chair and flipped through it page by page. Unlike the adoption memory books I had seen (and which Marissa also had), this was an interactive workbook that was to be completed by the child. Some pages of the workbook were educational, containing passages explaining why so many babies were relinquished for adoption in China, affirming that the babies themselves did nothing "wrong," and discussing the tough decision that the birth parents must have had to make to relinquish their child. When we reached this section, Marissa said that she liked that page and asked her mother if she did also. Based on Marissa's comfort in talking about the subject, it was clear they had talked about the issue together previously. Other pages were more specifically about China and the one-child policy. Some pages instructed the child to imagine and draw the birth mother and father. Marissa drew her birth mother with a striped shirt, long hair, and long eyelashes. On another page, she was asked to draw herself as a baby. She had drawn herself with a full head of hair, and I joked that she really didn't have that much hair when she was a baby.

Mary explained to Marissa that I had been with her in China when they first met and had taken the video that they sometimes watch. I remembered having taken that video, nervously making sure that I captured the moment as best I could, knowing that it would be something that Marissa would watch repeatedly. In some pages Marissa was asked to write down questions she would like to ask her birth family. She had written, "Did you cry when you left me?" "Did I cry when you left me?" "Was I sleeping when you left me?" She made sure I saw the extra page that she had inserted in the back of the binder, a piece of paper that had accompanied a necklace her mother had also given her for her Gotcha Day. The necklace incorporated a sun, moon, and star representing the birth mother, child, and adoptive mom. Marissa had worn the necklace so much that it was falling apart, so they were keeping it in a plastic bag until it could be repaired.

Marissa's adoption workbook drew upon the materials provided by her mother to help her create her own interactive narrative. The structure provided by the video and memory book that her mother had created for her had been necessary for her to be able to fill in the blanks and begin a dialogue about these issues. There were still some blank pages where she could insert photos of the adoption trip, but Marissa had already begun the process of creating her own new narrative. Her mother planned to revisit the book with Marissa before their homeland tour to help prepare her for some of the issues that might arise in China. Marissa's narrative remains open-ended, and some questions may never be answered. In fact, four months later, her mother told me via e-mail that Marissa had asked her to "keep my necklace a secret." Mary asked her if she had embarrassed her by telling other people about the necklace, and she had replied, "Yes, but that's OK." Mary apologized and promised not to mention it to others again. She's noticed that when other children ask her about the necklace, Marissa replies, "It's a secret," even to other kids who were adopted. She still wore it every day and told Mary that it makes her feel closer to her birth mom. Mary is not sure if doing the adoption workbook had made Marissa think more about these issues, or whether the trip they were planning to China the following March had caused her to start thinking more about her birth mother. She had read that at around age seven, children start forming "more concrete concepts about adoption," so perhaps this was just part of a normal process. However, Mary was proud of Marissa "for being so assertive."

Consumption

Marissa's necklace was purchased for her by her mother, and though it was produced for and marketed to adoptive families, it was instilled with more meaning for her than many other consumer purchases. It was meant to signify the importance that Mary placed on acknowledging that Marissa had both a birth mother and an adoptive mother, as well as the fact that the three would remain connected on some level through Marissa. During the China trip, Mary and the other parents had purchased many similar goods to give to their children in the future to represent their ties to China. Many families, such as Carla's, discussed earlier in this chapter, continued to purchase Chinese or Asian goods for their homes. Thus, for many of the families I interviewed, consumption played a key role in shoring up identity narratives, allowing families to display and perform identities with material objects to make the selective histories they crafted seem more tangible. Particularly for young children, these objects supplemented the adoption stories their parents and others narrated for them with tangible "Chinese" material culture, such as traditional outfits, chops, household decorations, Chinese language and culture DVDs, food, and music. These items, which provided visual, auditory, and other sensory means of understanding and participating in Chinese culture, constituted an important, albeit incomplete, archaeology of family origins that legitimized and reinforced family identity. The objects represented "Chinese culture" in ways that often reinforced its separateness from mainstream U.S. culture, as well as Orientalist ideas about China as a repository of exotic goods, people, and culture.

Adoptive parents often displayed items from the China trip, such as artwork and figurines, in the family home, not only as a way to represent Chinese culture but also as tangible artifacts that help illustrate the narrative of family origins. Rosene, mother of Stacey Brenner, who was profiled earlier, proudly displayed artwork and souvenirs from her four children's birth countries throughout her home. These included a set of bowls from India and a dragon tea set from Vietnam, placed on a table behind the sofa. There were collections of baskets from various countries near the hearth. A large, framed embroidered silk picture of the traditional Chinese theme of 100 children hung above the door in the front entryway. Rosene said that her children take pride in these items, which they sometimes bring to school for show-and-tell or lend to friends who are doing reports on these countries.

However, her children's exposure to their birth cultures was not limited to these material objects. Rosene said that she saw it as her responsibility to understand the history, current events, and U.S.-based communities relating to her children's countries of origin. The children have clothing, videos, history books, and currency from each of their countries. Rosene was also aware of the documentary *Daughter from Danang*, which chronicles the experiences of Heidi Bubb, a mixed-race Vietnamese adoptee who returned to Vietnam as an adult to meet her birth mother and who encountered more than the romanticized homecoming she had imagined, with her extended family expecting her, as a comparatively wealthy, overseas family member, to help support their mother. Rosene had adopted two children from Vietnam, and her knowledge of this video illustrated that she was interested in learning more about issues that her children might face that extended beyond knowledge of their birth cultures.

Many adoption critics have pointed out problems associated with focusing too much on the superficial consumption of cultural goods. Amy Traver's work details the role of consumption in the formation of middle-class ethnic identities. In the case of white adoptive parents consuming Chinese cultural objects, Traver observes that there is something absent from the context within which parents understand the celebratory purchase of these items:

> For most white parents, the display of Chinese cultural objects—much like the display of an ornamental shamrock or an Italian flag—is a celebratory act; one practiced to reveal and revel in the family's diverse origins and colorful immigrant histories. Missing, of course, is a critical understanding of the differential impact of race on these commemorations of ethnic diversity. While individualistic symbolic ethnic identities

(i.e., white European-American ethnic identities) are typically costless, voluntary, and, therefore, designed for overt celebration, racialized ethnic identities in America are, by definition, "socially enforced," "imposed," and stigmatizing. (2007, 212)

The Chinese Americans I studied previously (Louie 2004) displayed and practiced Chineseness through the consumption of popular culture items that are pan–Asian American or even pan-Asian and not necessarily rooted in the specific histories of their families and communities. However, they did so with acute awareness of what the purchase and use of these symbols meant both in the context of Asian American subcultures and in a broader U.S. context. As noted by Miri Song in the introduction, they strategically employed these symbols as ways to lay claim on particular identities or to redefine identities in specific ways. Transnational cultural flows played an important role in providing the repertoire for this selective display of identity elements. They consumed, used, and displayed products such as Hello Kitty knickknacks and Asian air fresheners, sometimes with a sense of irony (Louie 2004). Carla similarly explored this pan-Asian/Asian American popular culture when she went through her short-lived "Asian" phase. Indeed, these items are readily accessible for both adoptees and their parents, and as for the Chinese Americans in my previous study, attaching oneself to trendy popular culture flows emerging from Asia provided a way to demonstrate that one is both "modern" and "Asian."

Future Possibilities

In chapter 4, I discussed the ways that Asian American adoptive parents crafted identities for themselves and their children. To understand Asian American cultural production, it is important to take into account the broader power structures and histories that constrain the expression of Asian American identities, while remaining attentive to the dynamism inherent in processes of cultural production that allows room for Asian Americans to create alternative identities and histories. Lisa Lowe's model helps us better understand the tension that exists between the oppressive histories of racism and exclusion that have shaped Asian American cultures, and the ways that Asian Americans selectively draw upon these histories and modify them to produce new forms of cultural resistance. But the question remains as to whether these conceptions of Asian American cultural production can be applied to Chinese adoptees raised by white parents who have attempted to foster identification with China and Chinese culture in particular ways. As the climate of multicultural politics has shifted to encompass more "diversity" and as Asians are increasingly viewed as "honorary whites" whose difference (if any) is in the realm of culture and not race, what are some of the potentials and dangers in the shift toward culture as a means of managing difference? While the examples here illustrate that Chinese adoptees are beginning to craft and experiment with their own expressions of identity, will adoptees have the appropriate tools to deal with the issues of racism and exclusion that persist for Asian Americans in ever more subtle forms? The flexibility with which cultural symbols are decontextualized and recontextualized may make it easy for adoptees to play with new narratives of adoption and identity, but it may also serve to relegate their explorations of identity to the realm of the superficial "culture bites" about which Anagnost (2000) warns us, at the expense of attention to race.

My profiles of Asian American adoptive parents illustrated the great variability with which they conceived of their own Asianness, as well as the ways they modified these conceptions over time as they became adults and adopted their children from China. As in the case of Desiree, discussed earlier, conceptions of her Chineseness or Chinese Americanness shifted in relation to the changing position of China within the world power structure, changing demographics in the Bay Area that exposed her to a more diverse group of Asian Americans, and her own politicization as Asian American after the Vincent Chin incident in 1982. For her and many of the other Asian American adoptive parents I interviewed, their actions reflected a conscious negotiation between aspects of Chinese American or Asian American culture with which they had been raised and newly acquired practices that enacted their own evolving conceptions of what it meant to be Chinese American or Asian American. While some focused on language, others worked to implement practices that they felt reflected their family traditions. However, these practices were modified to suit new gender ideals and shifting generational values, and thus often differed from those of their

parents' generation. Even those practices they viewed as family traditions were modified or were assigned different significance by Asian
American adoptive parents and will likely be further modified by their
own children, who will enact them within their own contexts. Asian
Americans now occupy a different position within the U.S. racial and
social structure than they did in the 1990s, when Lowe's model was developed. While fears of Asians as an immigrant horde and Yellow Peril
still exist, the model minority stereotype has gained new strength, with
Asians increasingly being seen as honorary whites, and Asian cultures
gaining new cachet. The "Tiger Mom" (Chua 2011) phenomenon and
controversy are indicative of this shift. The dynamics whereby Asian
American cultures are appropriated and commodified have also shifted
in these intervening years. Alternative representations of Asians and
Asian Americans now exist, in large part fueled by transnational Asian
popular culture, the increasing representation of diverse Asian American characters in the mainstream media, and the growing availability
of forms of Asian American cultural production, including films, art,
literature, theater, music, and Asian American studies courses. However,
while representations of Asians and Asian culture are more readily accessed, they also often take complex forms that perpetuate Orientalist
and other Asian stereotypes. Because images of Asians as stereotypical
nerds, accented foreigners, dragon ladies, kung fu fighters, submissive
geishas, and so forth have been so prevalent, they have become an accepted part of mainstream culture. Not even Asian Americans themselves may possess the critical skills to dissect these images, which are
often not overtly negative and often couched as humor. However, it may
be possible to increase one's awareness of these issues.

Year after year, my students' scrapbook projects are filled with entries
analyzing contemporary movies, television shows, ads, and personal experiences that contain these stereotypical and often racist images. I am
also relieved to see increasingly positive images of Asian Americans,
including representations that challenge stereotypes or forms of creative
self-expression produced by Asian Americans that students are also able
to access, primarily through the Internet. Moreover, it is gratifying to see
that my students, most of them white Americans who admitted coming
into the class with strong stereotypical ideas about Asian Americans and
who had previously laughed at the same representations that they now

critiqued in their scrapbooks, had come to a much more historically informed and socially contextualized understanding of how to analyze representations of Asian Americans. I often tell my students that I wish all adoptive parents of children from Asia, whether Asian American or white, could be informed by similar perspectives so that they could then teach their children to critically analyze the multiple and often conflicting images of Asian Americans that circulate in popular culture and the media and that have real effects on how Asian Americans see themselves, as well as how others see them.

It is difficult for anyone to make concrete predictions about the future of racism and racialization in the United States. However, the recognition of Chinese identity as a racialized one can more easily exist in tandem with conceptions of culture as a set of meanings produced in the context of everyday life, as through these conceptions of culture individuals can begin to understand and address racism as similarly consisting of everyday actions and representations. This is not to say that it is not important to understand the historically rooted and structurally embedded nature of racism. And one can raise the concern that a focus on cultural production that emphasizes individual choice and agency may not allow for its systemic and embedded nature to be fully seen, and may foster more of the dehistoricized and essentialized experimentation with Chinese culture that many have seen as potentially distracting from issues of race and power. But, perhaps this is the "language" that must be spoken in order to effectively engage with the increasingly complex and multilayered ways that racist and stereotypical representations of Asian Americans circulate in our society.

In contrast to the not-so-subtle images of Chinese immigrants, African Americans, and Native Americans that were drawn in turn-of-the-twentieth-century political cartoons supporting Chinese exclusion illustrated in the book *The Coming Man* (Choy, Hom, and Dong 1995), portrayals of Asian Americans today, even negative and stereotypical ones, are found front and center in mainstream advertisements, television shows, and other forms of media and popular culture. The cultural and racial "difference" of Asian Americans is often merged in these representations, which are attached to historically rooted and powerful discourses about Asians as perpetual foreigners or model minorities. A controversial ad run by Republican senatorial candidate Dick Hoekstra and aired during the 2012 Super Bowl depicted a young, pretty Asian woman standing in the middle of a rice paddy with her bicycle, wearing a yellow shirt and a conical straw hat. The woman proceeds to speak in a generic "Asian" accent about how she is thankful to Debbie "Spend-It-Now" Stabenow (Hoekstra's Democratic opponent) for spending so much of Michigan taxpayer dollars to support the movement of jobs to Asia. In a smug manner, she talks about how China's economy is growing rapidly and becoming even stronger, saying, "Your economy get very weak. Ours get very good." This ad, with its "Oriental" music playing in the background, was clearly designed to touch a nerve among Michigan voters, many of whom were concerned with the outsourcing of manufacturing jobs overseas and the impact this has had on the local economy. The spot combines a number of strong stereotypes, including the exoticization and Orientalization of Asian women, the Yellow Peril connected to the rise of Eastern economic growth, and the generic lumping together of "Asian" images (rice paddies, bicycles, accents).

When I showed this ad in my class on Asian Americans, all of the students (the majority of whom were white students from Michigan) agreed that it was problematic. Its antiforeign sentiment reminded many of them of the Vincent Chin incident that they had learned about in class, which had occurred in 1982, a time of economic recession and U.S. competition with Japan in the auto industry, long before they were born. They were also surprised when it was later revealed that the actress featured in the commercial was Lisa Chan, a Chinese American, a recent graduate in sociology from UC Berkeley, and the winner of the Miss Napa Valley beauty pageant, who spoke unaccented English and was interested in issues of social justice and empowerment for underprivileged people.

When the ad was pulled, most of my students agreed that it had been inappropriate and that Hoekstra's message could have been conveyed in a different way. This example embodied on a number of levels the ways that historically rooted stereotypes are recirculated and gain new meanings within contemporary discourses about race, power, and difference. Through the completion of scrapbooks on current events, these students not only were beginning to recognize the prevalence of stereotypical and racist images of Asian Americans but also were beginning to connect these images to the histories and structures from which they emerged. It was only through searching out examples that they were able to connect to their own social worlds, and by analyzing them within the framework of the class, they were able to more fully understand the implications and impact of these broader structures. Many students discussed personal experiences involving these problematic portrayals of Asians or Asian Americans, and many also discussed their intentions to speak up when they witnessed such incidents in the future. Perhaps these individualized means of understanding the racism experienced by Asian Americans are an important first step in changing broader attitudes.

I am encouraged to see that there are now more opportunities for Chinese adoptees to produce their own forms of Chinese adoptee culture that reflect their individuality. The trick is to not let their efforts be absorbed as part of a broader mainstream (and Orientalist-inflected) appreciation of all things Asian. Carla went through an "Asian phase" in which she was "proud to represent," expressing an admiration for a variety of forms of Asian popular culture, including the Korean culture that her friends enjoyed. But she did not necessarily find this sense of cultural pride useful when, as mentioned earlier, another student made the racist and insensitive comment about Chinese babies during roll call. For this, she had to draw upon a different set of resources (including her Latin book) to stand up for herself and communicate to the boy that he had said something offensive.

My interviews with teenage adoptees, discussed in the next chapter, further elucidate some of the ways that representations of Chinese culture are lived and transformed into developing identities as children grow older, as well as the ways that Asian American cultural politics may be shifting. What is interesting and significant is that for all of these teens, being Chinese was not always central to their self-expressed identities; most of them were developing their own understandings of Chineseness, though to differing degrees still based on the backgrounds their parents had provided for them. Each adoptee had different (and often changing) degrees of identification with Chinese or Asian as a racial identity, which did not necessarily correlate with the extent to which they identified as Chinese or Chinese American or with how much they knew about Chinese culture.

7

Don't Objectify Me

Chinese Adoptee Teens

In the summer of 2008, in a crowded, noisy Bay Area café, I met Xiao Hua and her mother. We went inside to order drinks and find a table. Xiao Hua was fifteen years old, around five feet tall, and athletic. Xiao Hua's mother had told me that her daughter had been attending football practice all summer in the hopes of making her private school's team. I initially thought that her mother, who spoke with a British accent, had meant "football," as in soccer, but she clarified that she indeed meant American football. I tried to imagine Xiao Hua practicing with the high school boys, most of whom must have been much larger, and gathered that she must be one very tough young woman. I was also struck by the way she spoke. Although she had grown up in California, she had also spent some time with her relatives in England, and she had a British accent like her mother's.

After chatting about Xiao Hua's adoption story, her mother left so that we could talk privately. I asked her about how she identified herself. She said that her "voice" was English, her "culture" American, and her "background" Chinese. When I asked her to explain more about what it meant for her to be Chinese, she replied, "I like having the connection of being Chinese, but I don't really like act upon it, I guess? For me, it's just like an invisible link, it exists, but it's not really seen." In fact, she noted that her main nonacademic activity was Chinese lion dancing, an activity she started as a four-year-old, and for which she had talent. She is usually asked to be the "head" of the lion. "No fan dancing for me!" she exclaimed. She prided herself on being tough, something she imagines she had to be in the orphanage to survive, and she noted that perhaps she liked football because it brought out her "aggressive side." For Xiao Hua, lion dancing provided her main connection to Chinese culture. "I don't really want to go back to China, but I feel like I maybe should. . . .

I don't know. . . . Maybe when I'm older I might make a firmer decision, but right now it's a firm maybe. Right now I feel much more comfortable in Chinatown."

The fact that Xiao Hua felt a stronger connection to Chinatown than to China was not surprising, in that her lion dance troupe performed regularly in Chinatown and she had not been back to China since she was adopted as a young toddler. Her sentiment is shared by many Chinese Americans born to and raised by Chinese American parents, for whom China itself is a mysterious and unknown place. In my previous research with American-born Chinese Americans, for many youths raised in the suburbs, even Chinatown represented an unfamiliar "Chinese" space. Xiao Hua lived in a part of the Bay Area that is not as densely populated by Chinese Americans, though quite accessible to Chinese ethnic enclaves, and was raised by white parents. Yet interestingly, Xiao Hua (a pseudonym) has retained her Chinese name, which could be seen as representing a direct connection to China and Chineseness and, more specifically, the Cantonese dialect spoken in her region of origin. When she was adopted as a young toddler, she refused to answer to the English name that her parents had selected for her, shaking her head to say no.

In speaking with Xiao Hua, I realized that she was developing into a young woman with a very strong sense of self, and with attachments to Chinese culture and other anchor points of identity such as her British accent and tomboyish pursuits that perhaps her parents could not have predicted or purposefully shaped. Xiao Hua's Chineseness was intertwined with a more general perception of herself as a tough and individualistic young woman who did not fit the stereotypical feminine molds into which Asian women were often cast.

I begin this chapter with my initial impression of Xiao Hua to provide a launching point from which to discuss broader themes related to how Chinese culture is enacted, performed, and negotiated within broader U.S. identity politics. Throughout this chapter, I explore how Chineseness was just one of many factors these teens used to define themselves. Much of the literature on teenage transracial adoptees discusses their problematic identification with the white culture of their parents, peers, and majority society (Eng 2010; E. Kim 2010). The literature indicates that identification with whiteness may be at odds with the actual experiences of racism, discrimination, and marginalization that may also be experienced by these teens. However, most of these teens *are* part of white families, and they embrace the Jewish, Irish, or other traditions and values of their parents. As previously discussed, what further complicates this analysis of adoptee identities is both that adoptive parents have become increasingly aware of and concerned about potential forms of discrimination their children may face, and that many parents turn to culture as a way to address these issues. Therefore, unlike previous generations of Korean adoptees who have been portrayed as having had little or no exposure to resources to prepare them for dealing with issues of race or cultural identity, these newer generations of Chinese adoptees are growing up with differing degrees of access to this information, although at least initially it is filtered through the eyes of their parents. Still, some parents (whether white or Asian American) may still view racism and discrimination as blatant and overt acts and may not be as cognizant of the more subtle and often indirect forms they may take. Stereotyping, exclusion, and other forms of differentiation continue to affect Asian Americans, though often masked by model minority discourses—the idea that Asians are inherently smarter, better behaved, and more successful than other minorities or even whites—that serve to downplay their impact (Chou and Feagin 2008). The result, I argue, is that relationships to both whiteness and Chineseness/Asianness have become more complex for these teens who have been raised in the era of contemporary race-blind multiculturalism. As my interviews show, while their parents have to differing degrees provided opportunities for exposure to Chinese, Chinese American, or Asian American resources, these teens have also begun to negotiate their own complex relationships to their Asianness.

A vast literature in the field of psychology, social work, and family studies discusses the importance of "cultural socialization" for transracial adoptive families (Baden 2002; Freundlich and Lieberthal 2000; R. Lee 2003; Vonk 2001). However, much of this literature has not fully interrogated the categories and relations of difference used to describe the "Chinese" origins of Chinese adoptees, or the "American" contexts into which these children are brought upon adoption. In not viewing culture itself as a category that is constructed and negotiated, some of this literature has continued to rely on generalized or essentialized conceptions of culture that do not reflect the nuanced ways that cultural meanings shift and are often collapsed into racial essences. For example, Tessler, Gamache, and Liu, in their book *West Meets East: American Adopt Chinese Children* (1999), provide a valuable systematic sampling of adoptive families in the United States, including information on parental attitudes toward Chinese socialization. However, they do not deconstruct the supposed "dichotomy" between West and East (Chinese and American cultures) that these families are breaking down. In characterizing American and Chinese cultural influences as distinct and dichotomous, the authors create boundaries around notions of "Chinese" and "American" culture, thereby inadvertently essentializing both cultures and rendering each of them static and unchangeable. In de-emphasizing the broader social, political, cultural, or historical context within which people of Chinese descent are racialized in America (regardless of who their parents are), the very dichotomies that give power to ideas of racial difference in the United States may be perpetuated.

My findings speak to the need to further refine concepts such as bicultural socialization that are often used to describe the dual influences of "Chinese" and "American" cultures in the lives of Chinese adoptees. The work of Tessler and his colleagues (1999) is valuable for understanding from a longitudinal perspective the approaches and attitudes toward bicultural socialization by both adoptive parents and their children. Tessler's first survey profiled more than 300 adoptive families, and he has continued with follow-up studies, including ones with the now teenage children. In addition to providing demographic data on the parents (age, income, marital status, education), one study (Thomas and Tessler 2007) also measured the degree to which parents considered it important to provide Chinese cultural socialization for their children. The researchers administered a survey that asked parents how important it was that their children do things such as learn to say phrases in Chinese, visit China, keep their Chinese names, and visit Chinatown. The survey also measured the children's "Chinese cultural competence" by asking if the children had learned some Chinese words and phrases, had learned to count in Chinese, were able to write their name in Chinese characters, were able to speak some Chinese, and so forth. The study also looked at demographic information, such as the percentage of Chinese Americans in the respondents' communities, to help gauge respondents' access to

Chinese cultural resources and Chinese people. The researchers found that both parental attitudes toward Chinese cultural socialization and access to Chinese cultural resources in the community influenced the degree of Chinese cultural socialization experienced by their children.

A more recent study (Tessler and Gamache 2012) focusing specifically on the children, most of whom were about thirteen years old at the time of the survey, asked more specific questions about the teens' ethnic identities such as "How much do you think of yourself as Chinese?" "How much do you think of yourself as Chinese American?" "How important to you is getting to know kids whose parents are Chinese or Chinese American?" The study also asked questions about the importance of identifying as American and about contact with Chinese Americans.

These studies seem to provide a statistically valid, policy-relevant overview of aspects of Chinese cultural socialization and in this regard may complement more qualitative studies. From my perspective as an anthropologist, however, it is very difficult to distill the complex facets of identity down to specific questions without engaging in an open-ended dialogue to capture nuances. From my interview data, it is clear that it is possible to identify with and create new aspects of Chinese and Chinese American culture in subtle ways that cannot be easily captured in a survey format. These teens also strongly identified as not just American but also Irish American, Jewish, Catholic, and others, and like many other Asian Americans, some connected to Chinese American culture or Chinatown but not to China. Some were more interested than others in Asian American culture. Most of the teens with whom I spoke actively worked against any kind of essentializing of their identities as they carved out their own relationship to China, Chinese American, and American identities. One mother, Audrey, said that her daughter had become frustrated when filling out one of the surveys for the study that had asked, "Are you Chinese, Chinese American, or American?" She did not like having to choose just one identity and in the end decided to write in her own answer: "an eggplant."

The concept of bicultural socialization may be useful in that it acknowledges that, contrary to the melting-pot idea, other cultural influences do not merely melt into a generic "American" mixture. As noted throughout this book, for adoptees, acknowledgment of their birth origins by their adoptive families represented a departure from previous approaches that did not acknowledge adoptees' past. However, the concept of bicultural socialization does little to acknowledge the complex meanings surrounding notions of both "Chinese" and "American" and may even reinforce the false dichotomy between them. Some of the teens with whom I spoke may not have wanted to visit China or speak Chinese, but they nevertheless identified very strongly with other aspects of Asian (American) culture. This is not unlike one third-generation American-born Chinese American from the San Francisco Bay Area I interviewed for my earlier research, who felt he expressed himself as a Chinese American through his involvement in lion dancing, which was rooted in institutions in Marin County of the Bay Area where he lived. The concept of bicultural socialization does not easily encompass the variety of ways that people identify as Chinese American or Asian American, which involve more than just knowledge of ancestral language and customs. While the contact with adult Chinese and Chinese Americans that is often emphasized by adoptive parents is certainly important for adoptees, so are opportunities to meet, learn about, and be inspired by Asian American role models. In fact, cognizance of the ways that Asians have been and continue to be racialized as a single group is central to the formation of a broader Asian American identity, something that the model of bicultural socialization does not capture. As discussed in chapter 6, the influence of adoptive family ethnicity and other values is also significant and cannot easily be distilled into the general category of "American." These teens find various ways to contextualize these varied aspects of their identities as they continue to explore and express who they are or who they are becoming.

The ways these teens viewed themselves as Chinese and connected with China and Chinese culture were strikingly different. As a group, the young women I interviewed seemed open to exploring what it meant to be Chinese (or Asian) and adopted. They strived to do this on their own terms, and in ways that often actively disassociated themselves from stereotypical ideas about Chinese Americans or adoptees. In this sense, we are reminded that the constructions of Chineseness that parents create for their children do not play out in a vacuum, but rather within a real-world context in which Chineseness carries numerous, often conflicting meanings. On the surface, these teens' responses to being interviewed by an anthropologist they did not know well might to some extent have produced "model adoptee" responses. However, as I illustrate through-out this chapter, these interviews also provided insights into how these teens viewed themselves and wished to be perceived by others at a time in their life that was defined by a combination of peer pressure and the desire to express oneself as a unique individual.

These teens' responses allow us to further question exactly what "Chinese" or "Chinese American" culture is (or at least how it comes into play as a reference point for identity building), and how it can become a form of identity that securely grounds them but also flexibly changes. The flexibility of Asian American cultures may contribute to the creation of cultures of resistance as discussed by Lisa Lowe, but these cultures cannot be produced without contending with the hegemonic representations of Asian Americans that often make these representations oppressive. The variability and to some extent the unpredictability with which the teens I interviewed expressed and explored their identities illustrate their resistance to essentialization and stereotyping. It is striking to see that these young women have been deeply influenced by their parents and have also created their own meanings around the opportunities for exposure to China and Chinese culture that their parents had facilitated for them. Chinese identities, for them, were negotiated in the form of very specific and often evolving types of relationships to China and Chinese culture, including both selective identification and active disassociation with certain aspects often characterized as being Chinese or Asian in America. As such, their cases illustrate how identities are continually in process and are both highly individual and responsive to ever-changing anxieties, pressures, and desires.

At the same time, it is important to ask in what ways the ambivalent attitudes toward their Chineseness expressed by these teens have been shaped by the context in which ideas of Chineseness circulate and are enacted. Broader U.S. discourses both downplay the power and salience of race in the daily lives of people of color, and portray ethnicity as a matter of choosing ethnic options. To what extent do these teens who were adopted from China have the ability to shape their own ethnic (and racial) identities? To what extent and in what ways did having white or Asian American parents, or living on the West Coast or in the Midwest, affect these teens' perceptions of what it means to be Chinese? Did the specific approaches their parents have taken regarding issues of adoption and racial and cultural identity directly correlate with their children's attitudes? What other opportunities have these teens had to shape their awareness of issues of race and social justice or to form friendships and networks related to being Chinese/Asian or adopted? In this chapter, I aim to begin to address these issues through exploring the variety of approaches to being Chinese or Asian expressed by the young women I interviewed in both the Bay Area and St. Louis.

Varying Approaches toward Chineseness

After finishing my interview with Xiao Hua, I called Mei, the young woman I had arranged to interview next. She was to walk over from her school, which was not far from the café, and her mother would join us later, toward the end of the interview. My first impression upon meeting Mei, who was very poised and mature, was that she seemed older than her fifteen years. She was going into her junior year at a private school, where she pursued her numerous academic and extracurricular interests, including music (voice), poetry, horseback riding, and soccer. Mei had attended a bilingual Chinese immersion school until completing the program in the eighth grade and was fluent in Mandarin Chinese. She had traveled to China numerous times and had opportunities to meet children from her orphanage, her fluency in Chinese allowing her to communicate easily with them. She and her family had actually moved to the Bay Area from New York when she was three so that she could be enrolled in the bilingual school. She realized that her parents sent her there so she could be around other Chinese American students and learn about where she came from originally, and she was appreciative of the opportunity to do so. But although she was glad she knew Chinese, she especially liked learning in some of her upper grade level classes about contemporary issues, including the one-child policy, which gave her a better understanding of why her birth parents may have relinquished her for adoption.

Nevertheless, she clearly had mixed feelings about having attended the bilingual school and was thoroughly enjoying her private high school for the opportunities it provided her to express herself through poetry, creative writing, and music—in English. She had been frustrated that the English language classes at her former school had not been challenging or plentiful, and she believed this to be a casualty of the curriculum's emphasis on the Chinese language program. Still, for the most part she was glad that her parents sent her there and admitted that she "would not be the person" she is now, with her fluency in Chinese and the friends she made at that school, if she had gone somewhere else. She also felt fortunate to have more immediate familial connections to Chinese culture. Her uncle's wife is from Taiwan, and because of Mei's Chinese language fluency, they are able speak Mandarin together. Sometimes her aunt is mistaken to be her mother.

Upon entering high school, Mei said she was ready to move on to explore additional interests. Perhaps ironically, she said that she enjoyed the fact that her new school had fewer Asian students. She had always been afraid of being seen as a "nerdy Asian kid" because so many students at her previous school had fit that stereotype, but at her new school, she joined the Asian student organization and realized that one does not have to fit the nerdy stereotype. She observed that at her old school, "to me, being Asian was being them, and that scared me a little, and now to be Asian can mean so much more now, and I embrace it more now." Later, she added, "There are so many things . . . we talk about being hapa.[1] One of the girls . . . her mother was the first Western geisha. It's not just about being Chinese and eating dumplings at New Year's, and this is the kind of stuff that interests me, not just the stereotypical culture-type stuff."

Perhaps Mei had internalized negative stereotypes about Asian nerds, which circulate broadly. Were the Chinese American students at her immersion school different from the Asian American students at her new school, or was it because in her new school, Mei could choose which Asian students to associate with?

Mei noted that she enjoyed learning about other ways of being Asian or Asian American, and she found the students at her previous school to represent a very narrow range of what she now thinks it means to be Asian. In talking about how "being Chinese and eating dumplings" was no longer interesting to her, she was expressing her desire to go beyond a model of representing Chinese culture that was also predominant in FCC celebrations. While making dumplings may play a part in the household traditions and celebrations of many Chinese American households, what Mei seemed to be critiquing was the use of this activity as a clichéd means of signifying Chineseness, what she terms "stereotypical culture-type stuff." Rather, being Chinese American or Asian American takes place through the relationships that are formed and strengthened through such activities, particularly those that may more consciously explore the boundaries and varied manifestations that Chineseness or Asianness can take. As a Chinese adoptee, perhaps Mei identifies with hybridized ways of being Asian.

Like Xiao Hua, Mei is defining her own sense of what it means to be Chinese or, more broadly, Asian American, while also fostering her individual interests. She notes that she enjoys talking about Asian American issues, even those that do not affect her directly, perhaps because they reflect a more diverse vision of being Asian American.

The blending of traditional and contemporary elements of Asian American identity has become more broadly representative of celebrations of "diversity" under contemporary multicultural politics. While many Asian American students continue to express their identities using traditional symbols, they also feel a need to counterbalance these representations with demonstrations of their modernity that illustrate their connection to a broader community of Asian Americans. The cultural shows that are popular among Asian American college students illustrate this tension between honoring "tradition" and performing "modernity," all the while trying very hard not to appear too earnest about these displays of identity (something else that differentiates these celebrations from the dumpling-making sessions to which Mei refers). A biennial cultural variety show put on in 2006 by the Asian Pacific American students at my university exemplified these elements. It featured dance, spoken word, and skits by various Asian Pacific American student groups on campus, tied together by short performances by the emcees. The show took place in the school's large auditorium, which showcased a new sound system and spectacular lighting, both of which were used to their full capacity by the students in their lavish production. Each student group involved was allotted time for both "traditional" and "modern" performances. The traditional performances were most often symbolic of the groups' ethnic traditions in the home country, with students dressed in traditional costumes and accompanied by traditional music. The modern performances showcased hip-hop and break-dancing moves, stepping, and contemporary fashions, accompanied by contemporary music. This juxtaposition allowed students to show both their cultural pride and their place as part of a broader Asian American youth culture. As one of the emcees noted, "The dances show our Asian background, but also reflect that we are Americans. . . . We have the best of both worlds."[2]

Some skits, perhaps most notably the one by the Hmong American Student Association, were both a history lesson and a declaration of cultural pride, beginning with a clip from a documentary about Hmong involvement in and betrayal by the United States in the Secret War in Laos, followed by a moving spoken word performance, "I Am Hmong, Hmong Means Free." The latter recounted Hmong involvement in the Vietnam War and their flight from Laos, life in refugee camps, journey to America, struggles to adjust to American life, and finally the success of younger generations in being able to both take pride in Hmong identity and have the freedom to explore other aspects of identity. This group's modern performance consisted of a fast-moving hip-hop dance. The playful skit by the Asian American student group's executive board, titled "The Asian American Experience in a Nutshell," explored Asian Pacific American identities, both asserting the diversity of the community and playing with identity and stereotypes by asking whether things such as drinking bubble tea, listening to certain types of music, or eating sushi made someone Asian American. In this "performance" of identity, identity questions were playfully broached—in one part of the skit, an Asian American "Goldilocks" sampled three types of bubble tea, none of them being just right. In another, a student dressed as a piece of sushi, topped with orange balloons representing roe, was pursued across the stage by hungry students. The mixture of tradition and modernity, play with stereotypes, and declarations of identity within the show is characteristic of other Asian American cultural productions and adds depth of meaning and context to the colorful displays of traditional heritage. It was particularly evident in my previous work with American-born Chinese Americans, in which play with Chinese phrases (even by those who did not really speak the language) and Asian popular culture such as kung fu movies, popular music, manga, and anime, factored centrally in redefining and experimenting with the group's identity (Louie 2004; Maira 2002; Purkayastha 2005).

Sunaina Maira's (2002) work on South Asian American hip-hop also shows how youths take ownership of their identities by drawing upon and "remixing" traditions to signify both their racial and ethnic distinctiveness and their modernity as part of hip-hop and rap cultures. Today's Asian American youths are interested in multicultural spoken word performances by iLL-Literacy and hip-hop dance crews such as the Jabbawockeez, which are part of these popular genres but also involve Asian American performers.

Not wanting to be pigeonholed into an essentialized identity based on their Chinese backgrounds was a common theme expressed by other teenage adoptees I interviewed. Most I spoke with did identify with aspects of Chinese heritage and culture, but they did so selectively and intermixed their interests in Chineseness with other sources of identification. They performed Chinese "culture" through creatively and intentionally employing practices and symbols of Chinese, Chinese American, or Asian American culture, sometimes drawing upon decontextualized and dehistoricized versions of Chinese culture in inventing their own traditions. These form the scripts that people use in "shaping their life plans and in telling their life stories" (Appiah 1994, 159).[3] While Miri Song discusses Appiah's concept of "scripts of behavior" as being shaped and "upheld" by ethnic groups in relation to "dominant representations and discourses about groups in wider society" (2003, 50), I see these scripts as negotiated on a more individual level within the broader context of both dominant representations and multiple other currents of Asian and Asian American cultural production and youth culture more broadly.

The American-born Chinese Americans I studied previously (Louie 2004), many of whom did not speak Chinese fluently or know much about China before traveling there on "roots-seeking" journeys, employed decontextualized symbols of Chinese American or Asian American popular culture to bolster identity narratives that reflected both their modernity and their tenuous connections to both mainstream U.S. and Chinese societies. They consumed popular culture in crafting recontextualized versions of Chinese culture removed from hegemonic forms of cultural authenticity that denied them a social and cultural space of their own in the context of U.S. racial and multicultural politics (Louie 2004).

Adoptees' constructions of Chinese culture may draw both from the materials to which their parents exposed them and from the resources they are beginning to gather on their own. In some ways, these constructions may be purposefully decontextualized from their original sources, in part to intentionally remove them from their historical origins, which are often tied to oppressive and restrictive representations of China and Chinese Americans. The consumption and display of Chinese and Asian objects and the invention of new cultural practices played varying roles in these processes. This can be a risky move, as knowledge of histories of racism and exclusion of Asian Americans is an important part of combating these inaccurate representations. Too often, the culture of consumption results in the disassociation of material objects from their original contexts and histories, thus allowing for their easy appropriation. In the case of Chinese and Asian objects, this facilitates their use in the superficial ways for which white adoptive parents have been critiqued (Anagnost 2000; Traver 2007). The question becomes whether Chinese adoptees are able to find a way to create a new context within which they can effectively engage in the consumption of these objects as part of broader projects of identity-building, particularly if they are being raised by parents who may not be employing them in the same ways.

One thing that teens might have going for them is their desire to separate from their parents as they develop their own individual tastes and life goals. The next few interviews I describe illustrate these teens' dislike of being, as one put it, "objectified by other people" and their efforts to define various aspects of their identities within the context of their everyday teenage lives.

"Don't Objectify Me"

I interviewed Selina at her modest East Bay home, where she lives with her two mothers. She was a very mature fourteen-year-old who was going into the ninth grade at a private Bay Area school. Her parents had attended a talk on my research that I had given a few weeks earlier in Berkeley and had mentioned that their daughter was on a trip to England and Ireland, but that I could interview her when she returned. Selina and four other teen "Global Girls" ambassadors had traveled to

Great Britain, representing the organization Chinese Adoptee Links, run by Jennifer Jue-Steuck, a UC Berkeley graduate student and writer, who herself was adopted from China. The goal of Chinese Adoptee Links is to "to create a multigenerational social network for the 150,000+ Chinese adoptees living in 26 countries worldwide."[4]

There are eleven teenage ambassadors in total, representing different regions of the United States. In 2008, the ambassadors traveled to England to meet with local adoptee groups. According to Selina, while in England they had a picnic with a group of adoptive families, most of whom had younger children. In Ireland they held a panel discussion and stayed with host families. Most of the children in these families were around seven, and their parents had wanted them to be exposed to the perspectives of older adoptees. They asked the ambassadors where they were adopted from and at what age, and whether they felt more Chinese or American. Some of the teens responded that they felt "more American."

Selina noted that these British adoptees did not know many other adoptees or Asians in the surrounding areas, in contrast to her own East Bay community, which is quite diverse. She also learned that the other teenage ambassadors with whom she traveled, who were from different parts of the United States, represented a range of perspectives, from their political leanings to their opinions about whether they wished to go back to China to visit. One young woman had been back fourteen times, and Selina had been back five times, but some were not interested in going to China.

Selina recalled that in one panel discussion, she and her companions were asked to quantify how much they felt Chinese and how much they felt American. She replied that "it changes over time and it's definitely a mix of the two, but I can't give a concrete percentage." When I asked her to elaborate, she explained that she views Chinese American identity as continually changing, and does not "like being objectified by other people." Her conception of identity as fluid goes against the mainstream ideas discussed earlier about identity as fixed and unchanging, and as something that needs to be uncovered or discovered. For example, she does not like it when people make assumptions about her being adopted without actually asking her. During her trip, adoptive parents asked whether the teens liked Chinese food and Chinese clothes. To this, she would reply, "Well, I do like all that stuff, but it's not specifically because I'm Chinese."

One wonders whether Selina's fluid conceptions of identity and her insistence on not being labeled or stereotyped derive in part from living in such a diverse area and coming from a nontraditional family. She remembers that, as a child, she sometimes had to deal with being singled out for being Asian, having two mothers, or being adopted. She recalls, "I would just say I have two moms because I'm adopted. . . . It was a good diversion method." Her comments remind us that in contexts where parents cannot be present, the child is left to her own devices to deal with the inappropriate comments of other children and must work out her own ways to respond. However, Selina's parents had make a concerted effort to provide her with the tools and support to handle these issues. When I asked her mother Paula, whom I also interviewed, how the family addressed issues of racism, she noted, "She has a lot of knowledge, standupness . . . because we think that this is a responsibility. . . . We've taught her a lot . . . and things happen. . . . You can talk about it. . . . How do you as parents talk about that." Later she added, "We have to speak up. . . . We can't let her go out there and fight all these battles."

Chinese American Parents

While the interviews recounted thus far took place with teens who were adopted by white parents, the next few interviews I will discuss were conducted with teens with Chinese American adoptive parents. These teens might look more like their parents because they "match" racially, but many other factors also play into their identity formation. How their parents view their own Chineseness, and how they endeavor to incorporate it into their family's lives are highly variable, as are the ways these teens view their own identities. These profiles will further illustrate the variability and complexity of these teens' relationships to Chineseness (or Asianness more broadly), whiteness, and other racial and cultural groups. These portraits illustrate the impact of popular culture and peer influences on these young women but also how they strive to carve out spaces of individuality in their choices of extracurricular activities and their tastes in music and television. This does not exclude some level of identification with Chinese or Asian American activities. Nevertheless, it was clear that these teens often had specific reasons for making these choices, and they did not wish to be slotted into predictable categories.

I was greeted at the door of Nora's house by her small, loudly barking dog. Nora answered the door, and her mother, Judy, explained that the dog was blind and therefore felt especially threatened by visitors. Judy had told me that she had two daughters, an eleven-year-old and a thirteen-year-old. Not used to being around kids that age, when I first met Nora, a petite and bubbly girl, I mistook her for the eleven-year-old. Nora thankfully did not hold my mistake against me, and after she and her mother showed me their pet rats, we sat down at the dining room table for the interview.

The first thing Nora told me about herself was that she was very interested in Japanese graphic novels and manga. Her favorite manga are *Full Metal Alchemist* and *Inuyasha*, the latter of which she described, speaking a mile a minute and in great detail, as a feudal fairy tale about a half dog, half man. She then mused, "I'm starting to think I'm not really Chinese. I think I'm Japanese. My sister would think she's Mexican because she likes Mexican stuff." Nora had been introduced to Japanese pop culture by friends in her East Bay community. She also studied aikido, a Japanese martial art, at a local dojo. Her sensei, a well-known female aikidoist who trained in Japan, turned out to be the sensei of my former aikido teacher in Ohio, and we talked about this coincidence. Nora's interest in aikido had been inspired by her love of anime and manga and the fact that characters in these genres tend to "smash things," though we joked about how, perhaps ironically, aikido is a defensive martial art that uses the opponent's force against him or her. Through her (non-Japanese) aikido sensei, she has begun to learn some Japanese, and she admits that at this point, she is more interested in learning Japanese than Chinese.

Nora's parents seem OK with her not learning Chinese. Both of her parents are Chinese American, and her mother, Judy, who was quoted at the beginning of chapter 4, said that though she and her husband speak different Chinese dialects, their daughters are not interested in learning either of them. Judy emphasizes that she considers it most important to teach her children about what she sees as Chinese values, such as respect for elders and responsibility with money. Judy thinks that many white adoptive parents overdo Chinese culture in an effort to overcompensate for not being Chinese. While she has been very open with her daughters about adoption from the beginning, she has not involved them in adoptive family organizations, such as FCC.

Toward the end of our interview, when I asked her how she identifies, Nora said, "I'm just a normal Chinese girl who has been adopted by Chinese parents." In emphasizing both her normalcy and her Chineseness in the context of her other interests, Nora is claiming Chineseness as a flexible form of identity that can encompass varied tastes, including Japanese culture. In her self-description, she comfortably merges her own Chineseness, as a Chinese adoptee born in China, with that of her Chinese American parents. While her adoptive parents and her ancestral origins may make her Chinese, she has also had the freedom to develop her own distinctive interests while still considering herself to be Chinese, which in her mother's opinion is more a matter of values rather than language or involvement in specific activities. In this sense, this thirteen-year-old is exercising a nonessentializing view of identity that separates heritage from culture. The fact that she can explore Japanese and other cultures illustrates her efforts to move beyond the conflation of heritage, race, and culture. She prides herself on not playing "follow the leader" by, for example, following forms of music that "other people don't listen to," like K-pop, J-pop, or a Russian group called t.A.T.u.

However, Nora does not actively disassociate herself from her Chinese origins or her Chinese parents. One may ask whether her attitude is facilitated by her Chinese American parents, who do not view Chineseness as a package of race, culture, and identity but who nevertheless engage in some degree of essentializing Chinese values. Or does it instead parallel the efforts of the other teens I interviewed with white adoptive parents to define their Chineseness within the broader spectrum of their personal backgrounds, tastes, and identities?

Jennifer, another teen I interviewed, also seemed to be negotiating a fine line between being too identified with stereotyped notions of Chinese American culture, which she associates with parental pressure, yet still honoring her family's Chinese heritage and her relationships with other adoptees. I had a difficult time finding Jennifer's house along the row of homes in the Richmond District of San Francisco. Though it was the Fourth of July, it was a cool and somewhat foggy day, which would likely make it difficult to see the fireworks later that night. After locating Jennifer's house, I rang the doorbell, and Jennifer answered, explaining that her mother was busy helping her grandfather move. Jennifer graciously invited me in and made me some tea. We sat in the living room for the interview, which was informally decorated with photos of her and her mother, along with various stuffed animals.

Jennifer told me that she and her mother had lived with her grandfather in Chinatown when she was young, and Jennifer used to know how to speak some Cantonese and "knew Chinatown like the back of my hand." Despite her Chinatown upbringing, she describes herself as "loosey-goosey Chinese" in the sense that she speaks English and did not Chinese school. Similarly, she thought that though she "looks Asian," she does not act "super Asian" and, to her relief, also does not receive immense pressure from her mother to achieve straight As, as many Asian students do. She referred to herself as "a banana with a white background." In this sense, she is defining Chineseness or Asianness as less of a racial or cultural identity than a set of values, including an approach to academics that she feels differentiates her experiences from those of other Asians. This model minority stereotype of Chineseness or Asianness appeared to have some basis in her personal experiences with other Asian American students. She had attended Lowell High School her freshman year, a public high school with competitive admission standards and one to which many academically inclined students apply. According to Jennifer, Lowell was 58.2 percent Asian the year she attended, and I was surprised to hear her say that she initially had felt uncomfortable being around so many Asians, despite having grown up in Chinatown and the Richmond District, which were heavily Chinese areas of San Francisco. She eventually made more Asian friends and joked that she even began hanging around at the library. But the following year she ended up transferring to a private school that had fewer Asian students. At her new school, she felt that she no longer stood out. There, she decided to take Mandarin Chinese instead of French or Spanish, though she emphasized that she had been initially interested in all three languages and had arrived at Chinese through the process of elimination. She had ruled out Spanish because "everyone took it" and French because, though she thought the language was pretty, she had heard that "the teacher was scary."

While these comments may make Jennifer sound ambivalent about exploring her Chinese background, she also spoke very positively about other opportunities she had had to connect to Chinese culture. She mentioned enjoying playing piano and learning kung fu and thought that perhaps if she'd been adopted by white parents, she might not have had the opportunity to engage in these activities. It was interesting that she thought of these activities as being Chinese or signifying Chineseness, when in actuality, piano lessons and martial arts are popular activities for children from many backgrounds. However, in addition to mentioning being involved in these activities, she talked about how she appreciated having firsthand experiences with Asians and Asian culture through her Chinese American family members, which have given her access to an "inner circle of Asianness." In contrast, she thinks that white parents might not understand the "attached significance" of certain activities and values that "natural-born" Asians might. Though this statement is somewhat essentializing, merging biology and culture, it is interesting that Jennifer attributes a deeper level of significance to these activities when they are practiced in the context of an Asian community. She observed, "We celebrate the Moon Festival and Chinese New Year, and we still visit the [ancestral] grave in April, and we still do the incense thing outside the door. My grandfather has that . . . and we bring flowers to the giant graveyard . . . and [my mother's] devoted to the grandparents."

But while she values her familial connections to Chinese culture and traditions, perhaps her most significant connection is to her "sisters," the four other girls who were adopted at the same time from Hunan Province, and with whom she remains very close. As with other teens I interviewed, these relationships with other adoptees often remained meaningful as they grew up together, even if they do not see each other regularly. Interestingly, adoptive parents who create FCC events hope that these experiences will create just these types of relationships among their children. But while it is clear that relationships to other adoptees are important, it is also important to consider that this relationship building does not necessarily occur in the context of FCC events.

Perhaps these teens raised by Chinese American families may take for granted their exposure to these aspects of Chinese American culture. But their comments regarding their other interests are reminders that while these aspects may be important, they are not all-encompassing of their identities as Chinese or Asian individuals. In fact, adoptees appear to find it important that these activities and relationships be well integrated into their lives as a whole rather than compartmentalized and separated from other aspects of their lives. Indeed, that is how Chinese (or any other) culture should be—something lived and practiced as part of everyday life, something that is part of a broader worldview. Perhaps this is why these teens make de-essentializing moves that are similar to those of their peers who were adopted by non-Asian parents, reflecting a desire both to avoid common negative Asian American stereotypes and to express their individuality.

Laura's father, Daniel, who is quoted in chapter 4, was one of the few fathers who had responded to my general interview inquiry. In our e-mail conversation, he had commented, "She's your typical tweener; into Miley Cyrus and the Jonas Brothers." I interviewed Laura at her San Francisco home while her family kindly accommodated me around their dinner schedule, eating in shifts while I talked first with her parents and then with her. Laura was thirteen years old and attended a private school, where she liked to play volleyball and basketball. It did not take long for her to share with me that her primary extracurricular interests included following popular teenage music idols, such as the Jonas Brothers, Alicia Keyes, and Justin Timberlake. Perhaps more so than the other teens I interviewed, Laura expressed a strong interest in mainstream popular tween and teen culture, citing Disney Channel shows such as *Camp Rock* with the Jonas Brothers. She noted that her father has warned her about how the Disney Channel "draws you in," but she says she likes these shows because they communicate the message "be yourself." She said that she and her friends try to "act like themselves." They like to make up their own songs and dances. In contrast, she thinks that some of her friends at a Chinese church camp she attends do not always act like themselves. Laura described herself as being close to her family, sociable, adventurous, and outgoing, though she admitted that at times she can be introverted.

Though he had earlier stated that Chinese American culture is self-made and continually being produced, during my interview with Daniel, he seemed to have come to terms with Laura's interest in teenage pop culture. Nonetheless, he was not certain where it fit in with Chinese American culture, musing:

What is the purpose of identity anyway, with culture? It's got to fit in with the person, and the way that Laura will be will be based on not only how she sees herself but how others see her. I'm not sure where she's going to end up in terms of her comfort level. Right now I am not sure I know what Chinese American is . . . because I don't see it anymore. . . . I'm too old. . . . I wonder if it's that hip-hop thing. . . . She's perfectly happy with Hannah Montana and the Jonas Brothers. It seems very American.

Laura was adopted by her father and his ex-wife, who are both Chinese American, and has an older brother, who was born to her parents. After her parents divorced, her father married a white woman who had been previously married to a Filipino American and who had three children from that marriage who are half Asian. Daniel noted that Laura looks up to her older half siblings as role models because she shares musical and other tastes with some of them. She herself thought that she didn't have much Chinese cultural influence, given that her parents were born in America, but she said that her parents have talked with her about adoption, and that her mom used to go to Laura's class to teach about Chinese culture. On the one hand, it may seem as though Laura does not have much engagement with Chinese or Chinese American culture, and that her interests are similar to those of many other American teenagers. She also seems to conceptualize Chinese culture as being composed of Chinese cultural practices based in China, and not necessarily the Chinese American ones that her family practices. On the other hand, she has also been influenced in various ways by her half-Asian half siblings.

Daniel's earlier statements about the flexible and self-made nature of Chinese American culture raise interesting questions about what it means to identify as a Chinese American. For example, he questioned whether it was necessary for children to be sent to Chinese immersion programs to become fluent in Mandarin Chinese. In response to FCC e-mail discussions he saw about these programs, he remembered thinking, "I think they saw this as keeping them close to their culture, but it's like they're getting them ready for something they're not going to become." In other words, the children are Chinese American, not Chinese. He clarified that he is certainly not against learning Mandarin. In fact, Laura's older brother, Daniel's biological son, is now interested in studying the language in college. However, Daniel feels that the most valuable aspect of attending a Chinese immersion school might be so that the kids will be with other Chinese Americans. Indeed, the parents I spoke with (both Chinese American and white) who chose to send their children to immersion schools told me they did so not only for the language education but also for the opportunity to socialize with other Chinese Americans. However, as shared by Mei earlier, this does not always mean that the children will come to closely identify with them.

In Daniel's opinion, and whether or not Laura herself realizes this, Chinese American culture is something that his daughter will receive as part of her daily life, interwoven with their other interests: "As long as we do the things I did as a kid, we're passing it on . . . going to the cemetery, bowing three times, Chinese New Year, day camp in Chinatown each year, she is being exposed to Chinese American culture." He adds, "We do a lot of family things, . . . we have camping trips every year, with about forty people, mostly Chinese, . . . so that way they are with Chinese people, but I don't know how Chinese they are."

Interestingly, Daniel noted that he is not sure how "Chinese" the Chinese people he spends time with are. This contradicts his statement about Chinese culture being "self-made," but it is clear that he is grappling with what Chinese culture is. The fact that in many ways, it does seem very "American," infused with hip-hop and other popular culture forms, again raises questions regarding notions of Chinese cultural authenticity and the various ways in which Chinese American identities are expressed in the context of U.S. multiculturalism. However, Daniel's "privilege of authenticity" as a Chinese American allows him to feel confident that his children are being exposed to a Chinese American culture that has deep roots in the area. Not only did he engage in these activities as a child, but he still has a rich extended network of Chinese Americans with whom his family spends time.

"Jewish-ish" and Other Ways of Identifying

Though earlier I emphasized the varied ways in which Chinese adoptee teens with white or Asian American parents defined and expressed their identities, here I approach the issue of how they are negotiating their identities by painting in broader strokes the other forms of identification and interests that occupy their daily lives. As is the case for many other Chinese Americans and Asian Americans, the teens I interviewed did not necessarily view race and ethnicity as primary concerns on an everyday basis. While this might to some extent reflect their identification with the majority-white culture, through these examples I illustrate how their families' religious or ethnic backgrounds have shaped these teens in specific ways. As discussed in the preceding chapters, white ethnics are used to being able to exercise their ethnic options and may fold Chineseness into the mix in ways that critics sometimes deem as superficial. But when it comes down to it, all children adopted from China enter specific household and community contexts—they are being raised by parents with a variety of religious, ethnic, and political identifications that the children come to share and which are incorporated into their identities.

Arielle's mother had been very involved in their local FCC chapter since Arielle was a toddler, and I had gotten in touch with her prior to visiting the Bay Area. I arranged to meet them the day after I arrived in the Bay Area for my research trip, and their home was conveniently located about half a mile up the hill from where I was staying with my family. Their house, located on a quiet street not far from a busier shopping district in the East Bay, was filled with a number of items they had collected over the years. After speaking with her mother, I sat alone with Arielle and interviewed her. Fifteen-year-old Arielle described herself as athletic, having competed in gymnastics at a high level when she was younger, and joined the lacrosse team as a high school freshman the past year. She also told me that she did not think she was very smart but gets good grades because she works hard. "So why don't you think you're smart?" I asked, and she responded, "I just don't think I'm one of those really smart people who is really good at math. . . . I actually hate math." Though I had not made any assumptions about her mathematical ability, perhaps Arielle was responding to the common stereotype that Asians are good at math. I asked if she felt that she had been stereotyped, and whether the stereotypes bothered her. Ironically, she said, she had attended a small middle school where there were only twenty-nine students, most of whom were not Asian, and she did not feel that she had been stereotyped there. However, at her East Bay high school, which according to her is 40 percent white, 40 percent black, and 20 percent

Asian and Latino, she has encountered more Asian stereotypes. In fact, some of the stereotypes come from her Asian friends, who joke about eating rice, about being really smart, or about being FOB ("fresh off the boat"). Of course, it is important to differentiate between the playful mimicking of stereotypes in which some Asian Americans may engage, versus actually believing and deploying them. Arielle noted that most of her best friends are white, but she plans to join an Asian club at school to get to know more Asian kids.

Arielle said that her background is "definitely" Chinese, or Asian, and the fact that her mother is very involved with the local FCC chapter has factored into this identification. She usually does not just tell people that she was adopted but is often asked about her non-Chinese last name. Her mother told me that one day Arielle came home from camp wearing a T-shirt she had made that displayed the word "Jewish-ish." Arielle explained that she uses this term "because my Mom's Jewish so I guess that makes me Jewish, but I've never gone to temple or had a bat mitzvah." Later, she added, "I am not strongly Jewish, but I still like to identify myself with it." She and her mother celebrate Hanukkah and Passover but are very reformed Jews (so much so that they have a Christmas tree). Arielle also noted that she has a lot of Jewish friends.

Arielle's mother shared with me an essay on racial identity that Arielle wrote during her freshman year in high school. This essay reveals a number of insights that had not emerged during our interview, perhaps because Arielle did not know me very well. I had not been sure how the teens I interviewed felt about participating in discussions with me as an adoption researcher, particularly because I was older (though in most cases younger than their parents) and Chinese American. While I had been concerned that I would get "model adoptee" responses, I also wondered whether the teens could somehow relate to me as a fellow Asian American who was neither their parent nor a peer. I also understood that their self-presentations were subject to change. As Audrey, the mother of the teenager who responded to the Tessler survey with "eggplant," reminded me, their answers may differ if you asked them the same questions fifteen minutes later.

In her essay, Arielle discusses becoming aware of race about the time she could first talk. She remembers patting her mother on her face and asking, "Why don't you look like me?" However, growing up in her diverse East Bay community, she felt that it "wasn't a big deal." More recently, however, she realized that she was the only "nonwhite person" at her extended family celebrations on the East Coast. She reflects, "At first I thought it was weird and felt like it bothered me, but the more I thought about it, the more I like it. I am unique and I don't blend in." She felt uncomfortable when attending a country club wedding in Philadelphia where she noticed that the only other people of color were the wait staff, noting that it "really bothered me and made me feel awkward." In Berkeley, however, she feels that she is part of a community of families with children adopted from China. She reflects, "Even though I don't hang out that much with those people, having them there gives me a feeling of not being an alien."

Later in the one-page essay, Arielle says that she wonders if she is becoming "whitewashed" because most of the people she spends time with are white. But she notes, "Still I'm conscious of race and I realize I have always had friends who are non-white." She concludes her essay as follows:

> I don't think I have had an extremely hard time with identity and race growing up. I would identify myself as Chinese American, adopted from China, but just as American as anyone else, and as someone who doesn't speak Mandarin or Cantonese but still is connected to my heritage and my birthplace. In [my very large high school] I find that having an identity among the people you know is not hard. However I think that in the whole school, having an identity is extremely hard. Sometimes I feel like I'm being judged when I walk down the halls because of my appearance, but in reality I don't think people notice me or care and I'm fine with that. As for when I'm on the streets I think people just accept what they see, an Asian girl. But I don't really know what people are thinking. I would like people to see me for more than my appearance but for my personality as well, but if they don't know me then how can they make that assessment.

Arielle seems comfortable with and aware of her racial identity but still struggles at times with the daily process of negotiating her identity, which she thinks is hard on some level for all teens. She says she has come to some realizations of the ways that race does matter in the broader world, including how it often corresponds to socioeconomic status. Yet she is trying to carve out a comfort zone from which she can further explore both her Asian identity and her Jewish identity.

St. Louis Revisited

In St. Louis in the summer of 2009, I had the opportunity to reinterview some parents I had initially met during my earlier trips in 2001 and 2004; in some cases, I also was able to interview their children, who were now teenagers. Now an outgoing and poised thirteen-year-old, Amanda Kelley had been only five or six years old when her parents invited me over for dinner in 2001. I recalled that during my previous visit, she had climbed onto my lap while we were sitting at the dinner table. Her mother joked that that probably was not going to happen again this time.

I discussed Amanda and her family in chapter 5 in relation to the question of Chinese language education. Her father, Paul, had emphasized that his children were culturally Irish and American, in addition to being Chinese. He had petitioned the Irish government to grant Amanda Irish citizenship, which had not been given to her automatically because she was not his biological child. Now that Amanda was a teenager, her Irish identity indeed seemed to be very strong. When we met, she wore a hurling jersey with the words "Wexford Cheddar" emblazoned on it. When I asked her about her shirt, she tried to explain what hurling was; she also noted that Wexford was the town her father was from, and that she and her family had visited Ireland numerous times. She said that she is very proud of being Irish, and of being the first Irish citizen adopted from China. Her father has told her that she is Irish and American, and thinks that she even has a slight Irish accent from being around him. Her older brother, now seventeen, also told me that he identified strongly with Irish culture and also European sports and comedy because of the influence of their father. He had done some school projects on Ireland and also some on his trip to China when he had traveled with his mother when they went to adopt his younger sister.

Amanda did not necessarily make a distinction between Irishness as a "racial" and a cultural or national identity. To her, being Irish was related to her citizenship, her having spent time in Ireland, and her strong bond to her Irish father. Amanda also identifies with China, having traveled there with her parents three years earlier to adopt her younger brother. On the trip, they visited the police station where she had been found and the orphanage where she had stayed as an infant. She admitted that she had "zoned out" on that day, and that it didn't really hit her that she was actually there. She talked the most about her younger brother, with whom she had a special bond, perhaps, she says, because she was one of the first family members to interact with him. When I had visited her home eight years previously, she had really liked the story of Mulan, as did many young girls her age adopted from China. I asked whether she still enjoyed Mulan, and she said she's not as crazy about the story as she used to be. Her main interests at the time of our interview were art, music, reading, and writing poetry. She showed me some of the artwork she had produced at school, at art classes, or on her own. She had won second place in a contest for her drawing of a bird, which was displayed on her bedroom door. She told me that she would like to be an artist when she grew up. When I asked if she had ever felt singled out for being Chinese, Amanda answered that she has sometimes encountered the stereotype that Chinese people are smart and nerdy (and admitted that she somewhat fits the nerd stereotype), but that she had not experienced anything strongly positive or negative regarding being Chinese.

I first met the Hurleys in 2001 when they invited me over to their house for a Shabbat dinner. At that time, their daughter Emma was six, and her younger brother, adopted from Vietnam, was four. I remember Emma saying the prayers in Hebrew and hearing from her parents about her interests in ballet and gymnastics and her brother's interests in learning karate. I contacted the Hurleys in 2009 to see if I could interview them again, and perhaps also interview Emma, who was now fourteen. I spoke first with her parents, Ron and Ella, and then interviewed Emma afterward. Her brother was out of town. Ron and Ella told me that Emma had just had her bat mitzvah and was a straight-A student and a karate champion. She had become interested in karate when watching her brother's class and had continued studying it even after he had stopped.

Ella was going to represent the United States in the Maccabi Games in the girls' fourteen- to fifteen-year-old karate competition later that summer in Israel. The Maccabi Games, Ron and Ella explained, were like an

Olympics for Jewish athletes, and Emma, like all other participants, had been required to get a letter from her rabbi to prove that she was Jewish. They recalled that at the tryouts, the karate coach had said he had been wondering if Emma was really Jewish, and Ron and Ella assured him that she was. However, she would probably be the only Asian competitor at the games. Ron noted that Emma accepted that fact and tried to not let it bother her. He said that she also would most likely be the only Asian in her high school. He estimated that her high school district was 90 percent black and 10 percent white, even though their city's population was 49 percent white, 45 percent black, and 2.8 percent Asian.[5] He explained that most Asian and many white families pull their kids out of the city's public schools, but he and Ella felt strongly about supporting the schools and the local community. Emma has been with the same set of friends, boys and girls, black and white, and even one Republican, they joked, since kindergarten. Before deciding to send their children to the local public schools, they had done research and determined that some students who had graduated from that school system were attending top colleges. However, they are a little more concerned about her younger brother, who has had comments made to him about his short stature and about being Asian. He is often asked why his skin and hair are "different." He came home from school saying he wanted to sag his pants (his parents said no), and they remain concerned about whether or not he will be able to "cut it" in the public school system without being too distracted by his social life.

Ron and Ella also pointed out that their children have many friends who were internationally adopted, so they do not feel that they are alone in this regard. They said that Emma identifies with being Chinese, but emphasizes that her Chineseness does not totally define who she is. Her bat mitzvah invitations included her English name, her Hebrew name, and her Chinese name (designed to look like a Chinese name stamp produced by a chop).

Following my talk with her parents, I had a shorter conversation alone with Emma, after her mother excused herself to go make dinner. Emma described herself as "Chinese, teen, kind of short, athletic, happy." I asked her if she would include "Jewish," and she said she wasn't sure, though she noted that she had gone to Hebrew school since the third grade and had had her bat mitzvah. I inquired about her upcoming trip to the Maccabi Games, and she said that she was excited to see Jerusalem and the Dead Sea. While it was interesting to note the differences in the ways that Emma's parents versus Emma herself presented her identity, perhaps this also speaks to the various levels on which identities are constructed for and perceived by adopted children, or perhaps a more common gap between what parents see as important elements defining the identities of their children and how children view themselves. For Emma, the fact that she is the only Asian in a school system that is predominantly black may not seem significant because she has grown up within this context. Her Jewishness is also something that has been part of her daily life since she was very young. If anything, like many teens, Emma wished to emphasize not what makes her unique but what makes her similar to her peers. Though she included "Chinese" in her list of descriptors, she did not assign special significance to this aspect of her identity. However, it is important to remember that identity is always in process, and that various aspects may become salient at different times, whether or not they become a central aspect of one's self-description. As her parents pointed out, Emma's mother, Ella, had begun to explore her own Jewish background in earnest as a college student.

One of my final interviews in St. Louis was conducted with two sisters, aged twelve (almost thirteen) and fourteen. Their mother worked for a local adoption agency and had helped me to coordinate my research trip to China in 2002, but I had not yet interviewed her or met her children. This was the only teen interview that I conducted with siblings together. Many of the teens I had interviewed had been singletons or did not have siblings from China or siblings who were old enough to participate in my study, which required a minimum age of thirteen. Mara, the fourteen-year-old, was tall and mature for her age. She was soft-spoken but seemed comfortable sharing her thoughts. Marney was more petite, athletic (she had run the mile at school in 6:44), energetic, and funny. They were going into seventh and ninth grade, respectively, at a public school. They both said they were excited to return to public school after having attended a private Catholic school for a few years because the public school was more diverse, something of which they were acutely aware. Marney said she was the only Asian in her grade, and it had been four years since there had been a black student at their school. Mara related an incident in which the teacher brought in a newspaper story about a school alumnus who had broken a record for the mile. He was black, and most of the kids had been surprised that a black student had ever attended their school. The girls also looked forward to their new school because it was much bigger and there were more classes and activities available. Marney said that her favorite subject is PE, and her worst is science. Mara said that her favorite subject is math, but she also likes English and literature.

Interestingly, Marney's mother had told me that Marney sometimes identifies as black. She surmised that this was perhaps because her skin tans deeply during the summer. Her sister's does not. Marney had come home one day and mentioned that she was black, like another friend of hers, and her mother had corrected her, saying that she was Chinese. At the end of my conversation alone with the two girls, Marney made another comment about being black like another boy she knew. Unfortunately, I did not have time to question her further about this.

Mara recalled that at their private school, the other students believed many stereotypes about Asians—that they were smart and never gained weight—and that they were often singled out for being Asian. Marney said that her art teacher once asked her whether she spoke Chinese when they were doing a lesson on Chinese art. Marney had replied that she spoke a few words, though she told me she wasn't sure whether she learned them from one of the adoption coordinators who had stayed with them at their home or from watching *Big Bird in China*. She said that people have made fun of her because of her eyes and that she laughed right along with them because she thought it was funny. However, it is unlikely that she really did think being laughed at was funny.

Mara shared an incident in which a fellow student who was part Asian from Hawaii had told the rest of the class that people in China eat unwanted babies. The other kids had believed this student because she was Asian, and though Mara tried to tell the class that this was not true, her teacher just told her to "let it go." She felt that the girl's comments had been aimed at her, as an adoptee, but she had been unable to set the record straight without the support of her teacher. Both Mara and Marney dismissed the fellow student who had made the comment as a "wannabe" Asian who wanted attention.

Despite the negative associations that some of their peers had made with Chinese culture, both girls seemed proud to be Chinese. Mara said that being Chinese "added more" to her. In contrast, she thought that others she knew were just plain American and did not have ethnic backgrounds. Similarly, Marney said that it was "kind of cool" being Chinese and "not just American." They had attended adoption agency reunions and the Chinese Culture Days at the Missouri Botanical Garden. They told me that they like to look at pictures and videos from their adoption trip and like having Chinese things such as a big fan, Chinese Barbies, and Chinese yo-yos at home. In listing their Chinese possessions, Marney started to describe something that had a "big dude" with "little dudes" inside. I suggested that these were probably Russian nesting dolls.

Both girls said that they would like to visit China, but maybe just for a vacation. Their mother had mentioned earlier that they were not interested in visiting their orphanages. Marney said she wanted to see the Great Wall and to get a sense of how she lived when she was a baby in China. She added that she would like to see people practicing tai chi with swords, as she had seen in *Big Bird in China*.

The girls' cursory knowledge of Chinese culture may relate to Anagnost's (2000) critique of adoptive parents' approaches to Chinese culture as "culture bites," discussed earlier. In a sense, my asking them about the material cultural objects from China in their home was reinforcing the notion prevalent in contemporary U.S. multiculturalism that culture is something that is material and displayed. The girls have had other forms of contact with China and Chinese culture, such as through interactions with adoption coordinators from China who stayed at their home and with whom they occasionally talked on the phone. And though Marney often referenced *Big Bird in China* as her source of information about China, she was also curious about China in others ways. She had done a report on the Dragon Emperor for school. Mara had been interested in finding out whether child obesity and other health issues she had learned about in health class affect people in China. And while both girls had been singled out for being Asian and/or adopted at school and did not get support from their teachers in addressing these issues, they appeared to have a very strong sense that it was the others who were in the wrong.

I had been impressed by Mara's overall sense of social justice. After the interview had ended and I turned off the tape recorder, I continued to chat with the girls for a bit. I noticed that Mara was wearing a wristband that said "Stop Hate." When I asked her about it, she explained that it also said "Remember Matthew Shepard." She said that it had been available on the website of one of her favorite bands, and Marney had paid for the shipping for Mara's birthday. Mara said she liked the bracelet because it made a statement against hate crimes. She also mentioned that she had seen a video on meat production and was going to become a vegetarian, maybe a vegan (Marney said that this would be good because there would be more meat for her). Marney, on the other hand, seemed more interested in popular culture, which may in part explain the references to *Big Bird in China*. When I asked the girls what they knew about Asian Americans in popular culture, Marney had mentioned a number TV shows that featured Asian Americans, including *Heroes*, *Wendy Wu: Homecoming Warrior*, and *Kung Fu Panda*. Experts have emphasized the importance of Asian American children seeing representations of themselves on television and in the movies,[6] which signifies that they are part of mainstream society and provides them with role models. The fact that Marney had interpreted these characters as Asian illustrated her developing consciousness as an Asian American. Of course, she will also need to learn how to critically interpret these representations and the stereotypes contained within them, something that is not easy to do for many Asian Americans.

Though these sisters are only twenty months apart and were raised in the same household, their overall interests and even their racial identities are distinct. Perhaps they will also approach their identities as Chinese Americans and adoptees in different ways, while also influencing one another. It is difficult to gauge the full extent of their interests from my short conversation with them, but Mara's interest in social justice and Marney's in popular culture parallel two of the main trends I have seen in Asian American student approaches to identity. While a relative minority view Asian American issues within the context of activism and social justice, the majority enjoy connecting with other Asian Americans around shared popular culture and similar interests. Of course, some may be interested in both aspects of being Asian American, and their interests may change over time as a result of course work and mentoring by peers and student services personnel.

As the teen profiles I have shared demonstrate, there is a wide degree of variation in the ways that teens adopted from China express their identities—as teens, as adoptees, and as Chinese Americans or Asian Americans. There is no predicable pattern that explains how place of residence, parental background, or other factors shape these identities. And teenage interests, worries, and obsessions are always changing and will continue to do so. In many ways, adoptee identities may share similarities with hapa, or mixed-race Asian, identities. The work of Kip Fulbeck (2006), a hapa activist, artist, and scholar, emphasizes the importance of individual self-expression for hapa individuals, who are always being defined by others due to their sometimes ambiguous phenotypical features, which often defy easy racial categorization. In his Hapa Project, he photographed hapas from the shoulders up and asked them to describe themselves in their own words and handwriting. The photo and self-description were displayed on facing pages in his book, *Part Asian, 100% Hapa*. For hapas, cultural identities are equally complicated and may be a complex blend of Asian and other influences. Similarly, for adoptees, it is important to realize that neither their Chineseness nor their Americanness solely defines them. It is my hope that the varied portraits of the teens in this chapter illustrate the complexity of their identities.

8

Conclusion

A Global Network for ADOPTED, HAPA, & FOSTERED PEOPLE & FRIENDS Worldwide.

WHO WE ARE

We *are* Adopted, Fostered, & Hapa individuals *of all ages* from Hong Kong, Taiwan, mainland China, & across the globe. Some of us do NOT always *feel* "Chinese," even if our birthmothers happened to be in Asia when we were born. Some of us feel Jewish, British, Canadian, Spanish, Southern Californian, proud New *Yawkers!* or a mix of things. Some of us feel *very* Chinese, and maybe we speak Chinese quite well. Some of us *may* NOT speak Chinese at all. From Adopted & Fostered Adults of the African Diaspora to the Transnational & Transracial Adoption Group to our big sister organization The Mothers' Bridge of Love of the United Kingdom to Also-Known-As in NYC, we are proud sisters and brothers of Adopted, Fostered, and Hapa individuals around the world. All of us are human beings with hopes and dreams.

The preceding statement was found on the web page for Chinese Adoptee Links, the organization mentioned earlier that sponsored the trip to Ireland and England for its teenage "Global Girl" ambassadors. It emphasizes the connections between Chinese adoptees from various parts of the globe, but also the diversity that exists within this group in terms of relationships to both Chineseness and other axes of identity. It explicitly addresses the possibility that one may not feel very Chinese, despite the Asian origins of one's birth mother, but also the possibility that one might feel "very Chinese." The group envisions itself as a sister group to a number of other organizations that support internationally adopted or fostered individuals, including Also-Known-As, Inc., an organization run by adult Korean adoptees. The statement ends with an affirmation of the fact that "all of us are human beings with hopes and dreams." Founded by Chinese adoptee, writer, and scholar Jennifer Jue-Steuck, Chinese Adoptee Links speaks to the possible creation of what Eleana Kim (2010) calls a "counterpublic" in reference to the global activist movement of Korean adoptees. While this is an endeavor that has a broad vision, and is more limited in actual membership, it is important to consider how we have gotten to a place where such an endeavor is imaginable. How are adoptees creating space to express their varied identities?

My research shows that parents learn about issues of culture and racism to varying degrees—in some cases this reinforces existing Orientalisms, and in others parents begin to gain insight into how their children are being racialized. Meanings surrounding Chineseness are negotiated within the daily lives of adoptive families to varying extents. The fact that the daily schedules and multiple priorities of adoptive families result in the negotiation of Chinese culture activities might imply that Chineseness will be further excerpted and essentialized as it takes a back burner to other priorities. However, this "messiness" also may allow room for children to use and reinterpret these elements of Chineseness in their own ways.

As shown by the example of lifebooks in chapters 6 and 7, there is some space that opens up for children to begin to craft and shape their own identities. I do not want to imply that they are free to reshape identities as they wish, as the meanings surrounding Chineseness remain attached to historically rooted discourses that can be perpetuated when appropriated by white adoptive parents. But within this color-blind atmosphere, there remain ways for Asian adoptees to draw upon these decontextualized sources in making statements of identity that disrupt and provide alternatives to some of these images. This is demonstrated in chapter 7, which illustrated the ways that some teens' conceptions of Chineseness did not reflect the essentialized and static views that are characteristic of the Orientalist perspectives that their parents may have inherited and inadvertently perpetuated. Rather, they carved out a more fluid and de-essentialized relationship to Chineseness, mainstream white culture, and adoption, which reflected a resistance to being categorized or stereotyped based on these labels. While on the surface their responses may appear to represent model adoptee responses, their conceptions of Chineseness also illustrated the decoupling of associations between Chineseness as a racial origin, birthplace, and ethnic identity. Moreover, these teens also demonstrate that models of bicultural socialization that rely on essentialized notions of what is "Chinese" and what is "American" do not reflect the complexity of identities.

Asian American Parents

While it may initially appear that white parents have great flexibility in experimenting with culture, given that they are accustomed to exercising ethnic options (Waters 1990), the earlier examples show how Asian American adoptive parents retain the privilege of assumed authenticity, which may also grant them license to invent cultural traditions anew. The Asian American adoptive parents I profiled in chapter 4 illustrate that the process of Chinese identity construction is dynamic and ongoing, often involving the interpretation of practices and values as "Chinese." Some Asian American parents, particularly those who said that they were not making specific efforts to teach their children about China and Chinese culture beyond the mixture of traditions that they recognized as Asian or Asian American that they grew up with, may appear to be providing their children with even less overt Chinese cultural content than white parents who approach the issues in a more deliberate way. Of course, this begs the question of what constitutes Chinese culture, acknowledging, of course, that it is a construction and that no definitive versions exist. Is it the more tangible material items and ritual practices symbolizing Chineseness, or is it specific values (e.g., frugality, respect for elders, close-knit family) or daily practices that within a U.S. context may not be identified as specifically Chinese?

Most Asian American parents I interviewed saw Chinese American culture as adaptive, and to some extent a matter of selective choice, having observed how in the context of their own families, certain practices may have persisted, others may have come to represent new meanings, and still others might have been invented anew. But while some Asian American parents did not worry much about inserting Chinese customs into the home, this did not necessarily correlate with whether they addressed issues of adoption or racism. As I discussed in chapter 4, for many Asian American parents, direct experiences with issues of race and racism may result in different understandings of the relationship between race and culture.

But while some emphasized the importance of making their children aware of the positioning of Asian Americans as racial minorities, not all Asian American parents were concerned about the racism that they or their children may face. Many observed that particularly in the Bay Area, families like theirs were not unusual, and the Asian and Asian American presence was large. They did not recall their children experiencing much racism, though like the white parents in chapter 5, they tended to view racism as consisting of overt acts of discrimination and had perhaps internalized mainstream attitudes of color blindness with which they had grown up.

White Adoptive Parents

It is also important to remember the variation that exists among white adoptive parents. While some white parents who have not had much exposure to Chinese or Chinese American culture may take too many liberties with their constructions of Chinese culture, essentially removing it from any deeply rooted meanings attached to Chinese or Chinese American identities, others may become fluent in Chinese and know more about China and Chinese culture than some Chinese American parents. In the documentary *Somewhere Between*, Fang "Jenni" Lee's white adoptive mother had learned to speak Mandarin, and often spoke it at the dinner table along with her two daughters adopted from China. Interestingly, their non-Mandarin-speaking Chinese American father was left out of those conversations. Other parents may focus primarily on connecting to Asian American resources that help them deal with issues of racism and discrimination. Many white parents I interviewed also held nuanced conceptions of the relationship between Chinese and Chinese American culture and made efforts to connect to and draw upon the large and varied Chinese American and Asian American population in the areas in which they lived. In addition, other subject positions, such as coming from an immigrant family or being a minority due to one's sexual orientation, made some white parents more cognizant of the structural hierarchies within which meanings of race, class, and gender play out. One of Selina's mothers, Paula, described her wish to teach her daughter about Chinese culture to both reflect the diversity of the Chinese American community so that she will "feel comfortable in her own skin" and "know about what people in China do." Their productions of Chinese culture existed within a broader framework of other family traditions. Paula reflected, "I come from sort of a funny family. . . . We're Croatian immigrants, and on the Fourth of July my ninety-year-old aunt brings out the piñata. . . . This is her idea of how you celebrate the Fourth of July, and we have it while we're drinking our Slivovitz!"

When their daughter was little, they would hang up paper lanterns and other decorations to "make the images," but now the focus is more on traditions relating to family. Selina receives red envelopes on Chinese New Year and teaches her non-Chinese relatives how to make *jiao zi* (dumplings). Paula and her partner, Kelly, also try to expose their daughter to the "layers of culture" that make up the diverse Bay Area Chinese American community, and they have many friends who are part of bicultural Chinese American adoptive families. More important, they have tried to teach Selina to stand up against social injustices, whether racism or homophobia.

Audrey, mentioned earlier, had been centrally involved in parents' organizations from the time her daughter was an infant. She lamented to me that many adoptive parents prioritize gathering as a community of adoptive families with children from China, at the expense of fostering connections with the vibrant and varied Chinese American community in the Bay Area. She and her husband are conversant in Chinese and have provided opportunities for their daughter (also fluent in Mandarin after attending a Chinese immersion school) to maintain connections to her orphanage in China through repeated return visits and involvement in charitable and book projects.

St. Louis versus the Bay Area

Most of the Asian American adoptive parents I interviewed lived in the Bay Area, which is characterized by a multiracial politics in which Asians play a significant role. Though I also interviewed some white parents in the Bay Area, most of the white parents I interviewed came from St. Louis, and most of their attitudes reflected the predominantly black-white racial politics of that area. It might be tempting to speculate that because of the relative lack of resources on Chinese culture in St. Louis as a midwestern city, Chineseness will inevitably be put on the back burner and be replaced by other activities. But based on my research interviews in the Bay Area, despite the relative abundance of Chinese cultural resources there, many parents used similar approaches, seeking out other adoptive families and Chinese American friends and attending Chinese cultural events. Some Bay Area parents did have more options at their disposal—for example, many parents I interviewed sent their children to Chinese immersion programs and hired Chinese babysitters to further expose their children to Chinese culture and people on an everyday basis. At the Bay Area FCC playdates I attended, I would often see parents from both white and Asian American backgrounds participating and sharing knowledge about Chinese and Chinese American culture.

Thus, many Bay Area adoptive parents, both Asian American and white, said that because of the strong presence of Chinese and other Asian cultures in the region, they did not have to go out of their way to experience Chinese culture or to expose their children to it. This may have been true in a sense, depending on how these parents defined Chinese culture and conceived of its relationship to Chinese American culture or a broader multicultural, cosmopolitan environment. Does practicing Chinese culture mean observing particular traditions that are distinctively Chinese, interacting with Chinese or Chinese Americans on a regular basis in everyday life, or something else? Is culture something that people need to consciously try to practice, or is it part and parcel of one's everyday environment? As Mei observes in chapter 7, essentialized ideas were still implemented, often by Chinese Americans themselves, such as the parents and teachers at her Chinese immersion school. This is likely a by-product of trying to create a sense of Chineseness in the context of a U.S. society that subscribes to a particularly celebratory form of multiculturalism.

In St. Louis, I found that due to the demographics of the area, adoptive parents were more likely to seek out associations with Chinese people as cultural experts, for example, a local woman who taught cooking classes, another who owned a shop selling Chinese antiques, the woman who ran small group Chinese language and culture classes, the Chinese head of the local adoption agency, and the Taiwanese American adviser to FCC. It is difficult to say whether Jacobson's (2008) observation about the tendency for adoptive parents to seek out authentic Chinese from China as opposed to Chinese Americans was in operation here, as the line between "Chinese" and "Chinese American" is fuzzy. Many of these people had been in the United States for quite some time, even raising their children here, and held U.S. citizenship, yet it is unclear whether they saw themselves as Chinese American. Still, most of these Chinese culture authorities did speak fluent Chinese, which remains a marker of Chinese cultural authenticity. Parents also sought out experiences such as dining at Chinese restaurants, both as part of general cultural exposure and in an attempt to expose their children to other Chinese people. Many parents in St. Louis also brought their children to a Chinese pediatrician (from Hong Kong).

Ethnic Options Revisited?

Sociologist Miri Song (2003) argues that racial minorities can exercise some ethnic options as they strategically reframe negative images about their group that have been imposed on them by others or "reappropriate" them for the creation of new, positive meanings. Her application of Waters's concept of ethnic options to racial minorities politicizes the idea and gives it an instrumentality that differs from its use with white ethnics. As Chinese adoptees continue to craft their identities, the capacity to critically interpret and to (re)contextualize representations of Chinese or Chinese American culture will continue to be key. After all, whether they realize it or not, the versions of Chinese culture created by adoptive parents and adoptees through these processes of negotiation do not exist in a vacuum. Rather, they coexist with all of the other elements that constitute contemporary family lives, including their ethnic and religious identities. So what is at issue here, I think, is not whether "Chinese" culture is removed from any imagined original context but rather how elements of Chineseness are assigned meaning, politicized, and recontextualized within the context of adoptive families' lives. The seemingly decontextualized versions of Chinese culture that adoptees create may share similarities with those of other Asian Americans who are attempting to create identities that are removed from traditional and constraining conceptions of Chineseness.

Indeed, if we examine the diverse Chinese American community, we realize that there are a multitude of possible formations of Chinese culture, each combining elements of Chinese culture within an interpretive framework of family, values, and traditions. This begs the question of the extent to which newly invented forms of Chinese culture are bound by history and context. It is also important to remember that for Chinese adoptees raised by both white and Asian American adoptive parents, these processes do not occur in a vacuum, and that cognizance of stereotypes and processes of racialization is key to negotiating these new forms of identity, for the racial implications of Chinese identity, though they have changed throughout history, remain clear.

It is also clear that for adoptees, the capacity to critically interpret and to recontextualize representations of Chinese or Chinese American culture is key. After all, the Chinese culture created by adoptive families, whether Asian American or white, coexists with the Jonas Brothers, football practice, manga, Mexican food, and all the other interests about which the teens I interviewed were passionate, and which constitute contemporary family lives. Representations of Chinese Americans and China, both positive and negative, are found within popular culture and social interactions. They are framed by a politics of race and multiculturalism within which parents and children must construct meaning, and this meaning-making occurs in relation to these decontextualized (or recontextualized) aspects of Chinese culture and the consumption of cultural goods and symbols.

In deconstructing some of the cultural politics that underlie the processes of Chinese identity construction, we see how Chinese adoptees can claim both U.S. and Chinese American identities yet also express a tenuous connection to China. But while I argue that culture is pervasive as a mediating tool in discussions of identity in a U.S. context, I also assert that race cannot and should not drop out of the picture.

Final Thoughts

In what ways will Chinese adoptees participate in the creation of new Asian American subcultures? Eleana Kim's (2010) ethnography of

Korean adoptee activism points to a global movement that has been decades in the making. Fueled by a sense of shared anger, alienation, and marginalization, the Korean adoptee movement was facilitated by a combination of new technologies such as the Internet, and by the passion and persistence of groups of adoptees from the International Korean Adoptee Associations who organized the first Gathering and those that followed. They have rallied around a variety of issues, including gaining South Korean citizenship for Korean adoptees, supporting unwed mothers in Korea, gaining access to adoption records, and ending international adoption from Korea altogether. These movements exist alongside, and in some cases as alternatives to, parent-led Korean adoption organizations. Some Korean adoptees have played an active role in mentoring Chinese adoptees and their parents. Korean adoptees have also spoken out in the form of performance art and other creative forms of expression.

Will Chinese adoptees feel the same sense of urgency and alienation as earlier generations of Korean adoptees? Or does neoliberal self-fashioning allow room for Chinese adoptees to begin crafting their own forms of Chinese adoptee culture that enable them to channel their energies differently? Even though discourses of Chinese identity are framed by color-blind discourses that shunt discussions of Chinese identity into the realm of an often abstracted and aestheticized "Chinese" culture, Chinese adoptees are still able to work in dialogue within (or around) these discourses of Chinese culture as they craft their ever-changing relationship to Chineseness. As I have argued, processes of Chinese American and Asian American cultural and identity production are open-ended and inventive, often responding to or building upon the ambiguities left in the ways their own parents practiced Chinese culture. Though juxtaposing older generations of Asian American adoptive parents with Chinese adoptees is not an equivalent comparison, it may be productive to think about Chinese adoptee cultural production as similarly open-ended. Moreover, as Eleana Kim demonstrates, at least for Korean adoptee activists, Korean adoptee culture involves much more than the replication of Korean or Korean American culture, but rather is formed in relation to political issues that are particularly salient for them. Similarly, Chinese adoptee cultural production may involve both the practice of customs thought to represent Chinese culture and also those that modify or resist certain aspects of this culture. Just as Korean adoptee activism represents only a portion of organized Korean adoptee activities, and Asian American political activism is similarly limited to a relatively small percentage of the population, it is also likely that the majority of Chinese adoptees will express their identities in a variety of creative ways that are not overtly political in the sense of organized political action, but rather as forms of creative cultural production that speak to and possibly revise multicultural politics. These could include blogs, comics, creative writing, films, and other forms of expression.

In some ways, viewing Chineseness as a flexible form of cultural capital may liberate people of Chinese descent, whether adopted or not, to cultivate a sense of Chinese identity that is framed in a positive light and as something that is an asset rather than a liability. As illustrated throughout this ethnography, Chinese adoptees and their parents, whether Chinese or white, flexibly draw upon a variety of resources in crafting their Chinese identities. Some Chinese adoptees choose to create and maintain direct relationships to China through frequent travel there and involvement in charitable organizations. These activities are often encouraged and facilitated by their parents, including the fluent Chinese language skills that parents have helped them cultivate through bilingual immersion programs and other forms of Chinese language training, in addition to opportunities to travel to China. Mei, for example, had been back to her orphanage a number of times. Nevertheless, she found a different type of satisfaction in exploring Asian American identities that were nontraditional and crafted through her own friendships outside of a Chinese or Chinese American context.

Still others did not possess Chinese language skills and chose to engage with Chineseness in other ways, or sometimes by employing objects that signify Asian or Asian Americanness more broadly. Not surprisingly, in the context of globalization and increasing interest in Asia, many found that their peers without direct connections to China or adoption were also expressing interest in Asia and Asian goods. Of course, the concern for those who engage in the consumption of information and Asian objects is how to critically interpret what they see through the Orientalist lens that continues to permeate Western views of the East and is perhaps responsible for both seemingly positive and negative images associated with it.

This brings us back to the question posed at the outset of this book in relation to my own experiences but also more broadly: To what extent should a Chinese American be defined by his or her Chineseness, and what forms can Chineseness take in today's world, in which both authenticity and context can be called into question? We saw that Asian American adoptive parents experimented with Chineseness over the course of their lives, and these processes continued as they became parents. But ideas about what it means to be Chinese can be contested, and are often loaded, and this happens in particular ways for adoptees. As discussed previously, ideas about Chinese cultural authenticity can be used to lay claims on Chineseness as a form of capital and to restrict others from these claims. However, concerns remain about how the creation of versions of Chineseness that are largely decontextualized from broader structural realities will play out in the real world.

Although it would have been tempting to continue researching Chinese adoptee teens, this project had to come to a close. I am confident that this topic will not be left unexplored and will possibly by pursued Chinese adoptees themselves. But in other ways, this is a natural end point for this project, as many Chinese adoptees are now of college age and entering a new phase of their lives as they continue to pursue their varied interests and passions as young adults. Like the Asian American adoptive parents I interviewed, their identities are complex and continue to change. While adoption and Chineseness undoubtedly remain an important part of who they are, they are part of multilayered and multifaceted identities.

In this sense, I return to a theme discussed throughout this book—the importance of looking at Chinese adoptee culture being produced in relation to shifting and multilayered discourses on race, culture, and adoption that circulate around adoptees. Thus, rather than worrying that Chinese culture is being taken out of context, we might move beyond this to look for the new context within which these elements of Chinese culture are being produced and altered, as Chinese adoptees attempt to create their own meanings surrounding them. As Asian Americans who have historically been positioned between black and white, and as adoptees who have particularly complicated relationships to Chineseness and whiteness, Chinese adoptees are well positioned to speak to (and beyond) the black-white racial politics that currently define U.S. multiculturalism, though they may not do so directly. As they enter varied professions, becoming doctors, special education teachers, artists, and a myriad of others, they may speak to adoption, race, family, and identity in various ways, some direct and some indirect, through their actions, interests, and other choices they make. Some of these discussions may take place not at the center of but rather around the edges of parent-driven conversations about Chineseness and adoption, in new spaces that are being created at the intersection of race, culture, and adoption.

NOTES

CHAPTER 1. INTRODUCTION

1 I thank Sara Dorow for sharing this insight in her comments on a draft of my manuscript.

2 The term "birth culture" is often used by adoptive parents to refer to the culture of the country or region from which their children were adopted. While I understand that parents are trying to honor the ethnic origins of their child, the term is also problematic, as people are not born with culture. Rather, culture is a product of the environment in which one is raised. For this reason, in its first usage, I put this term in quotes, as it does not reflect my own conception of the term. Subsequent uses of the term will not be put in quotes.

3 Works by Yngvesson (2007) and Howell (2007) explore adoption from the perspective of new kinship and family formations.

4 These are sometimes overlapping categories.

5 I thank Sara Dorow (personal communication) for this observation and am borrowing her use of this term to discuss this phenomenon.

6 I was unable to find statistics for the number of Asian American adoptive parents.

7 Anagnost, an anthropologist, assures us that she is not concerned with the authenticity of cultural productions themselves. However, for many non-anthropologists, an implicit comparison to imagined authentic versions of Chinese culture appears to be at work.

8 Interestingly, my aunt and sometimes my mother make corned beef and cabbage around Saint Patrick's Day, though they will never be mistaken for Irish.

9 I thank an anonymous reviewer for this suggestion.

10 I thank the reviewer for NYU Press for pointing out that the scrutiny may be directed more toward the adopted child than toward the adoptive parents, as all parents experience scrutiny of their parenting actions (Hays 1996).

11 Thanks to an anonymous reviewer for NYU Press for this observation.

CHAPTER 2. A BACKGROUND ON TRANSNATIONAL AND TRANSRACIAL ADOPTION

1 I interviewed a total of thirty-five adoptive parents (because they were interviewed together, I count each couple as a single unit) in St. Louis, one of which was Chinese American. In eleven cases I talked with the husband and wife together, but in most cases I spoke with the mother alone. Of this group, five were

single mothers at the initial interview, though two later married. I reinterviewed seven of the St. Louis families and periodically interacted with many more over the number of years I visited St. Louis for research and through personal relationships I developed with some families. In most cases, families had at least one girl from China, though many families had adopted a second child, often a boy, from another country such as Vietnam.

In the San Francisco Bay Area, I interviewed a total of twenty-one adoptive parents, fourteen of whom were Asian American and seven of whom were white. I spoke with three men, who were interviewed as part of a couple. Of the Bay Area group, five were single mothers, and one was a lesbian (her partner was not at home at the time of the interview, but I had met her at a previous event). I also interviewed one adoption worker and another adoptive mother who had authored and coedited books on adoption.

I spoke with fifteen teens in all, all of whom were female. Nine were in the Bay Area, and seven in St. Louis. Of the Bay Area teens, five had white parents, and four had Chinese American parents. The seven teens I spoke with in St. Louis all had white parents, four of whom I had interviewed more than once; I had also associated with their families at numerous adoption events.

I do not claim that this distribution is representative of the adoptive population as a whole. Given the nature of qualitative research, I did not attempt to replicate a profile of the adoptive community in my sample. The sample is weighted toward St. Louis because I started my research there before it evolved to include the comparative element of Asian American adoptive parents and teens. Upon reflection, I realize that I could have conducted fewer interviews in St. Louis to provide a better balance with the San Francisco Bay Area data, but most interviews were conducted before the study evolved into a comparative one. Nearly all interviewees were from middle-class to upper-middle-class backgrounds, reflecting the demographic of China adoptive families more broadly. The balance of the emphasis of this book's chapters reflects the amount of data available on each group.

2   My sample was inherently biased, given that only those parents who were interested in talking about issues of Chinese culture and identity would respond to a recruitment notice from a Chinese American anthropologist who was asking about these issues. I made my personal background and my areas of academic interest and expertise (Asian and Asian American studies) clear in the recruitment notice.

3   I put the word "Chinese" in quotation marks to call attention to the different ideas of authenticity or lack of authenticity applied to the term in various situations. Thus, while to some people I may have appeared Chinese because of my physical appearance, I may not be viewed as culturally Chinese because I was not born and raised in a Chinese country and do not speak Chinese fluently.

4   In contrast to Jacobson's research, some parents were open to contact with Chinese Americans rather than only Chinese from China. However, one key

distinction may involve how to define Chinese versus Chinese Americans. Is it a question of legal citizenship? Language fluency? Length of time in the United States?

5 The "model minority" myth refers to the common perceptions that Asian Americans excel in education and the workplace, and also are well behaved, causing little trouble. The problem with this myth is that it does not hold true for all Asian Americans and is often used by conservatives to favorably compare Asian American achievements to those of other minority groups. Rooted in Orientalist ideas, the perpetual foreigner myth is based on stereotypes of Asian Americans as not assimilating to mainstream U.S. culture; it has resulted in suspicion of Asian American loyalty to the United States, such as in Japanese internment during World War II and the Wen Ho Lee case, in which a Taiwanese American scientist working for the Los Alamos National Laboratory in California was falsely accused of selling secrets about U.S. nuclear weapons to China.

6 Hopgood is the author of an adoption memoir titled *Lucky Girl* (2009). A former reporter for the *St. Louis Post-Dispatch*, she was invited to speak in May 2009 to the St. Louis FCC chapter about her book.

7 See http://quickfacts.census.gov/qfd/states/29/29189.html.

8 Ling discussed the significance of Chinese Culture Days in *Chinese St. Louis*, 222–24.

9 Knowledge and appreciation of Chinese cuisine are two symbolic markers of identification with China and Chinese culture, in a manner consistent with other forms of symbolic ethnicity in the context of U.S. multiculturalism. For example, Roger Rouse (1995) notes that popular ethnic street festivals involve public displays and associations with "traditional" foods and cultural products to represent the diversity within U.S. culture.

10 The very idea of birth culture conflates geographic and biological origins of culture, when in reality cultural practices are flexible and dynamic and sometimes do not correlate with ancestral origins.

11 Dorow (2006b, 216) notes that there is a range of approaches to Chinese cultural education, represented by the four key strategies practiced by adoptive parents she interviewed, which are assimilation, celebrating plurality, a balancing act, and immersion.

CHAPTER 3. BEGINNINGS

1 Dorow's chapter "Client, Ambassador, and Gift" (Dorow 2006b) also provides an ethnographic account and analysis of the two-week adoption trip.

2 A 2013 ban on Russian adoptions to the United States has since ended this flow.

3 These comments indicated that the transnational adoption of Chinese babies is gendered for both adoptive parents and locals. Though it was important to locals to establish whether or not the baby was a girl or a boy, and many adoptive parents told me that people often seemed relieved when they found out that a boy

was not being taken out of the country, the locals nevertheless saw the adoptive parents of these baby girls as being "lucky."

4 "Waiting parents" is a term used for parents who have submitted their adoption paperwork and are waiting to receive their referrals and travel to China to adopt their children.

5 "Double eyelids," which have a crease running across them, are common in most white people and in part of the Asian population. They are thought to make the eye look bigger, and some Asians and Asian Americans choose to have blepharo-plasty, or "double eyelid surgery," to achieve this effect.

6 Walmart actually has stores in China also.

7 The China-based agency employees accompanied the parents on each leg of their journal, and local guides in each city helped out with both paperwork and other logistics.

8 An official gift shop run by the government.

9 The Joneses ended up spending a semester in China with their two daughters in 2009.

10 I thank Sara Dorow for reminding me to articulate this point.

11 On a 2010 visit to Shamian Island, much of the area was under construction. While quite a few shops catering to adoptive families remained, many I had visited back in 2002 were no longer present.

CHAPTER 4. ASIAN AMERICAN ADOPTIVE PARENTS

1 A *cheong-sam* (Mandarin: *qi pao*) is a traditional long silk Chinese dress. Most of the dresses available for sale to adoptive families at souvenir shops are polyester.

2 Thanks to Sara Dorow for highlighting this part of his statement.

3 Thanks to Sara Dorow for encouraging me to emphasize this point.

4 Peranakan Chinese are the mixed-race descendants of Chinese immigrants to Malaysia, Indonesia, and Singapore.

5 Sara Dorow found similar experiences with the Asian American adoptive parents she interviewed in her 2006 study of Chinese adoption in the Bay Area and Minnesota.

6 Hawaii's multiculturalism of course relates to Lowe's conceptualization of forms of hybridity that emerge from colonial and other histories of unequal power.

7 Hop Sing was a stereotyped and always subservient Chinese character in the television series *Bonanza*.

CHAPTER 5. WHITE PARENTS' CONSTRUCTIONS OF CHINESENESS

1 Thanks to Laurie Medina for helping me clarify this comment.

2 See Dorow (2006b) and Volkman (2005) for discussions of the importance of birthplace for adoptive parents.

3 In their study of the approaches to race of parents of transnationally adopted Koreans, Shiao, Tuan, and Rienzi (2004, 8) identify three main approaches: "emphasizing the exotic yet non-threatening aspects of their child's racial

differences"; "acknowledging the significance of race and racism in America"; and "a color-blind approach in which their child's Asian-ness was essentially 'e-raced' or overlooked."

4 "Biracial" usually refers to a child who is black and white.

5 The transracial adoption of African American children has sparked controversy in the past, most visibly in the strong objection voiced by the National Association of Black Social Workers in 1972, which stated that white parents would be unable to raise black children to adequately deal with racism.

6 The perception that St. Louis had a large Asian community was of course a subjective one.

7 Due to the history of the term, discussed in the introduction, "Oriental" is considered to be a problematic label, particularly when used in reference to Asian people.

CHAPTER 6. NEGOTIATING CHINESENESS IN EVERYDAY LIFE

1 See also Anagnost (2000, 212).

2 I thank Michael Largey for reminding me to emphasize this point.

3 I thank an anonymous reviewer for this comment.

4 This process was shown in the documentary *Somewhere Between*.

5 Volkman (2005) builds on Oulette and Belleau's argument that birth/biological ties become part of a "deactivated, objectivized archive" that are replaced by adoptive ties.

CHAPTER 7. DON'T OBJECTIFY ME

1 The term "hapa," originally from Hawaii, refers to mixed-raced individuals. In the context of mainland Asian American culture, it has become a word used by mixed-race Asian Americans to describe their backgrounds, and in some cases as an identity base for empowerment.

2 Sumi Gambhir, "Students Discuss Asian American Stereotypes, Culture," *State News*, March 19, 2007.

3 I thank Brandt Peterson for suggesting this reference.

4 See http://chineseadopteelinks.wordpress.com/about/.

5 See http://quickfacts.census.gov/qfd/states/29/2975220.html.

6 See Adachi's film *The Slanted Screen* (2006).

REFERENCES

Adachi, Jeff. 2006. *The Slanted Screen: Asian Men in Film and Television*. Asian American Media Mafia.

Anagnost, Ann. 1997. *National Pastimes: Narrative, Representation, and Power in Modern China*. Durham, NC: Duke University Press.

———. 2000. Scenes of Misrecognition: Maternal Citizenship in the Age of Transnational Adoption. *positions: east asia cultures critique* 8 (2): 389–421.

Ang, Ien. 2001. *On Not Speaking Chinese: Living between Asia and the West*. London: Routledge.

Appadurai, Arjun. 1990. Disjuncture and Difference in the Global Cultural Economy. *Public Culture* 2 (2): 1–24.

———. 1991. Global Ethnoscapes: Notes and Queries for a Transnational Anthropology. In *Recapturing Anthropology: Working in the Present*, edited by Richard G. Fox, 191–210. Santa Fe: School of American Research Press.

Appiah, Anthony. 1994. Identity, Authenticity, Survival: Multicultural Societies and Social Reproduction. In *Multiculturalism: Examining the Politics of Recognition*, edited by Charles Taylor, 159–60. Princeton, NJ: Princeton University Press.

Baden, Amanda. 2002. The Psychological Adjustment of Transracial Adoptees: An Application of the Culture-Race Identity Model. *Journal of Social Distress and the Homeless* 11 (2): 106–25.

Bergquist, K. J. S., M. E. Vonk, D. S. Kim, and M. D. Feit, eds. 2007. *International Korean Adoption: A Fifty-Year History of Policy and Practice*. London: Routledge.

Bondi, Liz. 1993. Locating Identity Politics. In *Place and the Politics of Identity*, edited by M. Keith and S. Pile, 84–101. London: Routledge.

Bonilla-Silva, Eduardo. 2009. *Racism without Racists: Color-Blind Racism and the Persistence of Racial Inequality in America*. Lanham, MD: Rowman and Littlefield.

Borshay Liem, Deann. 2000. *First Person Plural*. Mu Films.

Bureau of Consular Affairs, U.S. Department of State. 2014. Intercountry Adoption, Statistics, Adoptions by Country. http://travel.state.gov/content/adoptionsabroad/en/about-us/statistics.html.

Ceniza Choy, Catherine. 2013. *Global Families: A History of Asian International Adoption in America*. New York: NYU Press.

Chou, Rosalind, and Joe Feagin. 2008. *The Myth of the Model Minority: Asian Americans Facing Racism*. Boulder, CO: Paradigm.

Choy, Philip P., Marlon Hom, and Lorraine Dong. 1995. *The Coming Man: Nineteenth-Century Perceptions of the Chinese.* Seattle: University of Washington Press.

Chua, Amy. 2011. Why Tiger Moms Are Superior. *Wall Street Journal*, January 8.

Clemetson, Lynette. 2006. Adopted in China, Seeking Identity in America. *New York Times*, March 23.

Cohen, Myron. 1994. Being Chinese: The Peripheralization of Traditional Identity. In *The Living Tree: The Changing Meaning of Being Chinese Today*, edited by Tu Wei-ming, 88–108. Palo Alto, CA: Stanford University Press.

Dirlik, Arif. 1998. The Asia-Pacific in Asian-American Perspective. In *What Is in a Rim? Critical Perspectives on the Pacific Region Idea*, edited by Arif Dirlik, 283–308. Boulder, CO: Rowman and Littlefield.

Dolgan, Gail, and Vincente Franco. 2002. *Daughter from Danang.* PBS Home Video.

Dorow, Sara K. 2006a. Racialized Choices: Chinese Adoption and the "White Noise" of Blackness. *Critical Sociology* 32 (2–3): 357–79.

———. 2006b. *Transnational Adoption: A Cultural Economy of Race, Gender and Kinship.* New York: NYU Press.

Dorow, Sara. 2010. Producing Kinship through the Markets of Transnational Adoption. In *Baby Markets: Money and the New Politics of Creating Families*, edited by Michelle Bratcher Goodwin, 69–83. Cambridge: Cambridge University Press.

Dorow, Sara, and Stephen Wunrow. 1997. *When You Were Born in China: A Memory Book for Children Born in China.* San Francisco: Yeong and Yeong.

Ebron, Paula, and Anna Tsing. 1995. From Allegories of Identity to Sites of Dialogue. *Diaspora* 4 (2): 125–51.

Eng, David L. 2003. Transnational Adoption and Queer Diasporas. *Social Text* 76 21 (3): 1–37.

———. 2010. *The Feeling of Kinship.* Durham, NC: Duke University Press.

Evans, Karin. 2008. *Lost Daughters of China: Adopted Girls, Their Journey to America, and the Search for a Missing Past.* Los Angeles: Tarcher.

Fong, Timothy. 2007. *The Contemporary Asian American Experience: Beyond the Model Minority.* 3rd ed. Upper Saddle River, NJ: Pearson.

Fong, Vanessa. 2004. *Only Hope: Coming of Age under China's One Child Policy.* Palo Alto, CA: Stanford University Press.

———. 2011. *Paradise Redefined: Transnational Chinese Students and the Quest for Flexible Citizenship in the Developed World.* Palo Alto, CA: Stanford University Press.

Frankenberg, Ruth. 1993. *White Women, Race Matters: The Social Construction of Whiteness.* Minneapolis: University of Minnesota Press.

Freundlich, Madelyn, and Joy Kim Lieberthal. 2000. *The Gathering of the First Generation of Adult Korean Adoptees: Adoptees' Perceptions of International Adoption.* New York: Evan B. Donaldson Adoption Institute.

Friedman, Hilary Levey. 2013. *Playing to Win: Raising Children in a Competitive Culture.* Berkeley: University of California Press.

Fry, Ying Ying, and Terry Fry. 2001. *Kids Like Me in China.* San Francisco: Yeong and Yeong.

Fulbeck, Kip. 2006. *Part Asian, 100% Hapa*. San Francisco: Chronicle Books.

Geertz, Clifford. 1973. *The Interpretation of Cultures*. New York: Basic Books.

Giroux, H. A. 1994. *Disturbing Pleasures: Learning Popular Culture*. New York: Routledge.

Gupta, Akhil, and James Ferguson. 1997. *Culture, Power, Place: Explorations in Critical Anthropology*. Durham, NC: Duke University Press.

Hall, Stuart. 1990. Cultural Identity and Diaspora. In *Identity: Community, Culture, Difference*, edited by Jonathan Rutherford, 222–37. London: Lawrence and Wishart.

Hays, Sharon. 1996. *The Cultural Contradictions of Motherhood*. New Haven, CT: Yale University Press.

Hopgood, Mei-ling. 2009. *Lucky Girl: A Memoir*. Chapel Hill, NC: Algonquin Press.

Howell, Signe. 2007. *The Kinning of Foreigners: Transnational Adoption in a Global Perspective*. New York: Berghahn Books.

Hsu, Madeline. 2000. *Dreaming of Gold, Dreaming of Home: Transnationalism and Migration between the United States and South China, 1882–1943*. Palo Alto, CA: Stanford University Press.

Hubinette, Tobias. 2006. Contested Adoption Narratives in a Swedish Setting. Paper presented at the Second Annual Conference on Adoption Research, University of East Anglia, Norwich, July 17.

Jackson, John L., Jr. 2001. *Harlemworld: Doing Race and Class in Contemporary Black America*. Chicago: University of Chicago Press.

Jacobson, Heather. 2008. *Culture Keeping: White Mothers, International Adoption, and the Negotiation of Family Difference*. Nashville, TN: Vanderbilt University Press.

———. 2009. Interracial Surveillance and Biological Privilege: Adoptive Families in the Public Eye. In *Who's Watching? Practices of Surveillance among Contemporary Families*, edited by Margaret K. Nelson and Anita Ilta Garey, 73–93. Nashville, TN: Vanderbilt University Press.

Johnson, K., and A. Klatzkin. 2004. *Wanting a Daughter, Needing a Son: Abandonment, Adoption, and Orphanage Care in China*. San Francisco: Yeong and Yeong.

Kelner, Shaul. 2010. *Tours That Bind: Diaspora, Pilgrimage, and Israeli Birthright Tourism*. New York: NYU Press.

Kim, Eleana. 2007. Our Adoptee, Our Alien: Transnational Adoptees as Specters of Foreignness and Family in South Korea. *Anthropological Quarterly* 80 (2): 497–531.

———. 2010. *Adopted Territory: Transnational Korean Adoptees and the Politics of Belonging*. Durham, NC: Duke University Press.

Kim, Tae-sun. 2009. Alien Asian: The Role of Racial Exclusion and Cultural Differentiation in the Identity Development of Transnationally Adopted Korean Americans. PhD diss., Michigan State University.

King-O'Riain, Rebecca Chiyoko. 2006. *Pure Beauty: Judging Race in Japanese American Beauty Pageants*. Minneapolis: University of Minnesota Press.

Klatzkin, Amy. 1999. *A Passage to the Heart: Writings from Families with Children from China*. San Francisco: Yeong and Yeong.

Knowlton, Linda Goldstein. 2013. *Somewhere Between*. Longshot Productions.

Lee, Barb. 2008. *Adopted the Movie*. Point Made Films.

Lee, Erika. 2003. *At America's Gates: Chinese Immigration during the Exclusion Era, 1882–1943*. Chapel Hill: University of North Carolina Press.

———. 2009. Asian American Studies in the Midwest: New Questions, Approaches, and Communities. *Journal of Asian American Studies* 12 (3): 247–73.

Lee, Richard. 2003. The Transracial Adoption Paradox: History, Research and Counseling Implications of Cultural Socialization. *Counseling Psychologist* 31 (6): 711–44.

Lee, Robert, 1999. *Orientals*. Philadelphia: Temple University Press.

Ling, Huping. 2004. *Chinese St. Louis: From Enclave to Cultural Community*. Philadelphia: Temple University Press.

Ling, Lisa. 2005. China's Lost Girls. National Geographic Video.

Louie, Andrea. 2003. When You Are Related to the "Other": (Re)locating the Chinese Homeland in Asian American Politics through Cultural Tourism. *positions: east asia cultures critique* 11 (3): 735–63.

———. 2004. *Chineseness across Borders: Renegotiating Chinese Identities in China and the United States*. Durham, NC: Duke University Press.

Lowe, Lisa. 1996. *Immigrant Acts: On Asian American Cultural Politics*. Durham, NC: Duke University Press.

———. 2003. Heterogeneity, Hybridity, Multiplicity. In *Theorizing Diaspora: A Reader*, edited by Jana Braziel and Anita Mannur, 132–55. Hoboken, NJ: Blackwell.

Lutz, Catherine, and Jane L. Collins 1993. *Reading National Geographic*. Chicago: University of Chicago Press.

Maira, Sunaina. 2002. *Desis in the House: Indian American Youth Culture in New York City*. Philadelphia: Temple University Press.

———. 2009. *Missing: Youth, Citizenship and Empire after 9/11*. Durham, NC: Duke University Press.

Mak, Liz. 2014. Chinese on the Inside. *New York Times*, March 3.

Malkki, Liisa. 1992. National Geographic: The Rooting of Peoples and the Territorialization of National Identity among Scholars and Refugees. *Cultural Anthropology* 7 (1): 24–44.

Manalansan, Martin. 2000. *Cultural Compass: Ethnographic Explorations of Asian America*. Philadelphia: Temple University Press.

Markowitz, Fran. 2006. Blood, Soul, Race, and Suffering: Full-Bodied Ethnography and Expressions of Jewish Belonging. *Anthropology and Humanism* 31 (1): 41–56.

Marre, Diana, and Laura Briggs. 2009. *International Adoption: Global Inequalities and the Circulation of Children*. New York: NYU Press.

Melina, Lois. 1998. *Raising Adopted Children*. New York: HarperCollins.

National Association of Black Social Workers. 1972. Position Statement on Trans-racial Adoption. The Adoption History Project. http://pages.uoregon.edu/adoption/archive/NabswTRA.htm.

O'Brien, Eileen. 2008. *The Racial Middle: Latinos and Asians Living beyond the Racial Divide*. New York: NYU Press.

Omatsu, Glenn. 1994. The Four Prisons and the Movements of Liberation: Asian American Activism from the 1960s to the 1990s. In *The State of Asian America: Activism and Resistance in the 1990s*, edited by Karin Aguilar San Juan, 19–69. Boston: South End Press.

Omi, Michael, and Howard Winant. 1994. *Racial Formation in the United States: From the 1960s to the 1990s*. London: Routledge.

Ong, Aihwa. 1999. *Flexible Citizenship: The Cultural Logics of Transnationality*. Durham, NC: Duke University Press.

———. 2003. *Buddha Is Hiding: Refugees, Citizenship, the New America*. Berkeley: University of California Press.

Ortiz, Ana Teresa, and Laura Briggs. 2003. The Culture of Poverty, Crack Babies, and Welfare Cheats: The Making of the "Healthy White Baby Crisis." *Social Text 76* 21 (3): 39–57.

Patton, Sandra. 2000. *Birthmarks: Transracial Adoption in Contemporary America*. New York: NYU Press.

Purkayastha, Bandana. 2005. *Negotiating Ethnicity: Second-Generation South Asian Americans Traverse a Transnational World*. New Brunswick, NJ: Rutgers University Press.

Rana, Junaid. 2011. *Terrifying Muslims: Race and Labor in the South Asian Diaspora*. Durham, NC: Duke University Press.

Register, Cheri. 1990. *"Are Those Kids Yours?": American Families with Children Adopted from Other Countries*. New York: Free Press.

———. 2005. *Beyond Good Intentions: A Mother Reflects on Raising Internationally Adopted Children*. St. Paul, MN: Yeong and Yeong.

Riley, N. E. American Adoptions of Chinese Girls: The Socio-political Matrices of Individual Decision. *Women's Studies International Forum* 20 (1): 87–102.

Rouse, Roger. 1995. Thinking Through Transnationalism: Notes on the Cultural Politics of Class Relations in the Contemporary United States. *Public Culture* 7 (2): 353–402.

Said, Edward W. 1979. *Orientalism*. New York: Vintage.

Schein, Louisa. 1997. Forged Transnationality and Oppositional Cosmopolitanism. In *Transnationalism from Below*, edited by Luis Eduardo Guarnizo and Michael Peter Smith, 291–313. Piscataway, NJ: Transaction.

———. 2000. *Minority Rules: The Miao and the Feminine in Chinese Cultural Politics*. Durham, NC: Duke University Press.

Segal, D. A., and R. Handler. 1995. Multiculturalism and the Concept of Culture. *Identities: Global Studies in Culture and Power* 1 (4): 391–408.

Shiao, Jianbin, and Mia Tuan. 2008. Korean Adoptees and the Social Context of Ethnic Exploration. *American Journal of Sociology* 113 (4): 1026–66.

Shiao, J., M. Tuan, and E. Rienzi. 2004. Shifting the Spotlight: Exploring Race and Culture in Korean-White Adoptive Families. *Race and Society* 7 (1): 1–16.

Shiu, Anthony. 2001. Flexible Production: International Adoption, Race, Whiteness. *Jouvert* 6 (1). http://english.chass.ncsu.edu/jouvert/v6i1-2/shiu.htm.

Simon, Rita J., and Howard Altstein. 2000. *Adoption across Borders: Serving the Children in Transracial and Intercountry Adoptions*. Lanham, MD: Rowman and Littlefield.

Simon R., H. Altstein, and M. Melli. 1994. *The Case of Transracial Adoption*. Washington, DC: American University Press.

Simon, Scott. 2010. Meant for Each Other: Scott Simon's Adoption Story. *NPR Morning Edition*, August 20.

Siu, Lok. 2005. *Memories of a Future Home: Diasporic Citizenship of Chinese in Panama*. Palo Alto, CA: Stanford University Press.

Song, Miri. 2003. *Choosing Ethnic Identity*. Malden, MA: Blackwell, 2003.

Stanek, Carolyn. 2007. *Found in China*. Tai-King Productions.

Steinberg, Gail, and Beth Hall. 2000. *Inside Transracial Adoption*. Indianapolis, IN: Perspectives Press.

Tchen, John Kuo Wei, and Dylan Yeats. 2014. *Yellow Peril! An Archive of Anti-Asian Fear*. New York: Verso.

Tessler, Richard, and Gail Gamache. 2012. Ethnic Exploration and Consciousness of Difference: Chinese Adoptees in Early Adolescence. *Adoption Quarterly* 15: 265–87.

Tessler, Richard, Gail Gamache, and Gregory Adams. 2009. Bi-cultural Socialization and Ethnic Identity in Daughters Adopted from China. *Journal of Social Distress and the Homeless* 18 (3–4): 131–67.

Tessler, Richard, Gail Gamache, and Liming Liu. 1999. *West Meets East: Americans Adopt Chinese Children*. Westport, CT: Bergin and Garvey.

Tessler, Richard, Huang Bang Han, and Jiang Hong. 2004. The Racial Attitudes of Chinese Adoptees in America: Comparisons with Children Being Raised in China. *International Journal of Child and Family Welfare*. 8 (2–8): 127.

Thomas, Kristy, and Richard Tessler. 2007. Bicultural Socialization among Adoptive Families: Where There's a Will, There's a Way. *Journal of Family Issues* 28 (9): 1189–219.

Traver, Amy E. 2007. Homeland Décor: China Adoptive Parent's Consumption of Chinese Cultural Objects to Display in Their Homes. *Qualitative Sociology* 30 (3): 201–20.

Trenka, Jane Jeong, Julia Chinyere Oparah, and Sun Yung Shin, eds. 2006. *Outsiders Within: Writing on Transracial Adoption*. Boston: South End Press.

Tuan, Mia. 1999. *Forever Foreigner or Honorary White?* New Brunswick, NJ: Rutgers University Press.

Tuan, Mia, and Jiannbin Shiao. 2012. *Choosing Ethnicity, Negotiating Race: Korean Adoptees in America*. New York: Russell Sage Foundation.

Turner, Victor. 1967. Betwixt and Between: The Liminal Period in Rites de Passage. In *The Forest of Symbols*, 93–111. Ithaca, NY: Cornell University Press.

Tylor, Edward Burnett. (1871) 1920. *Primitive Culture*. Vol. 1. New York: Putnam.

U.S. Census Bureau. 2012. State and County QuickFacts. Accessed June 11, 2014. http://quickfacts.census.gov/qfd/index.html.

Vandivere, S., K. Malm, and L. Radel. 2009. *Adoption USA: A Chartbook Based on the 2007 National Survey of Adoptive Parents*. Washington, DC: U.S. Department of Health and Human Services, Office of the Assistant Secretary for Planning and Evaluation.

Van Gennep, Arnold. 1961. *The Rites of Passage*. Chicago: University of Chicago Press.

Visweswaran, Kamala. 1998. Race and the Culture of Anthropology. *American Anthropologist* 100 (1): 70–83.

Volkman, Toby Alice. 2005. Embodying Chinese Culture: Transnational Adoption in North America. In *Cultures of Transnational Adoption*, edited by Toby Alice Volkman, 81–116. Durham, NC: Duke University Press.

Vonk, M. E. 2001. Cultural Competence for Transracial Adoptive Parents. *Social Work* 46 (3): 246–55.

Waters, Mary, 1990. *Ethnic Options: Choosing Ethnic Identities in America*. Berkeley: University of California Press.

———. 2004. Optional Ethnicities: For Whites Only? In *Rethinking the Color Line: Readings in Race and Ethnicity*, 2nd ed., edited by Charles A. Gallagher, 96–108. New York: McGraw-Hill.

———. 2006. Ethnic Options: For Whites Only? In *Origins and Destinies*, edited by S. Pedraza and R. Rumbaut, 444–54. Belmont, CA: Wadsworth.

Watson, James. 1975. Agnates and Outsiders: Adoption in a Chinese Lineage. *Man* 10 (2): 293–306.

Werbner, Pnina. 2009. *Anthropology and the New Cosmopolitanism: Rooted, Feminist and Vernacular Perspectives*. New York: Bloomsbury Academic.

Williams, Sue. 2008. Young and Restless in China. *Frontline*. Ambrica Productions and WGBH Educational Foundation.

Wu, David Yen Ho. 1994. The Construction of Chinese and Non-Chinese Identities. In *The Living Tree: The Changing Meaning of Being Chinese Today*, edited by Tu Weiming, 148–67. Palo Alto, CA: Stanford University Press.

Yancey, George. 2003. *Who Is White? Latinos, Asians, and the New Black/Non-Black Divide*. Boulder, CO: Lynn Rienner.

Yngvesson, Barbara. 2007. Refiguring Kinship in the Age of Adoption. *Anthropological Quarterly* 80 (2): 561–79.

Zhang, Li. 2002. *Strangers in the City: Reconfigurations of Space, Power and Social Networks within China's Floating Population*. Palo Alto, CA: Stanford University Press.

Zhang, Li, and Aihwa Ong. 2008. *Privatizing China: Socialism from Afar*. Ithaca, NY: Cornell University Press.

Zhou, Min. 2004. Are Asian Americans Becoming White? *Context* 3 (1): 29–37.

INDEX

Abandonment, 10–11, 33, 55–59, 83–84, 189

Adopted the Movie, 52–54, 104; as representation of transnational adoption, 54

Adoptee identity, 84, 144, 212, 254; and race, 250

Adoptees, 52, 81, 189, 244; adoptee narratives, 102, 186, 195, 214–15; and loss of birth family, 195; and teen identity, 40

Adoption, China to the United States, 37, 40, 59, 106; as experience, 80, 190, 256; mediation of, 82; as process, 10, 31, 61, 69, 71, 75, 83, 147–48; as transition to First World, 75. *See also* Trip to China

Adoption, race considerations/choice, 10, 54, 59–60, 144, 171, 269. *See also* Transracial adoption

Adoption decision, 10, 56, 72, 155, 161, 263n3. *See also* Adoptive parents

Adoption narratives, 40, 87, 107, 158, 186, 204. *See also* Identity: narratives of; Lifebooks

Adoptive families, 143, 189, 210, 260; and consumption, 63, 68, 79, 218; and identity, 80, 203; and parenting, 58, 86, 212, 229

Adoptive parents, 10, 50, 56, 58, 61, 179, 271n10; and China, 63, 83, 157; and Chineseness, 10, 42, 60, 63, 72, 86, 124, 143, 171, 185, 274n3. *See also* Orientalism; Transracial adoption

Affective labor, 187

African American stereotypes, 147

Agency, 223

Also-Known-As, Inc., 260

American melting pot, 163

Anagnost, Ann, 23–25, 171, 211, 221, 256, 271n7

Ang, Ien, 114

Asian American, 67, 95–97, 111–14, 130, 134

Asian American adoptive parents, 28, 88, 90, 124–29, 187, 261; adoption decision, 103–4; comparison to white adoptive parents, 20–21, 91, 137–38, 184; and cultural production, 91, 111; and inherited familial practices, 114. *See also* Ethnic options

Asian American and Chinese American subculture, 14

Asian American cultural production, 98, 188, 220

Asian American identity, 90, 96–8, 23; and hybridization, 235; in popular culture, 32, 128, 136, 149, 257; production of, 93; stereotypes of, 24, 91, 98, 147, 156, 255, 262. *See also* Orientalism; Race

Asian American studies, 6, 45

Asian American teen identity, 226, 257. *See also* Teens

Asian immigrants, 134, 170. *See also* Immigrant

"Asian invasion," 33

Asian Pacific American identities, 236

Authenticity, 113, 164–66, 261, 269, 272n2; inherent authenticity, 89. *See also* Chineseness; Cultural authenticity

Baby hotels, 74

Bicultural (socialization), 205, 230, 261; and adoptive families, 263

ABOUT THE AUTHOR

Andrea Louie is Associate Professor of Anthropology at Michigan State University, where she is also affiliated with the Asian Pacific American Studies Program. She is the author of *Chineseness across Borders: Renegotiating Chinese Identities in China and the United States* (2004).